A FLAMING SOUL

A FLAMING SOUL

A heart-touching account of
Swami Vivekananda's last years

CHANCHAL KUMAR GHOSH
Translation by N Bharati

Vitasta

Published by
Renu Kaul Verma
Vitasta Publishing Pvt Ltd
C, 29, C Block, Sector 7, Noida,
Uttar Pradesh - 201301
info@vitastapublishing.com

ISBN: 978-93-47098-86-4

First Edition 2026
MRP ₹450

Edited by Vichitra Goel
Layout by Shubhpreet Kaur
Cover Design by Smriti Maheshwari
Printed by Vikas Computer and Printers, New Delhi

Contents

To
My daughter Aruna, now Sannyasini, Pravrajika Chitprakashaprana. With all the warmth of a father's love and the quiet strength of a blessing.

Foreword

A Flaming Soul, as Chanchal Kumar Ghosh has titled it, may be called a biographical novel, but it defies the boundaries of a genre. It does not unfold like a conventional narrative; rather, it breathes like a living chronicle, capturing with lyrical grace the final year and a half of a towering, luminous life. Crafted with the precision of deep research and the tenderness of a poet's pen, the work radiates reverence and empathy. To bind it within the narrow confines of classification would be to diminish its spirit.

The book unfolds in delicately carved chapters, each adorned with evocative sketches that echo the soul of the narrative, lending a visual resonance to the text and deepening the reader's immersion.

The story opens on a wintry night—9 December 1900. The air is hushed, heavy with mist, when a horse-drawn carriage halts before the quiet lanes of Belur Bazaar. From it steps out a tall figure, clad in coat, trousers, and a gentleman's hat. At first glance, he might be mistaken for a European stranger. But then, with a quiet leap, he scales the locked gates of the monastery. As he lifts his hat, Sadananda's eyes widen with recognition, and his arms rise in uncontainable joy, 'Swamiji!'

Thus begins the tale. Following this first spark, the narrative glides onward, seamlessly weaving together moments and memories, reflections and revelations. Readers do not merely observe; they journey beside Swamiji, step by step, heart to heart, through the final chapter of his radiant earthly sojourn.

After hearing about the death of Mr Sevier, Swamiji set out for Mayavati despite his ill health. His heartfelt tribute at Mr Sevier's memorial, his journey to Dharmagarh with Mrs Sevier, and his spiritual connection to nature are all expressed in the phrase, *'Jo kuch hai so tu hi hai'* (Whatever there is, it is You), powerfully portrayed in the 'Mayavati' chapter.

In the next part, Swamiji forms the Belur Math Trust, lays down the rules for running the monastery, gives instructions for future activities to his fellow monks, and slowly steps back from his responsibilities—as if preparing for his final departure.

At first, it may feel like the author is simply telling a story. But upon reflection, it becomes clear that he is trying to express something deeper. The aspects of Swamiji's life that deeply moved and inspired him are what he is trying to highlight.

The author begins by saying, 'In the light of my own thoughts, I have tried to connect with Swamiji. His life is like a diamond—reflecting countless colours, scattering flashes of light. It is nearly impossible to capture him fully.'

Alongside deep themes, the book also includes enjoyable and readable episodes. For instance, the description of a steamer ride through East Bengal, and of *hilsa* fish and spinach, is written with real flavour.

Swamiji once visited the holy place of Langalbandh with his mother, Bhubaneshwari Devi. This name may not be widely known, but the author explores its mythological background—

blending past and present in colourful strokes.

The 'Durga' chapter is especially beautiful. Here, the goddess Durga's idol, the divine mother, and the living Durga, Sri Sarada Devi, come together. The description of the Kumari Puja is touching. The youngest girl is worshipped as the goddess, and it feels as if the divine mother herself has taken human form. Swamiji applies a *tilak* of red sandalwood to her forehead. It feels as though he has touched the goddess's third eye. He bows down and softly says, 'Bless everyone.'

Swamiji's friend, Josephine MacLeod, comes to Belur Math. Once again, Swamiji sets out—this time with MacLeod, Okakura, Nirbhayananda, and two young boys. They travel through Gaya and Bodh Gaya, heading towards Kashi. In Kashi, Swamiji hands over the responsibility for a youth-run service centre built on his ideals to the Ramakrishna Mission. 'Niranjanananda smiled and said, "Naren has done a great deed." Swamiji, suddenly lost in thought, quietly says, "This may be the last work of my life".' The author gently points out, we are now nearing the end.

Swamiji asks for a calendar. Yogan Maharaj falls silent, a shadow crossing his face, for Sri Ramakrishna too had once asked for a calendar just before his earthly departure. A tremor of remembrance stirs the air.

***

It is 2 July 1902. Sister Nivedita arrives at the Math. Swamiji, in an act of quiet grace, serves her the meal with his own hands, then gently washes her hands. Startled, she asks, 'Why did you do this?' Swamiji, serene as ever, replies, 'Jesus had washed the feet of his disciples.' Yes, Jesus had done so on the eve of his passing. And now, Swamiji, two days before his own, has done the same.

In the closing pages, the author paints the final moments of that luminous life with reverent tenderness. He offers no embellishment, only truth cloaked in awe. The sorrow is deep, but deeper still is the hush of divine peace that pervades the telling. He names Swamiji his *eternal friend*. And from Swamiji's own poem *To the Friend*, he invokes the final benediction: 'Love, love—this is all we truly possess.'

That love, unconditional, radiant, and undying, is the wellspring from which this entire book flows. And where love reigns, everything else falls away. In that truth lies the book's final, most precious gift.

Pravrajika Aptakamaprana
Editor, Nivodhata Patrika
Sri Sarada Math
Dakshineswar, Kolkata

Introduction

A Deep Life of Realisation, Love, and Struggle

It was probably 2010. I had just begun taking my first steps into the world of writing. I would often visit the library at Ramakrishna Mission for research. The librarian there was Pranab Goswami. I've been to many libraries in my life, but I've never met anyone as dedicated as him. He once told me, 'If possible, do some work on Swami Vivekananda.'

Since I primarily write novels, I thought maybe I could write something on Swamiji's wandering years. Pranab babu encouraged me, saying, 'I'll help with all the information you need.' So I began the work.

But God had other plans. For eight years, I journeyed along 2,500 kms of the Ganges River. That journey led me to write a series of books on the river's history.

Swamiji, it seemed, had faded away from my thoughts. About a year ago, I was in the office of a Bengali publisher. Beside me sat Sandeep babu, a teacher from one of Kolkata's oldest schools. During our chat, he mentioned a Bangladeshi writer who had written an outstanding book on the final years of poet Michael

Madhusudan Dutt. The publisher turned to me and said, 'Why don't you write something like that for us?'

I replied, 'Let me try.'

The teacher suggested, 'You could write about Swami Vivekananda.' Again, I said, 'Let me try.'

But time passed; months slipped by in the rush of other work. The publisher asked me a couple of times, but I couldn't give a proper reply. Still, something kept nudging me.

One day, my wife said, 'Every day I hear you say you'll start writing about Swamiji. When will you actually begin? What if you're not here tomorrow morning?'

Her words shook me. Time won't wait for me. That was the beginning.

Many essays and biographies have been written on Swami Vivekananda, but not a novel. So I started writing one. And for the next ten months, Swamiji didn't let me rest for a moment. I read many books, researched deeply, and wrote and rewrote countless times. I wasn't satisfied; I started over and over again.

At times, my body and mind gave up in exhaustion. Illness made me want to stop writing. Then it felt as if Swamiji stood beside me and said, 'Think of me—and of what I have achieved despite suffering from thirty different illnesses.'

That gave me new strength. I couldn't let this creation slip away. Swamiji's words echoed in my mind: 'Do your work; don't worry about the results.'

Another eminent person who came to my mind repeatedly was Ernest Hemingway, the world-renowned author. He once said that writing about human beings is the hardest thing on earth. It feels like hell. It takes everything from you. It pushes you close to death. Maybe then you can write something worthwhile.

When I finished the manuscript after ten months, it felt as

if the pain of childbirth had finally ended. All my doubts and fears were gone. I could feel the joy of creation wholeheartedly. Whether the final work is good or bad—I leave that to the readers; they are the true judges.

All I can say is I have tried to see and feel Swamiji in my own way. His life is like a shining diamond—full of colours, emitting flashes of light that are nearly impossible to capture. Perhaps only Kalidasa or Valmiki could have done complete justice.

While writing this novel, I have tried to use authentic sources carefully. Swamiji was a real person, not a fictional character, so I have avoided the intervention of imagination in shaping his character. I have made a sincere effort to stay true to history; a few descriptions and dialogues have been introduced to suit the story and the setting. Not all events are presented chronologically; some have been rearranged for the flow of the narrative. I hope readers will forgive me for that. This is not a history book, nor a biography—it is biographical fiction. In the words of the famous author Sharadindu Bandyopadhyay, this is not 'fictionalised history', but historical fiction.

If there are factual errors despite all my efforts, I can only say, even God can make mistakes, and humans are nothing compared to Him. If the need be, I will rectify them in the next edition on getting a chance by the grace of my readers.

The Bengali version of this novel, *Chiro Sokha Hey*, was released at the Kolkata International Book Fair. The overwhelming response from readers far exceeded our expectations. Many distinguished people have praised it. What more can an author ask for?

Many suggested publishing an English version of the work so readers worldwide could learn about Swamiji and enjoy the story.

Translating a novel is no easy task. Yet, someone took up the challenge without any honorarium. However, I can't reveal her name and identity due to certain reasons.

I requested Ms Renu Kaul Verma, MD of Vitasta Publishing, to publish the translated work and she gladly agreed. A mere 'thank you' cannot express my gratitude for her kind support. I also thank Somen, Saumya and all my friends at the publishing department of Vitasta; this beautiful edition would not have been possible without their tireless work. I offer my deepest respect and gratitude to Swami Vishnudhamananda who created the visual themes for each chapter of the book.

I thank my friend Jyanta Kumar Basu and Smt Sanghamitra Chaudhuri for helping me with various information while writing this book. But without mentioning her, everything would remain incomplete—she is my wife Sujata Ghosh. If she hadn't freed me from all household responsibilities and given me the chance to write, nothing would have been possible for me.

Revered Mataji, Pravrajika Aptakamaprana, Editor of *Nibodhata Patrika* of Sarada Math, graced my Bengali book with her attention, and was deeply moved by its spirit. At my humble request, she joyfully agreed to write the Foreword, a gesture of affection and blessing that I shall always treasure. To her, I offer my reverence and heartfelt *pranam* from the depths of my being.

The part of Swamiji's life that moved me the most was his deep love for humanity and his complete detachment, qualities that are now rare in today's spiritual and social world. Today, we speak of renunciation but live for comfort and pleasure. There is pain, despair, and darkness all around us.

And yet, we wait. May Swami Vivekananda be born again!

12 January 2026

Chanchal Kumar Ghosh

Kolkata–59

At the Ganga Ghat

He[1] stood at the ghat; his gaze turned westward, towards the setting sun. A gentle crimson glow lay across the waters of the Ganga. The tide was full and waves lapped upon the stone steps in rhythmic murmur. Two boats drifted by lazily, and he looked towards them. Yet, it was hard to say where his eyes truly rested. Perhaps, in the river's ceaseless current, the floating boats and their silent oarsmen, the trees lined across the far bank, the sky dotted with scattered clouds, and the dying light of day—he sought to stretch his own self into the expanse of all.

Serenity softened his eyes. His whole form bore the rustic simplicity of a village soul. He was middle-aged, of average height, with a slight build, his complexion the shade of worn brass. His face still carried the softness of a child, with a profound humility, and a glow, as if touched by divine bliss. He wore a *dhoti* draped just below the knee and an *uttariya* (a kind of shawl) around his shoulders. His hair was cropped short, with a youthful mix of

1 Shree Ramakrishna

black and grey in his beard. His arms, long and slender, reached his knees. His ears sat lower than usual on his head. Amid the natural peace of his surroundings, he appeared almost like a luminous sage from another realm.

A soft voice called out. He turned at once. A boy stood a short distance away, clad in *dhoti* and vest—a servant perhaps. He murmured something. The man listened. His mind, absorbed until now, seemed gently stirred. Perhaps he had been waiting for someone. Without speaking, he walked forward with quiet steps. A short way off was his modest cottage, surrounded by trees—palms, *bels*, mangoes. Their shade cloaked the earth. He walked along the gravel path, flowers blooming on either side. On one side was the Ganga embankment, and on the other, a temple dedicated to Shiva. There was no crowd of devotees now. Though morning chants once filled the air, now silence reigned.

A gardener watering plants spotted him, put down his can, and saluted with both hands to his forehead. He returned the gesture with a bow. Passing the Shiva temple, he turned a bend. There stood his cottage. He climbed the long steps and stepped onto the wide veranda. The floor was a mix of black and white stone, the ceiling high. From some hidden nook came the cooing of birds.

He crossed the veranda and entered his room—a modest chamber with two doors. Beyond the inner door stretched a corridor of rooms and a paved courtyard facing east. A western window stood open. A cot lay on one side, and aside from a few sparse furnishings, the room was nearly bare. A few people sat quietly on the floor. When he entered, they all rose at once, their faces lit with reverence.

He sat on the bed with simple grace, unwrapped his *uttariya*, and his childlike innocence shone through without a trace of pretension. The others also sat down. One of them asked him a question. He smiled and replied. He spoke of *dharma* without complication, plainly and clearly. Yet, his voice had a soothing sweetness that enraptured all who heard it. It was as though the sound of his words flowed from another realm, like a chant carried from beyond.

Soft footsteps broke the spell. He turned towards the door. A young man[2] stood there, just past nineteen, wearied by travel, his hair unkempt, his clothes dishevelled. There was nothing remarkable at first glance, but his eyes! In those eyes stirred the depth of an unfathomable sea. The rest of the world faded before that gaze, it was as if he floated untouched in detachment.

The elder's face lit up with sudden joy on seeing him, as if an unexpected treasure had appeared. He smiled, visibly stirred. The youth stepped inside, bowed low, and touched the elder's feet. Then he stood straight. Someone had lit a lamp; its glow gently fell across his face.

The elder looked up and, with emotion-laden voice, said, 'You've come? I was thinking of you all afternoon. I feel out of place amidst worldly folks. There's so much I wish to say to you.'

Like a child breaking into joy at the sight of his mother, he muttered something more, perhaps to himself. Then, glancing at those present, he said, 'Not today, dear ones. I will speak with you another day. Be well.'

All of them were struck with wonder. Who was this youth who moved the sage so deeply? Why this sudden urgency to send them away? No one asked. They bowed in silence and left. Now there were only two of them in the room—one aged, one young.

2 Narendra Nath Dutta

The elder asked softly, 'Did you come alone?'

The youth nodded. 'Alone,' he replied.

A glow of contentment lit the elder's face. He got off the bed and took the youth's hand. 'Come,' he said. 'Let's go somewhere else. Someone might come here, and I won't be able to speak freely with you.'

A flicker of unease crossed the youth's face. This was their third meeting. Despite his inner strength, he could not understand what lay within this simple man—what power pulled him with such force. The two stepped outside. The sun had already set. A red glow lingered in the sky. The southern breeze stirred gently. The shadows of the trees lengthened. A gardenia tree had bloomed nearby; its scent laced the air. But the elder did not pause. Holding the youth's hand, he walked on.

They passed the main gate. Beyond it, the shrine of Mother Bhavatarini[3] stood visible. A courtyard and a row of Shiva temples lay between them. Further ahead, a small pond nestled in an enclosed garden. They turned south. A few people, strangers to them, moved about with offerings in hand.

The youth walked on, as if entranced. What was it in this man's touch? It made him feel as if every iota of strength within him had melted. Was it enchantment? Or sorcery? It felt like an illusion. He asked, 'Where are we going?'

A faint smile touched the elder's lips. 'You'll see when we arrive.'

'I don't trust you,' the youth said, half-serious. 'I saw what you could do the other day.'

The elder burst into a laugh like a carefree maiden. 'That was nothing. I was simply testing you.'

---

3 Goddess Kali

The youth muttered to himself, 'Witchcraft! I didn't even know when I lost consciousness. It felt as though I wasn't within my own body. I drifted in space, screamed in terror. But he touched my chest, and everything returned to normal. But not today—today, no matter what, nothing will happen.'

The thought broke off as they reached a large garden, before a two-storied house. Trying to compose himself, the youth glanced around. 'Where are we,' he asked.

The elder, still walking, said, 'This is Jadu Mallik's garden house. He holds me in great regard. When I come, his guard opens the door. No one comes here. We'll be able to talk freely.'

The stillness of the garden spread all around. The watchman saw them and hurried to open the door. 'Come in, Thakur,' he called.

They climbed the stairs, passed the veranda, and entered the sitting room. Through the glass windows, the last rays of day filtered in, spreading soft hues across the room. A cot stood in the centre. They sat facing one another. For a long moment, neither spoke.

Then, breaking the silence, the elder asked, 'Who are you?'

The youth faltered. He hadn't forgotten the day they first met. The man had come to their neighbourhood, speaking of the soul and the supreme soul with such beauty, as though he had never heard such words before. The elder's gaze had fallen upon him, and something strange had sparked in his eyes, like one who had found a rare treasure. He'd asked for a song. The youth had obliged. He'd introduced himself, a wandering soul. This man might not even remember.

In a quiet voice, he began, 'I'm from the Simla neighbourhood....'

But the elder raised a hand. 'I'm not asking for that. I already know this. Everyone knows. I want to know, who are you truly?'

The youth looked startled. What identity was the man seeking?

Before he could reply, the elder pressed, 'Who are you? Where have you come from? Why have you come?'

The youth met his gaze. The elder's face was filled with infinite inquiry. He lowered his head and whispered, 'I don't know.'

'You don't know?' There was surprise in his voice. 'You don't know where you come from? That's not possible.' There was a teasing smile in the elder's eyes.

'I am like everyone else,' said the youth with a hint of irritation. 'I have no special identity.'

The elder smiled gently and moved closer. His face shone with calm brilliance, yet he was careful. Folding his hands, he said, 'I know. You have taken this form to lift beings out of their suffering.'

The youth grew agitated, 'What are you saying?'

The elder remained serene. 'Not everything can be said. You'll know when the time comes.'

The youth felt helpless before the man, drawn towards him despite himself. No matter how hard he tried, he could not dismiss him.

In the distance, a conch blew from some temple. The elder stirred, as if remembering an unfinished task. He rose and shut the door.

The youth didn't know what was happening and had no words to protest.

The elder sat again, calm and composed, as though sinking deeper into meditation. He reached out and placed his hand upon the youth's chest. It was like the touch of lightning. In a flash, the youth slipped from consciousness to something beyond. His entire self vanished.

The elder remained still. A strange expression came over him. Gradually, he felt he was no longer in this world. His mind went beyond the mortal realms, floating upward into the vast Infinite, with the sun, moon, stars, and planets, each circling around him in their orbit. Beyond them, higher still, his conscious soul rose. The layers of the cosmos fell behind. The bounds of earth ended. It was now in the realm of the gods, a world of divine beings and eternal joy.

He was awestruck. How far must he travel? He paused at the edge of this celestial realm. There was a boundary that even gods could not cross. It was the realm of the Undivided. Yet nothing hindered him. His path lay ahead. Before him shone a world of light. Seven sages sat in meditation. They had surpassed even the gods in wisdom, love, and divine power. He stood stunned, as if losing himself. He was no longer of the earth. He had become one of another world.

As he stepped forward, the foremost sage opened his eyes. Peace and love emanated from his gaze. He raised both his hands in welcome. He approached and stood before the sage, suddenly shocked. He had seen this sage before.

'Who are you?' he asked.

The sage replied, 'I am one of the seven Rishis.'

His face glowed with joy. 'I know you, Lord. You are that ancient sage, Narayana, in human form. You will descend to the mortal world to ease the suffering of beings.' A divine smile bloomed on the Rishi's lips.

In a trembling voice, he said, 'Will you come with me?'

'Where?' asked the Rishi.

'Upon the earth. For the good of the world. You shall flood humanity with the tide of your wisdom and love. The darkness will vanish, and the earth shall glow with garlands of light.'

A gentle joy spread across the Rishi's face. He said nothing. But the silence of his eyes expressed the unspoken vow, 'I shall go with you. My divine play shall unfold across the world. From the Infinite to the Greater Infinite, all things shall be swept along. I shall burn, age after age, as an unquenchable flame.'

Tears of joy welled up in the eyes of the elder man who bore the celestial form. Stretching his arms up towards the heavens, he cried out, 'For how many ages I have waited for you, Lord! Come, now. Spread your eternal light. Let your love fill every heart.'

The Rishi closed his eyes.

Across the cosmos, the auspicious conch rang out.

He Has Returned

It was 9 December 1899 in Belur, a quiet village by the Ganga in Howrah district. The winter night had fallen. A lone horse-drawn carriage came to a halt at the silent Belur market. The shops had long been closed. The streets were deserted. Who would linger outdoors on such a cold night after a day's toil? A few shuttered stalls stood at the bend of the road, lifeless behind their drawn blinds.

Out of the carriage stepped a tall man, clad in a coat and trousers, a cap drawn low over his brow. At first glance, he seemed every bit of an English gentleman. He carried a small bag in one hand.

The red road was paved with brick and mortar; worn and uneven, it was scattered with gravel. At intervals, stood lamp posts meant to hold hurricane lanterns, though none were lit. There were no shops along this stretch, only a few mud-and-thatch homes of the poor. Through the cracks of one or two windows flickered faint lantern light, casting dreamy shadows upon the road. No human voice stirred the silence, save for the occasional passerby cloaked in a shawl, melting into the night.

The tall stranger surveyed the surroundings. Darkness lay thick, yet the path was known to him. He moved unhesitatingly. Shrubs lined either side of the road, cicadas chirped in ceaseless rhythm, and the faint scent of wildflowers drifted through the air. A chill clung to the wind. The path ended here. The land rose and fell unevenly. Ahead stood a large iron gate. The visitor paused.

The gate was locked from within. He thought for a moment, then grasped the iron bars and shook them firmly.

Close by was the watchman's hut. Hearing the rattle, the guard emerged with a lantern in hand. 'Who's there?' he called out.

'I must enter,' came the deep, composed voice of the stranger.

The guard approached. He caught sight of the figure through the bars. Was it a *sahib*? What would an Englishman be doing here at this hour? He dared not open the gate without permission. 'Please wait,' he said. 'I'll go and inform them.'

And off he ran, across the open field, towards the river. Before him flowed the Ganga, vast and quiet, lapping both its shores. At its edge stood the newly founded Belur Math. A monastery in name, it was little more than two humble buildings upon a wide stretch of land. A few young monks lived there, practising their vows in silence. Some elders, too, were present.

Evening prayers and meditation had concluded. The dinner bell had just rung. The brahmacharis and monks were gathering one by one in the refectory, a rare moment of lightheartedness in their austere lives. The breathless guard arrived, his face flushed with excitement. A young novice spotted him and asked, 'What's the matter, Bholanath?'

'A *sahib* has come!'

'A *sahib*? Where?'

'Waiting outside the gate!'

A *sahib* at Belur Math, at this hour? A murmur rose among them, eyes turned upwards, inquisitive. A little apart stood Swami Saradananda—, the general secretary of the Math. Calm and thoughtful, he handled all affairs of the monastery. Someone informed him, 'Maharaj, an Englishman wishes to enter.'

'A *sahib*? What business would bring him here?' Saradananda's brows furrowed slightly. He knew well the British government's distrust of the Math. Rumours had reached the authorities that revolutionaries hid within its walls in the guise of monks. Though police had come before, never had anyone arrived so late. Friends at the local station would have surely warned them had something been amiss.

The watchman now stood before him, head bowed. Saradananda thought for a moment and said, 'I will go myself.'

He wrapped his shawl more snugly against the night's deepening chill and stepped out. A few monks followed. The watchman led the way. As they neared the gate, bathed in pale moonlight, they saw the figure of a man striding towards them, a *sahib* in appearance. 'That's him,' whispered the watchman.

Beside Saradananda stood Sadananda. He muttered, 'The gate was locked. How did the sahib get in?'

Saradananda peered closely. 'That walk...it feels familiar.'

By now, the man had come quite near. His cap still shadowed half of his face. Then, lifting it, he revealed himself.

With a shout of pure joy, Sadananda threw up his arms. 'Swamiji!'

All doubts vanished. The long, unkempt hair, the unmistakable glow, this sahib was none other than their beloved Naren, Swami Vivekananda.

Saradananda rushed forward and embraced him. 'Naren!

You! At this hour? From where?'

A young monk called out, 'Swamiji, the gate was locked! How did you come in?'

Swamiji laughed, 'I heard the dinner bell. I was famished! I feared I'd miss the meal. So, I climbed over the gate.'

Laughter rippled through the air. Saradananda exclaimed, 'Only our Naren! Not mountain, nor forest, nor river could stand in his way. And now, not even this great iron gate!'

A novice ran ahead to announce the news. 'Swamiji has returned!'

Inside, the disciples of Sri Ramakrishna—Swami Brahmananda (Rakhal Maharaj), Niranjanananda, Baburam Maharaj, and others—were just sitting for dinner. At the news, all rose as one. Their Naren, their very soul, had come home after nearly a year and a half abroad.

As he entered, it was as though moonlight had filled the room. Everyone gathered round, eager to hear him. But Swamiji said, 'All in good time. First, give me food. I'm starving!'

Chaos turned to cheer. A place was quickly made beside Rakhal Maharaj. A plate had already been set. A brahmachari brought a bowl of *khichuri* and some plantain curry.

Baburam Maharaj beamed, 'What will you have? Sit! I'll fry some *luchis*.'

But Swamiji's eyes lit up at the sight of *khichuri*. 'No, no!' he cried, taking his seat. 'Ah, how long it's been! This is *prasad*! Do you think one finds this in the West? Give me! I'll eat for ten men tonight!'

Rakhal Maharaj chuckled. He knew his brother's appetite well. 'Eat as you please. There's plenty. Nothing will fall short.'

As they ate, the stories began. Someone asked, 'Swamiji, how was this journey?'

His first visit to the West had lasted three years and nine months—from the Parliament of Religions in Chicago to his travels through England. After spending two and a half years in India, he departed again in June 1899, accompanied by Sister Nivedita[4] and Swami Turiyananda[5]. They visited London, America, France, and Egypt, before returning on 7 December via Bombay. The next day, he had taken the *Bombay Express*. Now, on 9 December, he was home.

Swamiji said, 'America received me warmly. Wherever I spoke, crowds came. Some of their misconceptions about India have begun to change. Our country's spiritual vision must be shared more extensively with the world. I have begun the work. The rest, I leave to you. As for me, now...I must rest.'

From a little distance, Niranjanananda[6] smiled meaningfully at Saradananda and said with a twinkle, 'Did you all hear that? Naren says he will *rest*!'

Saradananda looked at Swamiji and replied, 'The sun may rest one day and give no light, but Naren? That I cannot imagine.'

A gentle, wistful smile played on Swamiji's lips. In a faraway voice, he said, 'I have worked long. I wish to do more. But my body is no longer mine. Whatever time remains, I'll spend among you, in joy and laughter.'

Rakhal Maharaj placed a hand upon his back. The two of them, brothers of the soul, understood each other as no one else could. Rakhal could sense the weariness that had begun to shadow Swamiji's spirit.

To close the moment, he said, 'It's late. Time to rise, everyone.

---

4 Disciple of Swami Vivekananda
5 Disciple of Sri Ramakrishna
6 Disciple of Sri Ramakrishna

The cooks, the helpers, they too must rest.'

Saradananda stood up and said, 'Come, Naren. Let's go inside. We have much to talk about.'

With playful affection, Rakhal Maharaj said, 'I see, sleep shall elude us tonight. After all, how can anyone think of sleeping when Swamiji has returned home after so long?'

Midnight passed quietly. Words came to Swamiji with difficulty; his chest bore the weight of unspoken illness. His body, long battered, had quietly begun to break down; yet, never once did he reveal it to anyone.

Saradananda Maharaj rose to his feet and said gently, 'Let Naren rest now. We shall speak again in the morning. Sadananda, stay with him tonight, should he need anything.'

Sadananda nodded in silence. As others retreated to their quarters, Swamiji turned to him and asked, 'Tell me, Sadananda... how do I seem to you now?'

Sadananda remained silent for some time. To him, Swamiji was meditation, wisdom, and divinity incarnate. Even in the brief time he had spent close to him, it seemed Swamiji was beyond ordinary comprehension. But when the Master asked, he had to answer. After observing him, Sadananda said softly, 'Your health seems quite poor, Swamiji.'

Swamiji said nothing. His gaze drifted to the wall, where a photograph of Sri Ramakrishna hung, standing with one hand resting on a pillar, dressed in a black coat and a white *dhoti*. The picture, taken years ago at the Bengal Photographic Studio in Radhabazar, had captured the Master in a state of deep *samadhi*.

Swamiji, too, longed for such a dissolution, to merge as his Master did. Old memories stirred. He recalled how years ago, at the garden house in Kashipur, Sri Ramakrishna lay gravely ill. One day, young Narendra had asked him, 'Master, I want to attain the *nirvikalpa samadhi*. Show me the path.'

Sri Ramakrishna had smiled and said, 'If I recover, I shall give you whatever you ask.'

'And, what if you don't?'

With a hint of annoyance, the Master had replied, 'What are you saying? Why wouldn't I recover? Fine, what is it that you seek?'

'*Nirvikalpa samadhi*, like Shukadeva.'

The Master's mood shifted. His voice rose, indignant yet tender.

'Shame! I thought you would be a great tree—a vast banyan under which thousands would find shelter. You are meant to liberate others, not seek liberation for yourself! Such selfishness does not suit you. No, my child. I embrace all. I'll eat the fried fish, the boiled, the curried, and even the pickled! I see Him in all forms, formless or with form, I never tire. Do the same. Be both the sage and the lover of God.'

It felt like yesterday. Swamiji remembered sitting alone in the room downstairs at the Kashipur garden house. Upstairs, disciples attended to the Master. But his entire being ached for *samadhi*. Time went by. Then, suddenly, it was as though a great radiance had enveloped him. That light expanded, flooding the cosmos, dissolving all of nature into pure consciousness—unchanging, indivisible, and infinite.

His limbs felt as though they were vanishing into nothingness. In panic, he cried out, 'Where is my body?'

Disciples rushed in, alarmed. They stroked his head, touched his arms; everything was intact. Burologopal pressed Swamiji's limbs gently and said reassuringly, 'See, Naren? Everything is as it should be.'

Niranjan Maharaj hurried to the Master and, with great concern, said, 'Naren is shouting during meditation that his body is gone!'

Sri Ramakrishna's face darkened with irritation. 'Good,' he muttered. 'Let him stay like that for a while. He pesters me too much!'

Later that night, as Naren's body and mind returned to normal, the Master called him. His deep and luminous eyes rested on the beloved disciple. After a moment's gaze, he said, 'So... today the Mother has shown you everything. But the key remains with me. You still have work to finish. When it is done, I will unlock the door again.'

He was a seer of truth. With firm hands, he turned Naren away from the path of retreat and set him upon the great stage of the world. Not even for a moment did he allow him to rest. Like a divine puppet master, he kept the key to liberation in his own hand.

Swamiji returned from the realm of memory. Slowly, he raised his eyes to the image of his Master. From the deepest well of his being, he whispered, 'My Lord, my beloved...perhaps the time has come for you to unlock that door.'

He remained still, his eyes fixed. Outside, the wind howled. Cold as sharpened glass, it lashed against the windowpanes. He pulled the thick shawl closer around his shoulders. It seemed to him that the Master's face in the photo had softened into a smile, as though he had spoken something, something beyond understanding.

Swamiji slowly closed his eyes. The hours of the night silently marched onward.

The First Morning

Swamiji opened his eyes; the room was dim, touched by the pale shadow of the night's departure. Though he retired late, he always rose at *brahma-muhurta*, before dawn. It was a habit now—effortless and instinctive.

He sat up in bed and softly began to chant. In the distance, Sadananda slept, curled under a quilt on a wooden cot, his breath calm and steady. Swamiji looked at him with quiet affection. He cherished Sadananda, his disciple and son in spirit.

His mind wandered back. Thakur had left his body. Shattered by grief, the young devotees had scattered, their shelter lost. Swamiji too had departed, embracing the life of a wandering monk. From Vrindavan, he journeyed towards Haridwar and arrived at Hathras station—exhausted, starved, unwashed, having eaten nothing for two days. He slumped on a bench.

It was then that Sharatchandra Gupta, assistant station master of Hathras, passed by. The sight of the serene ascetic stopped him in his tracks. Never before had he seen such a radiant monk. Drawn by a sudden, inexplicable pull, he approached him and said gently, 'You look famished. May I offer you something to eat?'

Swamiji replied with grave simplicity, 'Your guess is right. I haven't eaten for two days.'

'Come to my quarters,' Sharatchandra offered. 'I'll give you whatever I can.'

At his home, he asked, 'What will you eat, revered one?'

Sharatchandra was stirred by something ancient and sacred. Quoting a Persian verse, he said, 'O Beloved, you are my guest. If need be, I shall cook you a feast from my own heart.'

Swamiji smiled. 'No need for the heart. Whatever you give, I will accept.'

Sharatchandra brought all he had, serving with care. He stayed near the whole day, listening to Swamiji and watching him. A thought struck him, could one not spend a whole life at this man's feet?

He begged Swamiji to stay. And so he did, for a few days.

One morning, Sharatchandra said, 'Swamiji, show me the path of life.'

Swamiji sang a song:

If wisdom is what you truly seek,
Smear ashes upon your moon-like cheek—
Else, go your way and do not speak.

Sharatchandra cast off all hesitation. He shed his office attire, covered his face in holy ash, and stood before Swamiji. He renounced everything, so easily, utterly. Surprised, Swamiji decided to test him.

'Take a begging bowl,' he said, 'and go door-to-door. Whatever you collect, we shall eat today as *prasad*.'

Without a flicker of doubt, Sharatchandra obeyed. Once a master among men, he now stood like a beggar before coolies and clerks—silent, humble, radiant. Swamiji saw it all.

'I shall give you *sannyas* (renunciation),' he said.

That was the beginning. Drawn irrevocably by Swamiji's magnetism, Sharatchandra became Sadananda. Renouncing everything, he walked alongside his guru.

That was years ago. Yet, in Swamiji's heart, it felt like yesterday.

He stepped down from his cot. The floor was biting cold. He slipped into the slippers beside his bed. It was time for *Mangal Arati* (the first worship of the day). The conch sounded from the temple. He loved this sacred moment, the fragile cusp where night kisses day.

He opened the door and stepped out. The Ganga shimmered through the mist, its gentle murmurs mingling with silence. Nothing could be seen across the river. A pale moon still lingered in the western sky. The fog thinned slowly; daybreak was near.

He bowed, hands folded. The river sang on. Down at the ghat, a monk stood waist-deep in water, facing east, chanting the ancient *Surya mantra*:

Om Jaba-kusuma-sankasham kashyapeyam mahadyutim,
Tamorim sarva-paapaghnam pranato'smi divakaram.

I bow to the sun—vermilion like the hibiscus bloom, son of Kashyapa, destroyer of darkness, great bearer of light, cleanser of all sin.

The monk came ashore. Swamiji recognised him, it was Shashi Maharaj (Ramakrishnananda), ever devoted to Thakur's service. Shashi didn't notice Swamiji as he passed. Swamiji turned indoors.

In the room beside the bed, a warm coat and shawl lay neatly folded, arranged by Sadananda, who stirred at the sound of Swamiji's steps. He sat up quickly.

Before he could speak, Swamiji said, 'No need to hurry. I'm going to the temple.'

'Shall I come with you?' asked Sadananda.

Swamiji smiled. 'Not yet so old that I can't walk that little distance alone.'

Sadananda flushed with embarrassment.

'Get ready and join me at the temple,' Swamiji added. 'I've been gone a year and a half. Let me see, what changes you've made.'

He did not wait. Downstairs, he stepped out into the river-washed silence. The old house stood near the Ganga. The monks in their cells murmured their *japa* (chanting). Peace hung heavy in the air. A few birds cooed softly.

Across the courtyard stood a second building, on the upper floor, the temple. Swamiji climbed up the open stairs. On the lion-throne rested Thakur's[7] image. The sight filled his heart with emotion. Thakur was inseparable from his soul. He loved Thakur more than anyone. Thakur alone had loved him without condition.

Days before passing, Thakur had called him near. As Swamiji sat, he felt a subtle current of power, like lightning, enter his body. When he opened his eyes, Thakur's gaze was wet with tears.

In a voice tender with infinite affection, Thakur had said, 'Today, I have given you everything and become a *fakir*. You will do great work in this world with this power. And when your work is done, you will return to your source.'

Swamiji knew that was the beginning of the end. Still, fifteen years had passed, and it felt like only yesterday. Thakur lived on—in consciousness, in dreams, in waking hours, in every breath of the ashram.

7 The devotees used to address Sri Ramakrishna as 'Thakur'

In the temple room, Shashi Maharaj[8] sat at the altar. On one side sat Shivananda[9]. Seeing Swamiji, he gestured that he come forward. He placed a seat beside his own.

Swamiji joined. The room held a deep stillness. Young monks sat cross-legged on rugs, their shaven heads bowed. A few had pulled shawls over their heads against the chill.

Five oil lamps were lit. One monk tuned the *mridanga*, two others readied the harmonium and *kartal*. Shashi Maharaj rose. The music swelled. The *arati* began.

The fivefold flame danced in front of Ramakrishna's portrait. Reverence flowed like a tide. With varied offerings, Shashi waved the lights. Last came the *chamara*. He laid it gently on the tray, and silence fell. Then, he took up the conch and blew it thrice. The sound echoed, ancient and profound.

Prostrating full-length, he then retreated to a corner and sat in deep meditation. The others followed, their bodies still, their minds absorbed.

After a while, Shivananda whispered, 'Victory to Thakur. Victory to the Mother.'

The spell broke. The monks stirred. Swamiji turned to Shivananda.

'Come, let's have some tea.'

Shivananda smiled. 'Here, in the prayer room?'

'What's the harm?' Swamiji's eyes twinkled. 'Our Guru never forbade anything.'

'That's for you,' said Shivananda, 'not for everyone.'

They stepped out onto the veranda. Dawn had not yet broken. But the sky in the east had begun to glow. Dew clung

---

8 Disciple of Sri Ramakrishna

9 Disciple of Sri Ramakrishna

to every leaf and blade. The *karabi* tree was heavy with white blossoms. A monk brought tea.

'This habit,' said Swamiji, taking a cup, 'began at the Baranagar Math. We rarely had proper meals; tea was our comfort. If someone came to visit, we offered tea.'

Three glasses steamed before them. Swamiji glanced at them and said, 'We're two. Who's the third for?'

'For me,' said Saradananda, dragging a chair under his bulky shawl.

Swamiji took a sip. 'There's one thing that won't let me rest—permanent arrangements for Holy Mother[10].'

Shivananda recalled a letter from Swamiji: *'First and foremost, I must make a place for Mother. If that happens, I shall worry no more. The land must be large. A clay house will do now. Later, we'll build better. No fear.'*

Before Shivananda could respond, Saradananda said, 'We're all concerned about Holy Mother. Every time she comes from Kamarpukur or Jayrambati, she has to stay in someone's home or in a rented house. Devotees keep coming. The small space is too much for her.'

Shivananda said, 'Now that Naren is here, there's nothing to worry about. He'll make it happen.'

Swamiji said nothing. He knew they relied on him for everything. But he didn't like to speak anymore. Yet, sometimes he had to, if only to lighten the heart.

'I think,' he said softly, 'I shall go see Holy Mother today or tomorrow. The last time I saw her was before I left to go abroad.'

Shivananda, hesitatingly but gently, said, 'When you go to

10 Sri Sarada Devi

Simla, do visit your mother, the one who bore you.'

At once, a shadow of deep sorrow passed over Swamiji's face, thinking of his greatest vulnerability in life—his mother, Bhubaneshwari Devi. He had done so little for her as a son. That silent wound had followed him through all lands, near and far, gnawing at his heart with its quiet ache. Years ago, he had written to his friend, the Diwan of Junagadh State, Shri Haridas Viharidas Desai:

> Dear Diwanji Saheb,
>
> I received your letter a few days ago. I was so glad to learn you visited my sorrowful mother and younger brothers. You have touched the tenderest chord of my heart. Please know, I am no heartless brute. In this vast world, if there is one soul I have loved most dearly, it is my mother.

Swamiji's tenderness for his mother was no secret to anyone. Sensing the growing heaviness, Saradananda swiftly changed the subject. 'Will Nivedita, MacLeod, and Dhira Mata be coming to Calcutta?' he asked.

Swamiji needed no explanation for the sudden mention of his foreign disciples. His life had become a crucifixion—each day marked by a fresh pang. The pain had turned his spirit to stone. His senses, once vivid, had now been dulled. A weariness settled in his bones. The vigour of body and mind was fading. Perhaps, he thought, these were signs of the impending farewell. Then suddenly, he realised Saradananda had asked something.

'You said something?' he asked softly.

Saradananda, sensing his purpose was fulfilled, said, 'Come, let me show you the new trees we've planted on the monastery grounds. Let me call Sadananda; he said he would join us.'

Even before he could call, Sadananda appeared. 'Let's go, Swamiji,' he said.

The four stepped outside. Their eyes were drawn eastward. A soft crimson light was spreading gently across the Ganga that flowed past the eastern border of the monastery. A few tall trees stood silhouetted in deep green, their gaps revealing slices of blue sky. The sun was slowly rising behind them. No darkness remained. Across the river, the fog still clung like a dream, veiling forms in gentle haze. The shadows that had nestled in corners were slowly melting into the advancing light. Small gardens flanked the path, bursting with blooms.

'Swamiji, Swamiji....'

Swamiji turned at the unexpected call. A boy of fourteen or fifteen came running and flung himself at Swamiji's feet. Swamiji recognised him at once; it was Hari, the cook's son, sweet-natured and affectionate. Swamiji had a great fondness for him. Taking his hand, he raised the boy gently.

'What are you doing here?' he asked with warmth.

Before Hari could reply, Sadananda said, 'He looks after all the cows and goats now.'

Swamiji's gaze followed westward. A few cows grazed at a distance.

'What do you feed them?' he asked.

'They eat grass,' Hari replied promptly.

'That's why your cows are so lean. Grass alone won't do. Give them leftover rice water from the kitchen, and some oil-cake. Only then will they grow strong and give more milk. Abroad, I've seen cows as big as little elephants.'

Saradananda laughed, 'Then take charge of the cowshed!'

Swamiji smiled, finding mirth in the suggestion. Glancing sideways at Saradananda, he said, 'Narendranath Dutta fears nothing. Just as I can interpret the Vedas and Vedanta, I can feed cattle too.'

Hari burst out laughing. 'If you go to feed them, they'll butt you!'

Swamiji laughed with him. 'Fine, I'll feed them tomorrow morning. Let's see how fierce these cows really are.' But he stopped mid-sentence, his eyes catching something odd.

'Why did you shave your head, Hari?'

Hari looked up solemnly. 'I want to be a monk like you.'

Sadananda said, 'If your father hears that, he'll thrash you good! Go, tend the cows for now. You can renounce later.'

As Hari ran off, something stirred in Swamiji. Running a hand through his own hair, he said, 'My hair's grown quite long too. That's one trouble with foreign lands. You never get a proper haircut. Half the barbers wouldn't even touch my head; they called me a Black man. I had to learn to cut it myself.'

'The barber should be here later in the day,' Sadananda replied.

They walked on. To the south, green fields spread out, scattered with young saplings. Further southeast stood neat rows of grafted mango trees, still young, but in another year or two, they would bear fruit. Banana plants stood further down, some heavy with hanging bunches. On the northern side, a fence enclosed a flower garden brimming with jasmine vines, clusters of bell flowers, mingling with foreign blooms: *tagar, kamini, konakchampa*. Creepers of *malati* wrapped the fence like garlands.

In one spot, cabbages were being grown; their wide green leaves spread like lotus pads, with tight heads nestled in the centre. Swamiji stooped and brushed a hand over one.

'Whose handiwork is this?' he asked.

Shivananda replied, 'All this—fruit, flowers, vegetables—you see around is the work of old Gopal Dada (Swami Adbhutananda), who is older even than Ramakrishna. Truly, were it not for him, the monks here would have survived on rice alone. There wouldn't be even a single vegetable dish with it.'

Swamiji said nothing. He knew the hardships his brothers had borne with a smiling face.

They walked on. The Ganga River lapped loudly at the shore. In many places, the earth had caved in and the bank was eroding. Swamiji paused, watching. In one spot, the water had eaten far into the land. A frown touched his brow.

Saradananda said, 'I've told Hari (Hariprasanna, later Swami Vijnanananda) to begin the embankment work as soon as possible. The trouble is money. What we've managed to raise will first go to the northern side, where the buildings and temple stand. This part will have to wait.'

Swamiji said nothing. There was still so much to be done, and there was the perpetual need for funds. People in this country speak endlessly of religion, but their hands don't open easily. The real help had come from abroad. They had given freely—Miss MacLeod of America, Mrs Sara Bull, Miss Henrietta Müller of Europe. The land of Belur Math was purchased with their funds. He had heard the criticism. He was aware of all the whisperings. But he gave no heed. He knew, good work brings its own thorns. Many speak, but only a few act. If one listens to every word, nothing can ever be accomplished.

The monastery bell rang for breakfast.

Saradananda smiled, 'Come, let's see what special dish has been made for Naren today.'

A Day Shrouded in Grief

Breakfast had ended—puffed rice, curried cabbage, and sugar-drop sweets. Everyone had eaten with quiet contentment. Swamiji, ever careful due to his diabetes, did not touch the sweets. But it was *prasad*, the Lord's offering; he gently touched a single sugar-drop to his forehead and then accepted it.

Seated beside him was Rakhal Maharaj—Swami Brahmananda, the first president of the Ramakrishna Mission—who was known for his fondness for food. Swamiji teased him, 'Son of a *zamindar*, your body was raised on royal feasts!' Rakhal Maharaj retorted, 'I've heard from Mahendra (Mahendranath Dutta, Swamiji's younger brother) that your household never lacked fine meals in your childhood either.'

A shadow passed over Swamiji's face. 'So long as Father lived,' he said softly, 'we knew no hardship. But then he passed away, struck down by the fever of renunciation. He was a lawyer; he earned much and spent even more. Not just on us, but on the entire extended family. He took every burden upon himself. And when he died, he left us a house…and an ocean of debt. No one wanted the debt, but everyone fought for a share of the house.

There were lawsuits, no income, and endless expenses. It was unbearable. I began seeking work to earn a few morsels of rice.

'Those who once considered themselves blessed by the Duttas' kindness turned their faces away. I wandered under the burning sun in search of a job. Often, I had nothing to eat the entire day. Sometimes, I'd spend the afternoon under the shade of the Monument. There was no food at home. I'd lie to my mother that I had been invited to a friend's house, and roam the streets all day on an empty stomach. Those days were cruel…unforgettable.'

He looked at Rakhal Maharaj, his voice low and steady. 'As long as my father lived, that was the only true joy I knew. Since then, only pain. First from the family, then from the world. I've found no peace, neither in my land nor abroad. My body is breaking, and the mind follows it. What began as a mere headache has now grown into a multitude of ailments. This body has become a house of disease.'

Rakhal Maharaj laid a gentle hand on his back. 'You've suffered much, my brother. Now, rest. Just rest for a while, and you'll see, your body and soul will recover.'

A young brahmachari entered. 'Swamiji, the barber has come.'

At once, the cloud lifted from Swamiji's face. 'Ah, good! Let's go! Where's the barber? Let him shave me clean and smart!'

Swami Shivananda called out from behind, 'You're already quite fair, and you've returned from abroad looking even fairer!'

Everyone laughed. Swamiji left the dining hall and walked to the courtyard by the Ganga, behind the house. The morning sun was gentle and warming. He cast off his shawl and then his light cotton shirt. Swami Saradananda was heading towards Belur Bazaar. On seeing Swamiji bare-chested in the chill morning air, he cried out, 'You're sitting like that in this cold?'

Swamiji grinned, pleased. 'In America and England, I've

roamed in -3° or -4°. Belur's cold can do nothing to me. By the way, are you off to the market?'

'Yes. Do you want me to get something for you?'

Swamiji paused. Then, almost wistfully, he said, 'Bring some *Koi* fish. The first time I left for America, Kalipada Haldar in Bombay served me a *Koi* fish dish. I haven't had any since.'

When the Swamiji desires something, it becomes sacred. Saradananda nodded eagerly. 'Don't worry. If I can't find it in Belur, I'll go all the way to Howrah.'

As Swamiji turned to speak, the barber warned, 'Don't move your head, Maharaj! I might cut you!'

The blade passed over his scalp. Tufts of hair fell to the ground. The beard was trimmed. Others had arrived and were queuing up for their turn. When Swamiji's grooming was done, he rose and headed for his bath. At the ghat, the tide had just come in. The Ganga shimmered, brimming to both banks in saffron-tinted swells. People crossed to the far side in boats, the oars cutting silver arcs into the golden water.

The stone ghat had a few short steps. At low tide, it would be all mud. Now, Swamiji stood poised above the holy river.

How tender, how sacred was the touch of the Ganga! For over a decade, he had seen the waters of countless rivers and oceans across the world, but none like this. No other water body held this centuries-old sanctity, this deep spiritual faith. Wherever he went, he carried with him a small pot of Ganga water.

Eyes closed, he stood in silence, then descended. In just five steps, the water rose to his chest. He bowed low, submerged himself once, twice, thrice. Each dip sent a shiver through his body, cool and purifying. Then, chanting the *Surya mantra*, he rose and slowly walked back up the steps.

As he turned towards the house, he noticed the barber

sweeping Swamiji's shorn hair into a heap.

'What are you doing?' Swamiji asked.

'Throwing away your cut hair,' the barber replied, dusting off his shawl.

'You threw it away?' Swamiji said, arching his brows.

'But what good is cut hair?' the barber asked, puzzled.

Swamiji gazed at him for a long moment, eyes narrowing. 'One day, people will clamour for a lock of Vivekananda's hair. Had you kept it, you could have sold it for a good price.'

The barber laughed. What strange things this holy man said! That people would one day fight over his discarded hair!

Swamiji changed into fresh clothes and returned to his room. During his absence, Sadananda had arranged all his letters neatly on the table. No matter how busy he was, Swamiji never neglected his correspondence. At least one letter each day, always.

He glanced at the pile. 'Any important ones, Sadananda?'

Sadananda had just returned after hanging Swamiji's wet clothes on the veranda. He stood silently for a moment, head bowed. Something was clearly weighing on him.

Swamiji's voice softened. 'What is it, Saradananda?'

'A letter has come from Mayavati,' he replied, still looking down.

'From Mayavati?' Swamiji repeated, his heart tightening. He hadn't received any letters from there in months, not that he'd expected any. For weeks, he'd had no fixed address, wandering like a nomad. He looked up slowly.

Sadananda raised his gaze and said, almost in a whisper, 'Mr Sevier is no more.'

Swamiji was stunned. The grief struck him like a thunderclap. 'Mr Sevier is… dead?'

'Yes,' Sadananda murmured. 'He fell ill suddenly. There

was no doctor in Mayavati. They had planned to take him to Almora...but he wouldn't go. He passed away at the ashram. Everyone performed the cremation according to Hindu rites. Mrs Sevier wrote to you, but the letter didn't reach in time.'

Swamiji was silent, paralysed by sorrow. He could not grasp that James Henry Sevier was gone. He recalled their first meeting in England, Mr Sevier and his wife, Charlotte Elizabeth. They were devout seekers, weary from the endless chase for spiritual truth across the West. One day, they heard of an Indian yogi lecturing in London. Driven by curiosity, they went to listen, and were captivated.

Swamiji's luminous presence, his radiant soul, had kindled something deep within them. His wisdom dispelled the fog of confusion they had long wandered in. That very day, he addressed Mrs Sevier as 'Mother'. From that moment, she became 'Mother' to all.

It was with them he had shared his dream—an ashram in the Himalayas, nestled among snow-capped peaks, where seekers could live in silence, devoted to meditation and service. 'Will you come to India?' he had asked. 'I wish to build a monastery devoted to *dhyana* and *karma*, where disciples from both East and West may live together and grow into true workers. Let the Eastern disciples go West and spread Vedanta; let the Western disciples stay in India and serve her soul.'

The Seviers had answered, 'Yes'. They came. And in a hidden grove, 50 kms from Almora, they discovered Mayavati—silent, shadowed by forest, ringed with peaks. On 19 March 1899, Sri Ramakrishna's birth anniversary, while Belur celebrated the spring bloom, Swamiji's dream took flight in the flowering heights of *Devabhumi*.

Built with the Seviers' support, the Advaita Ashram rose in

that wilderness. Abandoning the comforts of Europe, they chose this hardship as their path. They wore humble robes, worked with their hands, tended gardens, and carved out roads. They made Swamiji's vision real.

And now, one of them was gone.

Shivananda entered the room. Seeing the ashen grief on Swamiji's face, he asked gently, 'What has happened?'

As if rising from a trance, Swamiji looked up and said, 'Mr Sevier gave his life to India, to me, and I couldn't even be there at the end.'

Shivananda rested a comforting hand on his shoulder. 'I've written to Mother. Swarupananda and Virajananda are there. Everything has been taken care of.'

Swamiji sighed, long and heavy. 'I must go to Mayavati. Sadananda, write to Mother. Once we hear back, we'll fix the date of our journey.'

Shivananda added, 'I'll come with you. So will Sadananda. We'll take the train to Kathgodam. From there, it's 104 kms on horseback or *dandy* (a type of chair that can be carried by two porters). It is a rugged, mountainous path, but we'll manage.'

Sadananda said nothing. Where the Guru goes, the disciple follows.

On the Road to Mayavati

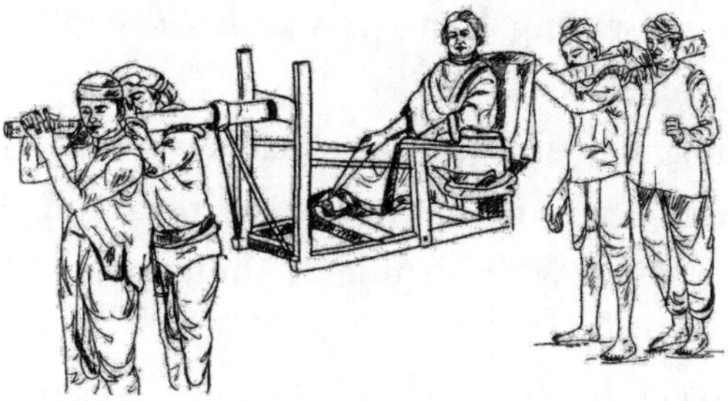

When Swamiji arrived at Kathgodam railway station, the night had nearly ebbed, and dawn hovered near. A light mist veiled the air, and a wind as cold as snow whispered across the platform. The train's journey ended here. It was a small station, just a single platform with a wooden cabin on one side, and no sign of any habitation nearby.

Before leaving Belur, a telegram had been sent to Sister Nivedita. Her reply was clear: Swamiji must inform her at least eight days in advance of his arrival at Mayavati. He chose 27 December for departure, planning to reach by 29 December. The message was dispatched accordingly.

Sadananda was worried. What if the telegram failed to reach in time? Swamiji, however, showed no concern. If no one came from Mayavati, he assured them, he would go to Almora and stay with his friend Badridas.

Three men disembarked from the train, burdened with no small amount of luggage. There was no rush; the train would halt there till night. After the two-day journey, they were slightly weary. The cold bit sharply. Swamiji glanced around. The platform lay empty. The last of the passengers had long departed. Suddenly, he noticed someone striding swiftly towards them from the distance—broad frame, overcoat reaching the heels, cap pulled low. The face was hard to see. But as the man drew near, there was no mistaking him—it was his disciple, Kalikrishna (Swami Virajananda).

Kalikrishna fell full prostrate at Swamiji's feet on the dusty platform. Then, rising, he bowed to Swami Shivananda. Swamiji's face lit up with a smile. 'I thought no one would be able to come,' he said.

With some embarrassment, Kalikrishna replied, 'We received your telegram three days ago. Snow has begun to fall in the hills. The roads are deserted. After much effort, I managed to gather a few porters and set off. We arrived at midnight.'

Swamiji gently patted his disciple on the back. 'Ah, now that is what I call my *chela* (disciple).'

Swami Shivananda asked, 'Where is everyone else?'

'Sleeping in a room behind the station. It's a two-day walk. One of them has fever.'

Swamiji pondered for a moment. 'Then let them rest today. We'll set off in the morning.'

Kalikrishna bowed. He, too, needed rest. 'Come, Swamiji. I've arranged a place for you to stay.'

After breakfast, Swamiji sank into a rickety chair on the veranda. He had not slept on the train. His body ached. Kalikrishna and Sadananda looked at him with concern.

Kalikrishna ventured, 'How do you feel now?'

Swamiji stared at him for a moment. Then, with a strange detachment, he said, 'I've lost the very sense of good or bad. Now I long only for peace and rest. No work seems appealing anymore. If I could spend the few days I have left in the seclusion of the Himalayas….'

Neither dared to speak. Swami Shivananda stood nearby, his *gurubhai*, nine years his elder. In a firm voice, he said, 'Enough of such idle thoughts. So much remains to be done. Thakur entrusted all his work to you. If you remain silent, who will tell the world of Him?'

Swamiji's eyes flared in an instant. He exclaimed, with sudden intensity, 'Who am I to speak of Him? If He wished, He could raise a hundred Vivekanandas!'

To dispel the storm, Shivananda changed the subject. 'Kalikrishna, what time do we set out tomorrow?'

'As early as possible,' Kalikrishna answered. 'We've arranged a dandy for Swamiji, and horses for the rest of us. One extra for the luggage.'

Sadananda laughed. 'You arranged all that in one day? I couldn't have done it!'

A quiet emotion lit Kalikrishna's face. Lost in devotion, he murmured, 'All by the grace of Thakur Sri Ramakrishna and Guru Maharaj's blessings.'

30 December

Morning passed in preparations. Swamiji, cheerful again, rode the dandy. Four porters hoisted it upon their shoulders. The others rode beside him on horseback—Shivananda, Sadananda, Kalikrishna. The procession moved slowly. The first stretch was level, then the hills began. The climb was gentle, but steady.

Swamiji turned to Shivananda, teasing, 'Tarakda, why don't you try the dandy? I can walk. After Thakur left his body, I wandered all of India on foot.'

Shivananda replied gravely, 'Old rice may taste better, but

you're no longer young. Asthma, diabetes, renal issues, stomach ailments, eye problems, toothache—you name it.'

Laughing, Swamiji said, 'And more! I never even noticed when all these diseases made a home in me. But I've never worried about illness, then or now.' There was a smile on his lips, but it held a quiet weight.

Shivananda knew the argument was futile. Silence was wisdom.

They passed a small mountain village. The porters, swathed in thick wool, caps on heads, marched with strength. Their leader, a stocky fellow with a long stick, kept up a steady stream of jokes, which Swamiji merrily answered.

They marched for three hours. At the roadside, they came upon a teashop, a few wooden huts, and hill folk milling around. Kalikrishna suggested a rest. A sign nearby read: Bhimtal. Narrow mountain paths, barely 10 ft wide, ran beside precipitous gorges. Wind rushed through tall trees, its voice a wild, haunting song.

By afternoon, they reached a roadside inn. A dak bungalow stood nearby, ready for the night. The porters rested and began cooking. Swamiji was in pain. But more than his own suffering, his thoughts turned to the Mayavati Ashram. Mr Sevier was gone. What if Madame Sevier closed it all and returned home? The entire institution had been built on their funds. He could not think long; nowadays, even brief thoughts exhausted him. Thakur was his only refuge. And there was another—She, who watched unseen, always. After Mayavati, he would go to Her.

31 December 1900

The final day of the year. The group set off in the morning. The sun peered out, but the cold had deepened. Swamiji joked as they went, 'Kalikrishna, Sadananda, if you were in England or America on a day like today, you'd see such joy and celebration! We don't have such a New Year's spirit. Those people live fully. We, on the other hand, neither know how to enjoy nor how to renounce.'

He stopped mid-sentence. Fog was thickening. The mountains ahead vanished in a veil of mist. Kalikrishna's face clouded with concern. Sadananda rode beside him. Though younger, their bond was strong.

In a low voice, Kalikrishna said, 'I think a storm's coming. If Swamiji were well, I wouldn't worry so much. I don't know what to do....'

Sadananda too felt the unease. Mountain storms were not to be trifled with. Shivananda's horse acted up. He controlled it with effort. They'd barely covered 4 kms. The next dak bungalow lay 15 kms ahead.

Rain began, light but needle-sharp. Kalikrishna had anticipated it and brought raincoats. Soon, snow began to fall.

The slope turned white. The porters stepped carefully; one slip could send them tumbling into the abyss.

Swamiji was disheartened. For a man of his strength to be carried on shoulders on a dandy was shameful. Yet he kept speaking, joking, hoping to ease the others' hardship.

The porter-chief, Chamanlal, middle-aged but full of spirit, occasionally chanted verses from the *Chandi*[11], mostly mispronounced, but Swamiji enjoyed it nonetheless, correcting him now and then.

'Chamanbhai,' he said suddenly, 'you are a scholar. I shall call you *Panditji*.'

Panditji beamed with delight.

'Who's at home?' Swamiji asked, turning towards him.

---

11 A Holy Book

'No one, Maharaj. Four times, I married. Four times, my wives died.'

Swamiji shook his head. 'Very sad. But marry again. This time, your wife will live.'

Chamanlal's face turned wistful. 'There is a girl I like, in the next village.'

'Then why the delay? Marry her,' Swamiji encouraged.

'How can I, Maharaj? Her father wants twenty rupees as dowry.'

Swamiji, with mock annoyance, said, 'That's all? I'll give you the money. Go, marry her!'

Chamanlal grinned so widely he could barely speak. He stretched out his hand in reverence and touched Swamiji's feet.

Rain thickened and the snow fell steadily. Kalikrishna lagged behind at times. He had already warned Swamiji that they must not stop before reaching the next bungalow. The road was long. They'd rest only at the destination.

They were midway now. The downpour eased. Water streamed down the mountain slopes, washing over the path. A village appeared ahead, with mostly wooden homes. A small tea stall stood by the road. The porters halted.

'Maharaj ji, we are drenched. Let us have some tea and a smoke.'

Swamiji's heart ached for them. Through snow and storm, these men had endured much. They still had a long road ahead. No matter what Kalikrishna said, they needed rest.

'Go. Drink tea,' he said. 'I'll pay.'

They lowered the dandy. Swamiji's legs ached too. He stepped into the stall—a tiny place, with a smaller inner room, crammed with goods. No one imagined then that this would be their shelter for the night.

After some time, Kalikrishna arrived. The porters were immersed in loud chatter. He began scolding them. 'We can't sit here! There's a long way to go.'

But once the porters sat, they were slow to rise. Evening had crept close and the rain had resumed. They got ready to move.

'Can we still go?' asked Shivananda.

Kalakrishna, now dejected, replied, 'No. It'll be dark soon. Snow will fall. We won't see a step ahead. We must spend the night here somehow.'

Swamiji had already surveyed the space. There was a medium-sized room adjoining the shop, with a sagging roof, a corner heaped with firewood, kitchen grime untouched for years, and a foul stench. But there was no choice. They would stay. There were no pillows, no bedding, and no blankets. A small corner was cleared for Swamiji to lie down.

He was suffering. And in his pain, his anger fell on Shivananda. 'You fools!' he shouted. 'If you feared snowfall, why did you bring me this way? Kalikrishna is young, but you, Tarakda, are old! You could've taken me to Almora. And you, Kalikrishna, you forced me to come to Mayavati. Now see what I suffer!'

Both men knew that when Swamiji raged, silence was safest.

When his anger ebbed, Kalikrishna quietly said, 'It's your fault. I warned you, not to let the porters stop. I knew this would happen. Because of their delay, we couldn't reach the bungalow.'

Hearing Kalikrishna's words, Swamiji fell silent for a while. Then, realising his mistake, he spoke with gentle affection, 'Ah, what's done is done. I scolded you; don't take it to heart. A father scolds both son and disciple. Tell me, what else can be done? Let's make arrangements to pass the night as best as we can.'

They ate coarse *rotis* and potato curry made by the shopkeeper, then spread cloths on the floor and stretched out their weary bodies. Cold wind seeped in through the broken door, so Shivananda leaned his back against it. Even so, the cold was relentless. Amid laughter and light-hearted chatter, the final night of the century quietly passed.

The next day was 1 January 1901. Snow had fallen through the night and now lay thick upon the roads. Everywhere their eyes turned, it seemed as though the world had been gently brushed with white paint. A pale golden light filtered through, and a blanket of ethereal beauty lay over the land.

Their journey resumed. By evening, they reached the Maurnalla dak bungalow. The arrangements were far better this time. Sadananda had arrived ahead of them to ensure Swamiji's comfort.

Swamiji, recalling the previous night's experience, joked, 'Poor shopkeeper, our endless stories kept him up all night! He must've feared we'd return again tonight.'

The journey resumed on the fourth morning. No fresh snow had fallen; what had been there had melted. After covering 33 kms, they reached the Dhunaghat dak bungalow. All day, Swamiji had sat in the dandy, and now his waist and back ached. A short distance before the bungalow, he got down and said, 'Kalikrishna, let's walk the rest of the way.'

They had gone barely half a kilometre when Swamiji stopped. His chest rose and fell heavily, breath coming in great gasps. He said with quiet anguish, 'You see, once I could walk 40 kms without a thought. Now look at me, how weak I've grown. I can't even manage this little stretch. It pains me.'

Kalikrishna, too, could sense Swamiji's failing strength, though he tried to encourage him. 'This mountain road wears on everyone,' he said.

A wistful smile touched the corner of Swamiji's lips. His

gaze drifted towards the snow-covered peaks ahead, distant and forlorn. To Kalikrishna, it felt as though Swamiji was peering beyond them—into another world, into the realm that lies across the veil.

Swamiji began to speak softly, as though to himself. 'I've come to the final edge of life. This is how it is in the end. Nothing feels like mine anymore. Everything seems to belong to the great universe. There's nothing left to seek or to give, only the waiting remains… for the last farewell.'

Kalikrishna said nothing. A solemn stillness fell over him. It seemed to him that such great souls perhaps do glimpse their own destinies, as though they can see beyond the ordinary horizon of men.

Mayavati

For several hours now, Swamiji had been seated in the dandy. This was the fifth day since they had left Kathgodam. In these past days, rain, snowfall, and the strain of trudging mountain paths had left him utterly weary. But today, the weather had turned. Sunlight streamed across the world, golden and gleaming. It danced upon the tree branches and leaves, and upon the crests of distant peaks. The sky was scattered with patches of white clouds. On either side of the path, the hills were cloaked in deep green. A few streams flowed gently down the slopes. The road was nearly deserted; scarcely a soul was seen.

Swamiji felt light of heart. He hummed softly to himself:

Return, O mind, to your own abode.
Why wander needlessly, draped in the garb of a stranger,
In this foreign land of illusion?

He remembered that the first time he met Sri Ramakrishna at Dakshineswar, he had sung this very song. As he sang, the Master had been overcome, lost in divine ecstasy. When the song ended, Sri Ramakrishna had risen, taken his hand, and led him to the northern veranda. 'Why have you come so late?' he had said. 'I have waited long for you.'

Swamiji hadn't understood him then. But over time, he had come to realise—the Master was the very embodiment of divinity. Everything he had, his power and purpose, was a gift from Sri Ramakrishna. Even that momentous journey to America, where he had raised the banner of India high, had been through the strength the Master had bestowed.

Lost in thought, he barely noticed the rhythmic clatter of hooves approaching from behind—the gentle trot of a mountain pony, the soft clang of a bell. Soon, Kalikrishna appeared, smiling. Swamiji assumed the others were scattered along the way. The porters, worn from the climb, moved slowly.

'How much farther?' Swamiji asked Chamanlal.

'We are almost there, Maharaj,' came the reply. 'Once we cross that last hill, we will see the monks' retreat.'

A quiet unrest stirred within Swamiji. What would happen to Mayavati in Mr Sevier's absence? They barely had the means to sustain this ashram. Now, all was in the hands of the Divine. He himself had no strength left to do more. If only he could live the rest of his days in solitude, in the heart of the Himalayas! No more work. The burden had grown too heavy. He longed only for peace and rest. However many days remained to him, let them be days of silence.

The mountain path curved gently. The body no longer felt the fatigue. The beauty of the way dissolved all weariness. Hills surrounded them on all sides. Snow shimmered white on a distant peak. Below lay a forest of deodar. Above, the sky was deep, impossibly blue, as though someone had spilled indigo across its canvas.

The porters, slowed by days of travel, trudged on. Swamiji

grew inwardly eager. How long before they reached the ashram? As they rounded a bend, his eyes turned to the right, and in an instant, they came alive. The word slipped from his lips, 'Mayavati.'

Across the gorge, built into the mountainside, lay a stretch of level ground. And there, nestled in its heart, stood the ashram. There were the monks' cottages, a garden of flowers, and all around—deodar, oak, rhododendrons, and trees of every kind. Swamiji gazed, entranced. This was his dream—Mayavati. A deep satisfaction washed over him, the joy of arrival. He felt a yearning to merge into the vastness of nature, into infinite peace.

The ascent was over. Before him, the world opened wide. Kalikrishna galloped up, laughing. 'Can you see it, Swamiji? That is Mayavati.'

Swamiji smiled. 'You have done much.'

Kalikrishna lowered his gaze. 'It is but a beginning, Swamiji. Much remains.'

By the roadside stood a stone, set upon a pedestal. A narrow footpath led down from it into the valley. Kalikrishna pointed. 'By that stone, Mr Sevier's funeral rites were performed.'

'Stop the dandy,' Swamiji said at once.

No one knew why he had suddenly asked them to halt. 'What is it, Swamiji?' Kalikrishna inquired.

His face had clouded like a sky darkened by storm. He simply said, 'I will go down.'

Kalikrishna had thought Swamiji would first go to the ashram to rest, and later return to this spot. But when he expressed his wish, there was no question of dissuasion. He ordered, 'Lower the dandy.'

Swamiji stepped down and, without a word, began walking towards the descending path. Kalikrishna followed quickly. 'Let me come with you, Swamiji.'

The trail snaked along the mountainside. Loose stones underfoot, patches of soft soil crumbling. They moved carefully.

The trees were sparse. The valley spread wide at the bottom. Shrubs grew thick all around. A small stream flowed, clear as glass. At one spot, stones were arranged like an altar.

'This is where Mr Sevier's cremation took place,' Kalikrishna said. 'He had been ill for months. We wanted to take him to Almora, where treatment was better. But he refused to leave Mayavati. He was in great pain. On Sunday, 28 October 1900, he passed into eternal peace. The next morning, we brought his body here to the banks of the Sarada River. It was his wish to be cremated according to Hindu rites. The fire was lit in a wooden pyre as Vedic mantras were chanted.'

A pain twisted through Swamiji's chest. He had felt it, felt Sevier's passing across oceans. He remembered that on his return from the second trip abroad, he had been in Egypt. A strange unease had come over him that evening. And that night, in a dream—or was it something deeper?—he had sensed that Mr Sevier was no more. It was 28 October. He had told no one, but confided to MacLeod that he wished to return to India at once. Back in Belur, he heard the news.

He stood still. Then, bending down, he cupped his hands and lifted water from the river, pouring it over the stone. He gently scattered a few wildflowers over it in a silent offering, a remembrance for one dearly loved. Then he sat down upon a rock.

The scent of leaves filled the air. Not a sound. Only silence—endless and vast.

He remembered those early days. How he had told Mr Sevier: 'I wish to build the Advaita Ashram in the solitude of the Himalayas. Here, where the voice of Vedanta first rang through the heavens, a haven must arise for the study and realisation of the non-dual truth. No rites of superstition, no dependence on others—only self-reliance, pure truth, and deep contemplation. From here, strong and noble souls shall be born.' And it was Sevier who had made that dream a reality. And yet, before it could all be completed, he had departed.

Swamiji had slipped into a space between consciousness and reverie. Kalikrishna's voice brought him back. He raised his head slowly, as though waking from a dream.

'What is it, Kalikrishna?'

'Let us return. Everyone awaits you at the ashram.'

Swamiji stood, shook off the weight of sorrow, and placed a hand on Kalikrishna's shoulder. 'Yes. Let's go.'

They climbed slowly back up. The porters lay resting by the roadside, stretching limbs, snatching what respite they could. Kalikrishna's horse waited nearby. A bell rang from the ashram. Its sound echoed off the mountains.

'What bell is that?' Swamiji asked, suddenly alert.

'The meal bell,' Kalikrishna smiled.

In a moment, Swamiji's face lit up with childlike glee. The man who had just sat in silent mourning now transformed utterly. 'If I go by dandy, we'll be late! There'll be nothing left for us. I'm going ahead. Kalikrishna, come on foot!'

With a leap, he mounted the horse and spurred it forward. The ashram lay ahead, his dream world, awaiting him.

He crossed the mountains. The horse came to a halt in the ashram courtyard. Swamiji looked up; he had arrived in Mayavati, the realm of his meditation. The entire courtyard was adorned with leaves and blossoms, as though anticipating a sacred arrival. A few monks stood there, waiting. The moment they beheld Swamiji, a cry of joy rose from them, and with fervent voices they declared, 'Swamiji has come!'

Within moments, all those in the ashram abandoned their tasks and rushed forward. Many among them had never seen him before, yet through tales often spoken, an image—part saint, part divinity—had formed in their minds.

Swamiji dismounted. The first to step forward was his disciple, Swami Swarupananda. Swamiji held great affection for him; he was as devoted in spirit as he was steadfast in duty. His birth name was Ajayhari Bandopadhyay. Though married, his heart had never taken root in worldly life. Once, he had attended a religious gathering where Swamiji was speaking. So deeply was he captivated by those words that, at the end, he stepped forward and said, 'I wish to renounce the world.'

Swamiji had gazed at him for a moment, then spoke gravely, 'Ajayhari, can you uphold the severe disciplines of *sannyas*? If I ask you to walk into the jaws of a serpent, into the maw of a tiger, into the mouth of a cannon, will you go without a quiver in your heart, knowing death awaits, but unmoved by fear or doubt? You must seek no comfort, no gold, and no desire. You must cleave your heart from all tender bonds, abandon all dreams of name or fame, for such things are but filth. Can you do this? If you can embrace all of this, only then may you take the vows of renunciation. Otherwise, remain in the world and live out your life as you are.'

Ajayhari had not flinched. The fire of his spirit, his resolution, and energy were remarkable. Swamiji initiated him into sannyas and gave him the name Swarupananda.

Now, Swarupananda knelt before Swamiji, touching his feet. One by one, others followed. Swamiji blessed them all, asking gently, 'Is all well with everyone?'

With a serene smile, Swarupananda replied, 'Yes, Swamiji. For the past two days, we have been awaiting your arrival. We felt your hardship on the journey, ceaseless snow, relentless rain....'

Swamiji nodded. 'The fury of nature, there was no choice.' He spoke, but his gaze drifted elsewhere.

Perhaps Swarupananda sensed for whom his Master's heart was restless. He said softly, 'Come inside, Swamiji. Mother is waiting.'

They passed through the veranda into a spacious room with wooden walls, shrouded in curtains. A fireplace glowed in one corner. The moment Swamiji stepped in, he saw Madame Sevier, a vision of quiet maternal grace. Her face calm, her eyes deep with peace. No trace of sorrow or despair. At once, Swamiji felt that she had accepted the passing of Mr Sevier with serene fortitude. The long road travelled in anxiety and dread found a moment's peace.

He approached slowly and took both her hands in his. And gently he spoke, 'Mr Sevier... and Goodwin[12]... both are gone. They've taken with them half my heart.'

Madame Sevier showed no outward agitation. The sorrow she had locked away in her soul—never once did she let it rise. But now, standing before Swamiji, who was not just her Guru, but her very God, she could not hold it back. Tears streamed down her cheeks.

Swamiji knew that within those tears of sorrow lay a balm of peace.

After a few quiet moments, Madame regained herself and, a bit embarrassed, asked, 'Was your journey very difficult, Swamiji?'

'Oh, that was nothing. I am simply happy I could come,' Swamiji replied, his voice warm with emotion.

12 He was the stenographer of Swamiji.

The sound of many voices could be heard outside. The others had arrived. Swarupananda, mindful of all things as the ashram's head, said, 'It has been a long journey for many. Food is ready. Let us eat first. We can speak afterwards.'

Madame's face lit up, a flicker of joy dancing in her eyes. 'Come then! If we delay, the food will get cold.'

To lift the lingering pall of sorrow, Swamiji spread a smile across his face and said, 'Come, come, everyone! Five days of cold food on the road have left even my bones frozen. Swami Shivananda, come along. Sadananda, Kali, you too. After we eat, we'll sit and talk at length.'

Swarupananda added, 'We've arranged a room for you upstairs. We can talk there.'

A large chamber was prepared upstairs for Swamiji. But as he stepped inside, he felt the air strike colder than below. The room was nearly bare, except for a bed. He walked to the window and drew aside the heavy curtain. Before him spread the vast expanse of the sky. Above, lay coiled masses of white and blue clouds, the infinite form of the cosmic Mother.

In an instant, Swamiji was absorbed in still meditation.

He felt it then; this sacred Himalayan land was the perfect field for the practice of Advaita. These snow-covered, shining peaks were the purest manifestation of the formless Brahman. Here was a realm for divine contemplation.

'With a thousand peaks and arms
You speak in silence—
The ancient assurance of the seers.
Hear it, O world,
I have known — I have known!'

Entranced by the majesty of the Himalayas, Swamiji could not remain long in the upstairs room. The cold was unbearable. As night fell, his asthma worsened. He had to descend. He rested by the warmth of the fireplace, and spoke of all the tales of India and of distant lands. The gift of storytelling he possessed was magical. All who listened, listened spellbound.

So much snow lay around, none could step outside. Days passed within the shelter of walls. In the midst of it all, a feast was held one day. Virajananda brought a block of ice from the lake.

Swamiji asked, 'What will you do with that?'

'Ice cream.'

'Truly?' Swamiji's face lit up like a child's. 'Make it well, then! Let it be like real ice cream.'

Sadananda said, 'Will you eat ice cream, Swamiji?'

'Why not? What's wrong with that?'

'You'll catch a cold.'

Swamiji thought for a moment. 'Then heat it up!'

Madame Sevier, standing nearby, smiled gently. 'That would be best. Swamiji will have hot ice cream.'

That night, seated by his bed, Swamiji wrote a letter to Dhira Mata, the gentle Miss Sara Bull, wife of Norway's great violinist Ole Bull:

> This ashram at Mayavati is beautiful. Those who dwell here have lovingly made it even more so. The grounds stretch across several acres—all a gift from Mr and Mrs Sevier. Today I walked a long way through the snow to survey the land. The surroundings are exquisite, lovely paths, fruit gardens, and everything is a feast for the eyes. In Calcutta, my asthma was troubling me greatly. Here in the Himalayas, I feel well. The two days of cold on the way here even helped. Are you soon

departing for America? If not, I hope to meet you in London within three months. Everyone here sends you love.

Ever your loving child,

Vivekananda

Several days passed. That morning, the sun glinted and gleamed in a sky without blemish. After breakfast, Swami Swarupananda asked gently, 'Swamiji, would you like to go somewhere today?'

At once, a gleam of delight lit up the Master's face. Though his body ached and his strength was failing, his spirit had never taken well to confinement. 'Where would you take me?' he asked, eager as a child.

'Not far,' replied Swarupananda. 'There's a place atop a hill. From there, the view of the Himalayas is breathtaking. Many go there to meditate. The locals call it Dharmagarh.'

'Let us go then!' Swamiji said, his eyes shining. 'We shall spend the whole day at Dharmagarh.'

Madame Sevier had been suffering from severe leg pain for two days. Yet, she knew that to walk by the Master's side was no ordinary journey; it was to move in the light of something beyond the self. He animated every path and filled every mile with presence. She said firmly, 'I will go.'

Swarupananda and Kalikrishna hesitated. 'Will you be able, Mother?'

Her voice rang with certainty, 'Swamiji will be there. I am not afraid. I shall reach.'

Swamiji strongly believed that no power in this world surpassed the power of the soul. With that alone, even the impossible could be overcome. Had he not seen pilgrims to Amarnath, some even without feet, leaning on staves, ascend to the snowy shrine with indomitable spirit? He said gently, 'Yes, Mother, you shall come. We are all with you. There will be no trouble.'

Dharmagarh lay 2.5 kms from the Mayavati Ashram. They set off together. The path was steep, winding along the hillside, more of a suggestion than a trail. Uneven stones lay scattered underfoot. At every step, they had to choose their footing carefully. Pines, deodars, oaks, and countless nameless trees lined the way. At times, the forest thinned, with bare slopes marked by landslides and fallen branches. Behind the brush, rivulets tumbled down the mountain; their flowing music sounded like a subtle melody in the symphony of nature. Something deep stirred in the heart in response to that sound.

Two young brahmacharis walked ahead, tapping the ground with their staffs. The sound rang clear through the still air, sending wild animals scurrying away.

Midway through the climb, Madame Sevier faltered. Her leg pain became unbearable. She leaned against a large stone and said, 'You go ahead. I will rest here.'

Swamiji paused, then walked to her side and took her hand. 'Come,' he said, 'you are not broken.'

Something within her shifted at the gentle touch. The pain, the fatigue, all seemed to melt away. It was not the hand of man, but the hand of the divine upon the heart of a devotee. The touch of the Swami's right hand—vast, compassionate, powerful—had brushed against her. It was the greatest blessing of the earthly realm. She thought of receiving it not with gratitude, but as a prayerful surrender. Let all that is his, all that is best in him, be worthy of acceptance.

Slowly, she stood. 'Come, Swamiji. I will manage.'

A smile dawned on his lips. 'I knew you would.'

Wildflowers bloomed by the roadside. One of the companions picked a blossom and offered it to the Master. Swamiji took it with joy, humming to himself as he walked. The path twisted and turned. Wherever the eye wandered, the green garment of the mountains spread in endless folds. Now and then they paused for breath. Then onward again.

At last, they reached the summit.

Before them spread a wide plateau. At the centre stood a stone platform with a simple tin canopy above. Someone laid down a mat.

'Please be seated, Swamiji.'

With wonder-lit eyes, Swamiji gazed northward. In the distance, stretching across the sky, stood the mighty snow-veiled peaks of the Himalayas—Panchachuli, Nanda Devi, Kamet, Nilkanth, Nandakot—resembling still, white-robed goddesses in silent meditation. The deep blue sky poured its radiance upon them. Swamiji sat unmoving for a long time, immersed in an otherworldly joy, as though he had given himself, wholly and without remainder, into the Infinite.

Turning at last to the young brahmacharis beside him, he spoke softly, with deep feeling, 'If you truly wish to know God, sit before these mountains and meditate on the Vast. Leave behind the cities, the crowds. Sleep beneath this sky. Here, the beauty of the Lord will reveal itself. Everywhere you look, the Infinite has laid His seat. The hand of the Creator has passed over all this. Victory be unto Him.'

The air pulsed with presence. The whole morning passed in a quiet ecstasy, as though they had discovered themselves anew. But as noon wore on, clouds began to gather on the horizon.

Swarupananda said, 'We must go, Swamiji. If rain starts on this mountain path, it will be hard to descend.'

Reluctantly, Swamiji stood. Placing a hand on Swarupananda's shoulder, he said, 'If only we could build an ashram here, where the eternal flame of truth might burn day and night, consuming every superstition and delusion in the fire of knowledge. It would be a place where the great truth could resound throughout the world: God alone is real. Apart from God, nothing exists.'

No one spoke. Swamiji now seemed like a star from a distant realm—visible, perhaps even near, but beyond touch or grasp.

Silence surrounded them. And then, softly, Swamiji began to sing to himself:

Tujhse humne dil ko lagaya, jo kuch hai sab tuhi hai.
Ek tujhko apna paaya, jo kuch hai sab tuhi hai.
Dil ka makaan sabki maki tu, kaunsa dil hai jismein nahi tu,
Har ek dil mein tune samaya, jo kuch hai so tuhi hai.

To You alone I gave my heart—for all that is, is You alone.
You are the one I made my own—for all that is, is You alone.
The heart's abode—You dwell in all—Is there a heart where
You are not? In every heart, You are contained—all that is,
is You alone.

The Sanctum of a Dream

The drawing room of the monastery house was quiet. Inside, Swamiji sat, surrounded by Brahmananda, Saradananda, Vigyanananda, Niranjanananda, and a few others scattered about the room.

It had been five days since Swamiji and Sadananda returned to Calcutta from Mayavati. Swami Shivananda had remained behind in Uttar Pradesh to preach the word of the Master and collect funds for the monastery.

Since morning, Swamiji had not felt well. His feet were swollen, making walking painful. He had bouts of breathlessness. Of late, he had grown increasingly weary of his failing health. A restlessness had crept into him, a discomfort that would not leave. And so, after the evening arati, he had summoned everyone downstairs to the drawing room.

Two hurricane lamps flickered in the room, casting a soft glow. Outside, a dense darkness pressed close. Somewhere nearby, a jackal cried. In this leafy neighbourhood, jackals could be seen even in daylight. Brahmananda felt an uneasy chill. His bond with Swamiji stretched back to their boyhood. At twelve, he had met Naren as a student of Calcutta's Training Academy. Though Naren was only nine days older, Brahmananda still could not claim to fully understand him. Even amidst all, he remained apart—as an enigma.

So when, after the arati, Swamiji had quietly said, ' Let's go to the drawing room. I have something to speak to you about, ' Brahmananda had immediately sensed that something of weight lay behind his words.

The cold had grown bitter these past few days. Saradananda sat wrapped from head to feet in a shawl. He too waited, watchful and silent.

Swamiji cast his eyes around the room, then, without preamble, began: 'I have something to say regarding the Belur Math Trust.'

No one spoke. All were now listeners.

Swamiji leaned forward from the comfort of his chair. His voice was calm but direct. 'The land and house of Belur Math, everything, has been purchased in my name. Legally, I am the owner. Given my health condition, anything could happen at any time. If that were to occur, then, by law, all this would pass to my family.'

Both Saradananda and Brahmananda recognised the unassailable logic in his words. After all, the funds used to purchase the land had come entirely through Swamiji's personal efforts. His family could, quite justifiably, claim ownership. Until he finished speaking, neither of them said a word. Their eyes remained fixed on his face.

Swamiji continued in the same composed tone:

'I never wished for anything to be bought in my name. I am aware there is a quiet discontent among some about this. The problem is, the donors from abroad do not know anyone here.

Nor do they have a particularly high opinion of our people. But they know me. They respect me as a Guru. They trust me.'

Brahmananda knew well that it wasn't just the outsiders. Even among their own brother-disciples, some could not accept Swamiji's greatness. In their hearts, they were doubtful. They believed his work with foreigners was not in keeping with the Master's will.

He remembered well—once, long ago, their brother-disciple Yogananda had said to Swamiji, right to his face, 'Whatever you say, whatever you do, the Ramakrishna never gave such instruction.'

Swamiji had replied, 'Don't try to bind the Master within your narrow frame. It is He Himself who works through me like a machine, making me act according to His will. I do nothing.'

But that hadn't stopped others—Yogananda, Adbhutananda, Turiyananda—from believing that Swamiji had strayed from Sri Ramakrishna's ideals. They felt he was overly infatuated with foreign lands and people, intoxicated by their money and adulation.

Back then, Swamiji had been in America. It was just after the Parliament of Religions in Chicago. His name echoed across continents. And yet, back home, even Baburam (Swami Premananda) had not spared him biting remarks. One night, seated in the Baranagar Monastery, he had declared in agitation: 'Naren is puffed up with pride! He flaunts his name everywhere, hungry for fame. Gathering disciples to build himself up as some grand Mahant! He is so full of himself that in his speeches, he doesn't even mention Sri Ramakrishna! He speaks only of himself! It's all about promoting his own philosophy now!'

Many present that night had flared up in anger. Only Rakhal (Swami Brahmananda) had not. He knew many more would speak such things. How many mouths could be shut?

Instead, with a wry smile, he'd teased, 'Oh, Baburam! Did you hear the latest news? They say Naren's dining with the Western ladies now! And guess what? He's planning to marry some rich white *memsahib* and settle abroad for good! He won't even return to see us anymore!'

Of course, Baburam had not taken long to realise his mistake.

But for Swamiji, these barbs, soft or sharp, were the price of his path. It was a path that bore the Master's fire, though few could see the flame.

All this while, Brahmananda had remained silent. Now, fixing his eyes directly on Swamiji, he spoke in a quiet but firm voice, 'No work can please everyone, Naren. What was it you were saying?'

Swamiji stilled the doubt within him and tried to speak plainly. He knew well that whatever he proposed would be accepted without resistance, yet he had no desire to impose his own will upon others. He said, 'I wish for the Ramakrishna Math and Mission to rise as a distinct and self-governing institution. All that we own—house, land, temple—should become its property. All future activity should bear the name and seal of the Order.'

To Saradananda, this rang wholly true. The individual is here today, gone tomorrow; the institution endures. And more urgently, there were already whispers; people thought Belur Math was simply Naren's garden house. Not long ago, the Bally Municipality imposed a tax of Rs 207 on the land at Belur. They refused to see it as a spiritual retreat, believing it instead to be a commercial venture. No argument could persuade them. To them, the Math was a suspect—foreign ladies coming and going, being entertained and fed, men and women mingling freely, money flowing in pounds and dollars. 22 bighas of land—who but a king or zamindar could afford such a thing? And these monks, who called themselves renunciants, had no lack of anything. 'It is a monastery in name only,' they said. 'In truth, it is Vivekananda's pleasure-garden, and the men in ochre merely actors in costume. Their real aim is to attract foreign memsahibs and their wealth.'

With no recourse left, they had taken the matter to court, Vivekananda versus Bally Municipality. Swami Brahmananda had overseen the case. Every day the courtroom overflowed with curious onlookers, and the air was thick with murmurs and accusations. The municipal lawyer had uttered such vile things in open court that they were scarcely bearable to hear. Brahmananda had borne them in silence. The case was won in the lower court, and for a moment, they had hoped it was over. But the government would not concede so easily. To them, it had become a matter of pride. The case was taken to the higher court, and an official was sent to inspect the Math. He left deeply moved. In time, by Thakur's grace, the land was declared exempt.

Saradananda did not wish to dwell on those days. What Naren said now came not from impulse, but from careful thought, and it was logical. He turned again towards him and asked, 'What were you saying about the trust?'

Swamiji replied, 'I have drafted the deed of a *Devottar*[13] Trust. In it are laid out the mission of the Math, the regulations for its governance, the names of future members, and the scope of its work. If you all go through it and share your thoughts, I will consult with Solicitor Pramatha Babu. This must be done; it is vital.'

He reached for the table beside him, pulled out a few folded

13 For God

pages, and handed them to Brahmananda. The latter drew the hurricane lamp closer and, after a glance through the papers, said, 'I'll read it aloud; everyone listen carefully. Then we'll discuss.'

The reading was deliberate, the words echoing clearly in the stillness. The deed was thorough, each line precisely written. Except for a few minor points, everyone gave their assent. Saradananda said with a smile, 'At times I feel, Naren, if you hadn't chosen to be a monk, you would've become a lawyer of nationwide fame.'

Swamiji laughed quietly. 'Fate offered me nothing beyond the path of renunciation. And so, I became what I am. As for the deed, I've written what I felt needed saying. You all agree. Now the responsibility of registering is on you, Sharat.'

Saradananda nodded. 'You needn't worry. I'll meet Pramatha Babu tomorrow. He's at the High Court, very experienced in such matters. I don't foresee any difficulty.'

Brahmananda, who had been sitting beside Swamiji all this while, gently laid his hand on his and said in a calm voice, 'This Ramakrishna Math and Mission, all of it, is yours. Thakur entrusted it to you, knowing your worth.'

Swamiji did not speak. A long silence followed. Then a quiet sigh. Barely audibly, he said, 'All for Thakur and Holy Mother. I am but a vessel.' He spoke no more. Rising without a word, he left the room in deep stillness, not glancing at a single soul. He walked soundlessly towards the stairs.

Time passed.

Strange reverberations stirred within his chest. What once had belonged to him alone now belonged to all. And yet, there was no one in the monastery before whom he could pour out his full heart.

On the table lay a letter from Mrs Ole Bull. His Dhira Mata.

A woman who had given like a mother, with open hands. Perhaps she was the one to whom he could confide it all.

He pulled the letter paper close and reached for his pen.

Dear Dhira Mata,

It is becoming increasingly clear to me that I must relinquish all concerns of the Math... And now comes to me the highest renunciation of all, to give up ambition, leadership, and the thirst for fame. My mind is prepared; the austerity must be done. I now see Jo and Nivedita's dreams through the lens of reality. Let them shape those dreams on my behalf, I no longer claim them. I wish to make a Trust deed.... I will do so as soon as Sharatchandra hands me the documents. Then I shall be at peace.

What I long for is rest, a little food, a few books, and space to study and write. The Mother is showing me this Light now. She had already shown it to you, but I had not believed.

I trust your guidance more than my own. Jo and Nivedita's hearts are noble, but now, the Light that must guide me lies in your hands. Are you seeing it? What is your advice?

I realise I shall never again speak from a public platform... and I am content. I do not feel weary, but what lies ahead is no longer speech, but something finer—the silent touch of the miraculous, as it was in Sri Ramakrishna....

Your eternal child,
Vivekananda

Looking Back

In the darkness of the night, Swamiji sits alone in his room. It feels as though he has finally laid down the burdens of life and found release. A deep tranquility, like the infinite sky above Mayavati, settles over him. Thoughts ripple silently through his mind, like waves in still water. Within them, there is nothing, nothing but two faces. Clear and vivid.

One is of a woman, eternally adorned with the parting in her hair, clad in a white saree with a red border. She has Rudraksha beads around her neck, bangles on her wrists. A divine glow radiates from her face. Beside her is the ever-smiling face of her husband, no longer of flesh and blood, yet alive in the hearts of all. The two seem to have become one, inseparable.

Within his heart, a voice seems to whisper: *I know you. For ages, you have crossed the river of time to reach me. I have seen all that is yours. I know all. There is nothing unknown.*

No one is in the room. Swamiji shuts the door and enters meditation. A deep blackness drapes the world outside. The wind stirs the leaves of the mango, jackfruit, *bel*, and neem trees. Slowly, he floats back into the distant past. Amidst them, one image stands out clearly: Mother Sarada walking alone through a desolate land. Swamiji sees her with his inner eye. One by one, scenes from the past unfold like a picture-scroll.

Mother Sarada had gone to Bodhgaya. Four years had passed since Thakur (Sri Ramakrishna) left his mortal body. His disciples were rootless and shelterless, living in hunger and half-hunger. The world around them offered only ridicule and mockery—young men doing nothing but begging for food. Mother Sarada's heart cried out in pain.

At Bodhgaya, she was overwhelmed. Two and a half millennia ago, the Blessed Buddha had walked there, and meditated in silence beneath the Bodhi tree on the banks of the Niranjana River. The Bodhisattva Siddhartha became the Enlightened One—Buddha. That sacred ground had become a holy place for all Truth seekers. Around it had sprung countless monasteries, temples, hospices, and *viharas*. There was no shortage of food, clothing, or shelter. Everything was abundant.

And yet, what did her children have?

How long would they continue to roam the streets like this?

Mother Sarada's heart filled with sorrow. She turned her wounded spirit towards Thakur[14]. Tears welled in her eyes.

'Thakur, my sons have no place to rest. They don't even get to eat. They go door to door, wandering. If only they had a place like this to live, they would not have to suffer so much. Give them a roof, give them food. They have no wealth, no support. Where will they go?'

Though bodiless, Thakur remained present. To him she prayed. In the dark night of the soul, he stood as a beacon of

14 Sri Ramakrishna

light to the lost traveller as his salvation.

A few months after returning from Bodhgaya, Mother Sarada was travelling by boat from Ghusuri to Dakshineswar.

The boat was midstream, gliding through the full Ganga. She gazed at the beauty of the two riverbanks, with trees, villages, and temples peeking through. Then her eyes drifted towards the open stretch of land at Belur. There was nothing there, just weeds and wilderness.

Lost in thought, she was suddenly startled. Who was that she saw? There, on that very land, Thakur, walking alone, deep in thought. So far away, and yet unmistakable. Bare-chested, slightly stooped, moving with that familiar gait, as though strolling through his own home.

Why had Thakur come there?

In that moment, her heart leapt with joy. All her worries melted away. Thakur himself had found the place for his children's shelter.

Fragments of the past floated into Swamiji's mind like autumn clouds. It all felt like yesterday. None of it is forgotten.

Thakur passed away on 16 August 1886. His young disciples, once united, now stood bewildered. They had to leave the garden house. They had no home. Scattered, some went on pilgrimages, others returned to their families. There was no hope or certainty.

But Thakur had dreamt of a monastery by the Ganga, where his ashes would be enshrined, and his disciples would live—a sacred refuge. A confused Narendra Nath (not yet known as Swami Vivekananda) feared that the dream would go unfulfilled. What would happen to the responsibilities Thakur had entrusted to him?

Above all, they needed a shelter. After much effort, they found a house. It was a house in name only; the locals called it a haunted house. A crumbling garden home on Paramhansa Road in Baranagar, overgrown with weeds, with broken floors, no windows, and a foul pond behind. And the rent? Rs 10. Thus, began the Ramakrishna Monastery on 19 October 1886.

The next chapter unfolded in Antpur. On 24 December, the disciples went to the home of Baburam's mother. What followed was unprecedented, etched forever in the history of the Ramakrishna Order.

That evening, under an open sky, a sacred fire was lit. The stars glittered above, and below, the renounced sons of Ramakrishna plunged into deep meditation. Later, they discussed God. Narendra Nath spoke movingly of the life of Jesus—his sacrifice, his austerities, his tireless mission. He spoke of Christ's disciples, their struggles, and their surrender. And how the light of Christianity had spread across the world.

This was the true meaning of life. All must dedicate themselves to the welfare of the world, like the Lord Jesus.

There was such power in Narendra Nath's voice that all rose to their feet. Standing before the leaping flames, they took a solemn vow. They surrendered everything at the feet of the Lord. Thakur had given them the ochre robes, now they formed a brotherhood.

Niranjanananda too re-dedicated himself that night, feeling a new beginning stir within his soul. Thakur had already blessed them with *sannyas*. Now the *sangha* was born.

After a week at Antpur, the disciples returned to Baranagar and resumed their austere lives. They called themselves *Danas*—a word meaning 'demon,' to reflect their extreme way of living. Balaram Babu and Surendra Babu helped with occasional donations, but these were meagre. All were sons of respectable families, and too proud to ask for help. Why should those who renounced everything for Thakur depend on others?

With no steady food supply, they began to beg. Whatever rice they received, they boiled and laid out on a cloth. Sitting around it, they ate with salt and chilli water. A single bowl held the spicy broth, another held water. Each took a mouthful of rice, dipped into the broth. If the heat got too much, they cooled it with another handful of rice.

Some days brought a single meal. Other days, none at all. They had no plates. The garden grew banana and gourd leaves, but even plucking them invited angry abuse from the gardener. Eventually, they turned to leaves of *taro* or *arum*—scratchy and irritating to the throat. Yet, none complained. Worship, meditation, chanting went on.

Their sleeping arrangements were worse still. Two mats on the floor of a hall. Pillows made of soft bricks. Swami Shivananda would joke, 'The bricks are soft enough, try one under your head.' No blankets, no quilts. On winter nights, they would wake up and huddle for warmth. Narendra Nath was no exception; he too walked that same path.

Sri Ma Sarada, seeing their hardships, would say, 'The boys have tested Thakur thoroughly before letting him go.' At Baranagar, how many days they had gone half-fed, absorbed in their devotions.

One day, they said, 'We've given up everything for Thakur. Let's see if staying in his name brings food. If Surendra Babu comes, we'll say nothing. We won't even go out begging.' With that, they wrapped themselves in shawls and entered deep meditation.

The whole day passed. Night fell. Then, someone knocked at the door. Narendra rose and said, 'See who it is. First check if he has anything in his hands.'

They opened the door, and there he was, a man from

Lalababu's[15] temple, bearing platters of delicious food. Everyone was overjoyed. They had felt Thakur's grace. That night, after offering the food to Thakur, all partook of the sacred *prasad* together.

There was no trace of anger, no shadow of complaint. Days passed in meditation and quiet chanting. Sometimes, they would go out for alms; they ate what little they received, if not, they fasted. Not indulgence, but renunciation was the path to liberation. Yet Narendra was restless, troubled by a persistent thought: What use was there in sitting silently in this dilapidated house, immersed only in meditation and hunger? How long could the young disciples endure such hardship before losing heart and returning to their homes? If that happened, all that Sri Ramakrishna had taught would be rendered meaningless. The Master's ideals had to be carried to every corner of the land, or all would be in vain. Desperate, like a man possessed, Narendra wrote letters across the country, seeking funds. A plot of land, a temple, these would require thousands. But who would give so much money? It was not only for the monastery; Mother Sarada, too, needed a place of shelter. How long could she, the embodiment of the Divine, wander uninvited from place to place?

Narendra set out, walking the length and breadth of India, seeking help. Then came a call from the Parliament of Religions. He felt it was time to step beyond his homeland and reach the court of the world. And what a storm he raised! Europe and America beheld the luminous soul of India in the garb of a monk. Disciples gathered around him—foreigners with hearts

---

15 A devotee of Krishna

awakened. Funds came. Perhaps this was God's will. With the goodwill of the world, the monastery transformed into a universal refuge.

He wrote to Swami Ramakrishnananda:

> First, we need a large piece of land. The rest, buildings and everything, will follow. Our monastery will grow slowly. Do not worry.... If you tell me whose name I should send the money to, I will send it today itself. As soon as you receive it, purchase the land—initially in my name. Later, find an adjacent plot, so that the two may be close together. Even if it is a little far from Calcutta, do not worry; wherever our monastery stands, it will become a place of great stir. Do not forget—two plots. Also, write who among you will take responsibility for this. Consult with Girish Ghosh and Atul. And remember—'arthamanartham'—money should remain with one whose custody arouses no envy.

So began the search. One day, Swami Vijnanananda and Swami Niranjanananda were travelling southward by boat along the western bank of the Ganga when a stretch of uneven land caught their eye. There were a few one-storied houses with verandas. They disembarked to look around. A small channel like a creek wound through the wilderness, shallow and still, where boats were docked for repair. The place was utterly silent, save for a large timber depot nearby. No habitation, only the murmur of trees and birds. The land was called Belur, once where the Darvabhadra river met the Ganga, now a sandy delta left by time. Someone gave the landowner's name, Bhagavat Narayan Singh of Bakshi Mohalla, Khazkalla, Patna.

At that time, Vivekananda still hoped to purchase the Kashipur Garden House, sanctified by Sri Ramakrishna's final days. So he asked them to leave Belur's land aside. Moreover, Miss Müller had reservations—this ground was too uneven, full of pits and hollows.

But the birth anniversary of Sri Ramakrishna was approaching. Until now, it had always been held at Dakshineswar. However, after the 1897 celebration, the temple authorities barred Swami Vivekananda from entering the Kali temple. Urged by time and necessity, he again turned his attention to Belur. The Kashipur land was beyond his means. From Lahore, he wrote to Swami Brahmananda:

'Keep a quiet eye on that large tract of land. Do all you can so that this year's celebration may take place there.'

Efforts began in earnest. Finally, a plot was secured beside the Ganga at Belur. On 3 February 1898, they paid Rs 1,000 as an advance. It was decided that the remaining Rs 39,000 would be used to complete the registration within a month.

Twenty-two days later, the monks were staying at Nilambar Mukherjee's garden house on the bank adjoining the land. After the Alambazar Monastery fell into disrepair, this had been rented. Here, the renunciate children of the Master gathered—Vivekananda, Brahmananda, Saradananda, Shivananda, Yogananda, Shuddhananda, Sharatchandra Chakraborty, and others. Sri Ramakrishna's birth anniversary had arrived. With Dakshineswar closed to them, all were concerned about where the celebration could take place.

Swami Yogananda, frail and silent, raised his eyes and softly proposed Dey's house at Bali. They were good people—recently, Purna Dey himself had expressed a desire to host the celebration. Brahmananda agreed, 'If that be the Master's will, then so be it.'

But Vivekananda said, 'I want the worship to be held on the land we are buying, this Sunday.'

Saradananda hesitated, 'But we are not yet the legal owners. We've only placed the deposit. Vivekananda brushed it aside, 'And what of that? The land has come into our hands by Master's will. We will register it in a few days.'

Brahmananda, more spiritual than practical, said calmly, 'If Naren wishes it, let the worship be held there. There will be no obstacle. And if it is also held at Bali, there's no harm in that.'

A smile lit up Vivekananda's face. 'This is why I like Rakhal so much. He knows how to resolve a situation. Was it for nothing that the Master said he could rule a kingdom?'

Uncomfortable with the praise, Brahmananda closed the topic with gravity, 'Very well. Let the preparations begin.'

The eve of the festival arrived. All were awake before dawn. So much to do. The mangal arati had already been completed in the sanctum. Vivekananda rose from bed and stepped out into the veranda. Darkness still cloaked the world. The Ganga flowed before him, its gentle waves kissing the banks. Southward, the large garden loomed. Beyond the trees, darkness filtered through the leaves in pale streaks. Soon, it would lift, and all would be visible.

He stood in silence, perhaps seeing nothing, lost in stillness. In a soft voice, he uttered, 'Shiva, Shiva.' His soul reached out to that unborn Lord, the eternal ascetic, Shiva, the soul of India, the highest of the gods.

Footsteps approached. It was Sharatchandra, the householder disciple. Bowing low, he asked, 'Shall we go to the shrine, Gurudev?'

The Master's seat had been prepared in a room below. Vivekananda paused. Today was the sacred day of Sri Ramakrishna's birth. He would worship him with a purified body. 'I must bathe,' he said.

A young brahmachari, barely past boyhood, responded

instantly. His eyes still held the innocence of a child. To him, Vivekananda was Sri Ramakrishna incarnate. Awed, he asked, 'Did you call me?'

Sharatchandra said, 'Bring Guruji's garments and accompany him to the ghat.'

In the courtyard, Swami Nirbhayananda greeted Vivekananda with a reverent bow. He had not known him long, but understood his needs with quiet sensitivity. 'Are you going to bathe?' he asked.

'Yes,' said Vivekananda. 'I shall bathe and then sit for the worship.'

At the shrine door stood Swami Premananda Baburam, who had prepared everything meticulously. Vivekananda smiled, 'This is why I love you so, Baburam. You always know exactly what I need.'

Premananda said nothing, but his face glowed with joy.

At the ghat, darkness veiled the sky. The rising tide now touched the southward-flowing Ganga. Water lapped against the steps. Across the river, the world was shrouded in mist. The moon had set in the west, and the morning star still glittered like a diamond in the eastern sky. A faint glow spread there. A few indistinct fishing boats floated by.

Vivekananda stood still. Cold wind bit the air. Those with him were wrapped in thick shawls. Sharatchandra said gently, 'I have brought warm water for you, Swamiji.'

Vivekananda turned, surprised. 'Warm water? Why?'

'In this *Magh* cold, bathing may harm your health.'

Vivekananda smiled faintly. 'I've bathed in the frozen waters of Amarnath. I shall be fine in Calcutta's Ganga.'

He bent, touched the sacred water, and sprinkled it upon his head. Then slowly, he stepped in. At chest depth, he dipped thrice and emerged, trembling slightly.

Nirbhayananda stood ready with cloth, towel, and shawl. Before anyone could speak, he dried and dressed him in fresh garments and wrapped him warmly. Comforted, Vivekananda whispered, 'Come, let us go to the shrine.'

Premananda still stood by the shrine door. There was never the slightest fault in his arrangements. Still, Vivekananda asked, 'Have you brought flowers?'

Premananda's face shone. 'By the Master's grace, today we have so many; you won't be able to finish offering them all.'

Swamiji did not utter a word. In silence, he entered the shrine room. On the altar rested an image of the Master, beside which stood a small copper urn containing the sacred ashes from the Master's funeral pyre—an object of profound reverence and rare sanctity. Swamiji called it Atmaram's casket, and it was everyone's unshakable belief that the Master still dwelled within it.

At the foot of the altar lay the Master's sandals. Swamiji took his seat upon the ritual mat, performed *achamana* (a purification ritual), folded his hands, and bowed low in concentration, softly reciting the invocation. The quietude of the surroundings seemed transformed into a sphere of worship. With both hands, he gathered flowers and gently strewed them upon the sandals. Overcome with emotion, his body trembled—he was no longer the man they knew, but someone transfigured. Outside the sanctum, everyone remained still, holding their breath.

After a long silence, he began to chant in a deep, resonant tone:

Om hrīmṛtaṁ tvam achalo guṇajit guṇedyaḥ
naktam divaṁ sakaruṇaṁ tava pādapadmam.
mohāṅkṣaśaṁ bahukṛtaṁ na bhaje yato'haṁ
tasmāt tvameva śaraṇaṁ mama dīnabandho!

The voice, rich and soaring, seemed to belong not to a mortal man but to a divine presence descended upon the earth. Standing at the side was Sharatchandra, who remembered how Swamiji had once handed him some handwritten hymns, asking him to check for metrical flaws. He hadn't had time to read them properly, but from what little he saw, he thought, if Swamiji had not been a monk, he could have been a great poet, like the seers of old.

When the prayers were complete, Swamiji rose, lifting the copper urn reverently to his head with both hands. The onlookers broke into jubilant cries, 'Victory to Sri Ramakrishna!' The quiet grove reverberated with their voices.

As Swamiji stepped out of the shrine, none could tell what he intended next. But Premananda knew. Stepping forward, he touched Swamiji and declared in a loud, clear voice, 'At last, the wish of our Guru will be fulfilled! Blow the conch! Ring the bells!'

Behind Swamiji walked the *sannyasis* and brahmacharis. The air was charged with festivity. They passed through Nilambar Mukherjee's garden house and arrived at the land of the monastery. Swamiji's eyes shone like the sun. The darkness of night had lifted, and dawn's golden light touched the Ganga, the earth, and the trees.

A narrow canal flowed ahead, crossed by a bamboo bridge. One by one, they crossed carefully. Among them were disciples of Sri Ramakrishna, disciples of Swamiji, disciples of the Holy Mother—all devotees of the Master. Suddenly, Swamiji looked about, as though seeking someone.

Saradananda stood behind him. 'Is something the matter?' he asked.

'I don't see Shivananda,' Swamiji said.

Until then, no one had noticed his absence. Premananda

added, 'I've been at the temple; I haven't seen Shivananda for quite some time.'

A brahmachari quickly spoke up, 'I saw Maharaj heading to the kitchen, some time ago.'

'What's he doing there?' Saradananda asked. 'Go check. Don't delay. We'll move on. Naren, come.'

This side of the land was damp with the tide's retreat, but not muddy. At the mouth of the canal lay a broken boat once used for repairs. Shrubs and undergrowth dotted the landscape, but Swamiji saw none of it. Absorbed in reverence and emotion, he walked on, holding the urn aloft, as if entrusted with the most precious object in the world.

Sharatchandra walked by his side. As they moved, Swamiji turned to him and said, his voice choked with feeling, 'Thakur told me, "Wherever you take me, I shall go and abide, be it beneath a tree or within a cottage." That is why I am bringing him to this new land of the monastery. From here, he will bless the world for ages to come.'

To Sharatchandra, it seemed that Swamiji no longer belonged to the mortal world, he dwelled among the gods.

They crossed the canal and proceeded farther. A slender stream joined the Ganga nearby. The spot was clean and serene, with a neem tree beside it. 'This place is beautiful,' Premananda said. 'I saw it yesterday.'

Swamiji's face lit up. 'Then let the Master reside here,' he said, his voice trembling with emotion.

Nirbhayananda stepped forward, cleared the space with the hem of his cloth, sprinkled Ganga water, and laid down flowers. A seat was arranged for Swamiji, and he sat. Then, with trembling hands, he placed the urn upon a *bilva* leaf. Tears streamed from his eyes. He bowed low. One by one, the others followed and offered their respects. Mats were laid on the earth. Everyone sat down.

Swamiji began chanting mantras:

'*Sthāpakāya ca dharmasya sarva-dharma-svarūpiṇe avatāra-variṣṭhāya Rāmakṛṣṇāya te namaḥ.*'

(To the establisher of *dharma*, the embodiment of all faiths, the greatest among the incarnations—salutations to you, Ramakrishna.)

What a voice! Noble and full. The entire grove seemed to resound with it.

Panting, Swami Shivananda arrived with a vessel of *payasa* (rice pudding). He had been cooking it for the Master. His face was radiant with joy, and tears welled in his eyes. The offering was placed upon the earth. The sun now climbed the eastern sky, spreading golden light across the world. The morning chill had lifted. The breeze carried the murmur of the Ganga. Sand was strewn upon the ground for the *yajna*. The sacred fire was lit. Swamiji, chanting mantras, offered offerings into the flames.

Swami Brahmananda sat gazing at him with a steady look; his eyes filled with wonder and awe. This was the same Naren from his boyhood, now transformed into Swami Vivekananda. How radiant was his form! Amid the open sky and burning fire, he looked like a being descended from the heavens, a divine soul. Shaven head, fresh and beautiful, fair-skinned, strong and graceful. Eyes like blooming lotuses—beyond compare. One felt compelled to say, 'Salutations to you, lotus-eyed one—*namah pankaja-netrāya namah!*'

The yajna ended. Swamiji offered the final oblation and intoned in a thunderous voice:

'Om pūrṇam adaḥ pūrṇam idaṁ
pūrṇāt pūrṇam udacyate.
pūrṇasya pūrṇam ādāya
pūrṇam evāvaśiṣyate.
Om śāntiḥ, om śāntiḥ, om śāntiḥ.'

Slowly, all rose to their feet. Swamiji's voice was choked with emotion. Taking Brahmananda's hand, he said, 'Today, a great burden has been lifted from my shoulders. For the past twelve years, one thought alone weighed on my mind—how to find a place for Thakur, how to enshrine him in a home of his own. And now, by his will, all has come to pass.'

He paused briefly, then turned to the gathered assembly. No one spoke. A profound silence hung in the air, charged with a strange exaltation. A new path had been opened; the journey had begun.

The New Helmsman

Swamiji lay in his room, eyes closed, reclining against the cushion of his easy chair. A little distance away, Sharatchandra sat cross-legged on the floor. Before him, atop a low stool, rested the latest issue of *Prabuddha Bharata*.

Lately, Swamiji's eyesight had weakened so much that he could barely read for long. The words would blur, and strain his eyes, causing discomfort. *Prabuddha Bharata*, published from Mayavati, was now edited by Swami Swarupananda, in whom Swamiji had unwavering trust. 'A tireless worker like Swarupananda is worth more than a thousand gold coins,' he would often say.

Sharatchandra was reading the editorial, aloud. A gentle smile played on Swamiji's lips; it was clear he was pleased. As the reading ended, Swamiji remarked, 'That boy writes so well. Thakur's blessings rest upon him. Whatever task he takes up, he completely surrenders himself to it, without evasion, or pretence. That zeal is sorely lacking in our people. They put on airs of virtue outwardly, but are dead stone within! How can such lifeless clay serve the world?

'I went to Europe and America and saw the energy in their lives; so much drive and vigour. And here, our people seem paralysed. No blood flows in their veins, no strength in their limbs, no fire in their hearts, no spark in their minds. What can be done with these inert bodies? I want to shake them awake, rouse them! I was born to sound this clarion call, *Uttisthata! Jagrata!* Rise! Awake!'

There was a flash of intensity in Swamiji's eyes and voice. Just then, footsteps were heard outside. He stopped mid-sentence and looked up. Saradananda stood at the door, dishevelled, a bag slung across his shoulder.

'What is it, Saradananda?' Swamiji asked, after a brief glance.

Without a word, Saradananda entered and sat down on the empty stool before Swamiji. Sharatchandra could tell Maharaj was tired. He quickly brought him a glass of water. Saradananda took it with a weary hand, drank it all, wiped his face with a corner of his cloth, and said with quiet frustration, 'It didn't work out.'

Swamiji, already anticipating this, asked calmly, 'What didn't?'

'They wouldn't accept the registered trust deed.'

Till then, all of Belur Math's land, buildings, and property had been in Swamiji's name. He had now written everything over to the trustees—the disciples of Sri Ramakrishna.

'Why not?' Swamiji asked.

'They refused to accept the authority you had granted me to sign on your behalf. They insist you appear in person before the registrar and sign everything yourself.'

Swamiji gave a faint smile. 'Even when I try to free myself, you won't let me go.'

'We have no power to let you go. But you can, if you wish, leave us.'

A melancholy shadow passed over Swamiji's face. In a quiet

voice, he said, 'I wish I could let everything go and retreat to the solitude of the Himalayas for the rest of my life, but I cannot. Leave that aside. Tell me, when must I go?'

'Tomorrow.'

'Then I'll take Rakhal with me. These government offices —who knows what they'll demand next. Bangal,' he said, calling Sharatchandra by the nickname he used for him, 'what were you reading?'

Saradananda could tell that Swamiji no longer wished to speak about the Math's property. He rose quietly. There was much to do; he would have to return to Howrah the next day.

At the veranda of the Howrah Sub-Registrar's office, Swamiji sat with Brahmananda, Sadananda, and Nityananda. Saradananda stood a little away. They had been waiting for a long time.

It was an old colonial building, with rows of benches, rooms on either side, shadows and dim corridors. Most of those who came here for land registration were householders. A group of ochre-clad monks gathered like this was rare. Curious clerks peeked in, whispering. Some recognised Saradananda from earlier visits. One leaned in and whispered, 'You're from Belur Math?'

Saradananda nodded.

'Is that Vivekananda, the one who became famous in America?'

Saradananda knew where such recognition led—endless questions, none worth answering. He deflected the query, asking, 'Do you know when Sub-Registrar Ramendralal Mitra will arrive?'

The man, clearly annoyed, replied curtly, 'No idea.'

Swamiji had been sitting in silence for some time. Lawyer Paltu Babu stood nearby, a High Court advocate and a devout devotee handling many of the Math's legal affairs. Swamiji turned to him and asked, 'When will your Registrar arrive?'

'With government officials, Swamiji,' Paltu Babu said, 'there is no telling when they come or go.'

A quiet irritation crossed Swamiji's face. 'But they're never late on payday,' he said dryly. 'That day they all come on time. Everyone wants everything without effort. That is why our country doesn't progress.'

Paltu Babu could see Swamiji's discomfort but was helpless. 'Perhaps he's caught in some work. He should be here soon.' As he spoke, the registrar's carriage arrived.

Ramendralal Mitra alighted—a man of middle age. Crossing the veranda, his eyes fell on Swamiji. He halted, folded his hands, and said, 'Pranam, Swamiji. I am sorry I'm late. I will call you right away.'

He entered his office. Soon, a peon summoned them in. Swamiji, Saradananda, and Brahmananda entered the large room. Several chairs were arranged for them.

Ramendralal said respectfully, 'Apologies for troubling you, Swamiji. But you understand, I must follow official rules. Please sign these documents.'

Swamiji appreciated the man's sincerity. As he signed, he said, 'Do come to Belur Math someday. You'll be served *prasad* at noon.'

Ramendralal smiled gently. 'We are sinners, Swamiji. Even knowingly we commit many wrongs. How can such a sacred place suit people like us?'

Swamiji's face grew grave. 'No one is a sinner. God dwells within every soul. The more you remember Him, the more your sins are washed away. Do you know what my Master, Sri Ramakrishna, used to say?

"A cave shrouded in darkness for a thousand years, light a lamp, and the darkness vanishes in an instant. A flock of birds resting on a tree, clap once, and they scatter. So too can the impurities of the mind be dispelled in a moment, if you will it."'

Ramendralal folded his hands. 'Two more years in service, then I shall be free. I've resolved to dedicate the rest of my life to God.'

Swamiji rose to go. Ramendralal said, 'There is no need for you to come again. I will sign the trust deed and send it to you within two days.'

They stepped out into the open. Brahmananda asked, 'Naren, won't you eat something? You've had nothing since morning.'

A line of roadside stalls bustled outside the office. Food lay exposed in the heat, flies swarmed, filth lingered. In one corner, there were *jalebis* being fried.

Swamiji's eyes lit up. With a chuckle, he said, 'Those *jalebis* look tempting!'

'I'll get some,' offered Sadananda.

Brahmananda snapped, 'Don't you dare! Naren may have conquered the world, but he's still a child at heart. Diabetic—yet wants *jalebi*!'

Saradananda gave Swamiji a sideways glance and smiled. 'No worries. I'll fry you some *jalebis* in the evening, without sugar. Eat as much as you like.'

Swamiji, with mock despair, said, 'Fine, I'll eat that. I'm in the hands of madmen now, whatever they feed me, I must eat!'

Right on time, the trust deed arrived. Swamiji glanced through it; everything was in order. A great weight seemed to lift from within. Now, only one task remained: to pass on the mantle formally.

It was Sunday morning. During breakfast, Swamiji said, 'Let all the brother-disciples gather in the downstairs office at eleven.'

'Is there something urgent?' asked Trigunatitananda.

Swamiji, who had become more solemn of late, simply said,

'Come. I'll explain everything then.'

Out of all of Thakur's disciples, eight were at Belur. The rest were away. One by one, they assembled with serious faces and quiet expectation.

Once everyone had taken their seat, Swamiji came straight to the point. His eyes swept over them briefly, then he said, 'Yesterday, the trust deed arrived. From now on, Belur Math's entire responsibility lies with the Board of Trustees. According to its rules, you must now elect, from among yourselves, a President and a Secretary. They shall oversee everything. You must decide who will take up these responsibilities.'

A new helmsman was to be chosen. The voyage would go on.

All eyes turned to one another, seeking direction. Shivananda spoke first, 'You decide. We shall all abide by your word.' Swamiji knew well that when he spoke, his counsel was often taken as law. Yet, he also foresaw future murmurs—how Naren had imposed his own will upon them. Calmly, he said, 'I have laid down the rule myself: by unanimous consent, the President and Secretary shall be elected in due course. And shall I be the one to break my own law? You tell me.'

Premananda spoke, his tone, hesitant, 'Shall I speak?'

'Certainly,' Swamiji encouraged. 'I wish for you all to step forward freely, not merely echoing my voice, but taking responsibility independently.'

A flicker of eagerness stirred among them. Though renunciates by vow, their hearts still bore many desires. Without hesitation, Premananda fixed his gaze on Brahmananda and declared, 'Rakhal is the most worthy among us. Let him be President.' Shivananda nodded his assent.

Swamiji inquired, 'Does anyone else have words to offer?'

Saradananda spoke up, 'Shashi has done much for the

monastery and mission. His name, too, deserves consideration.'

Maharaj, the youngest among them and ever fond of Subodhananda Shashi Maharaj, said, 'Shashi Dada is worthy of the Presidency.'

A faint smile curved at the corner of Swamiji's lips, unnoticed by all. 'Any further opinions?' he asked. 'Do not hesitate. Decisions made through mutual consultation will surely bring welfare to all.'

Then Brahmananda raised his hand, 'I wish for Sharat to be President. His qualifications surpasses ours.'

Swamiji replied, 'Three cannot hold the Presidency at once. Let us vote.'

A subtle discomfort spread among them. To hold a vote among comrades long united was unsettling. Latu Maharaj, quietly seated aside, muttered with irritation, 'I do not like all this.'

'You too are a trustee board member,' Swamiji reminded.

Latu waved off the remark. 'I do not know how to read or write. What use is membership to me?'

Saradananda reassured, 'You need do nothing but lend your name.'

'I know only the names of God and Guru,' Latu said. 'All this talk tires me.'

Swamiji felt no purpose in vexing this simple soul further. 'Let Latu be as he is,' he said gently. 'The rest, write down your names and hand them in.'

Though Brahmananda felt uneasy, his heart leaned more towards spirituality than practicality. He knew no good came of resistance. Swamiji acted solely for the monastery's welfare.

Swamiji tore a sheet of paper into slips and handed them out. None spoke further. Each wrote their name and folded the paper before Swamiji.

He gathered all the slips, eight in total. Opening them, he saw five votes cast for Brahmananda. Others had received only a couple of votes each.

A smile dawned on Saradananda's face. The Master was gone, but the spiritual heir had become the head of the Ramakrishna Order. Could there be greater joy?

Premananda said, 'I believe Sharat (Saradananda) is the most suitable for Secretary. The one who takes that office must bear great responsibility.'

Maharaj agreed, 'I concur with Premananda.' Shashi Maharaj nodded in assent.

Swamiji declared, 'Then all accept Saradananda as Secretary?'

Every hand rose in approval.

Swamiji rose to his feet. 'Rakhal, Sharat, from this day onward, I entrust to you the entire responsibility of this monastery and mission. You shall carry forward the work with all. I have no further duty here. I think I shall visit Mother this afternoon. How long it has been since I last saw her! My heart longs deeply for Mother.'

Mother

Once upon a time, there were many silk cotton trees in the Simla neighbourhood. That was why everyone called it Shimulia. From that came the name of the street and the neighbourhood—Simla. At the junction of two streets stood a large house, Number 3, Gourmohan Mukherjee Street. At the southern face was a massive entrance gate made of sal wood. Inside stretched a spacious courtyard paved with polished tiles. To the west stood the temple hall with five arches resting on round pillars made of rubbed red bricks. On the upper floor of the temple hall, the large main hall lay to the south; the northern room was the meeting room. The southern room was the deity's chamber. Below, to the south, was the meditation room. On the outer courtyard's west side stood another tiled building, the cowshed. Behind the house, within the inner courtyard, was a pond for the women to bathe. On the meeting room's walls hung painted murals; above, bell lanterns and pot lanterns swayed. On one side of the house loomed a giant *bel* tree.

Crossing Karnawali street, Swamiji stopped in front of the house. This house had been built by Rammohan Dutta, father of Thakurda[16] Durgamohan. That was long ago. Whenever he came here, a heaviness filled his heart. From birth, countless memories were intertwined with this home. How mischievous he had been in childhood! Mother Bhubaneshwari Devi had ten children in all, six daughters and four sons. Except for daughter Swarnamoyee and three sons—Narendranath, Mahendranath, Bhupendranath—all others had died young. As long as father Vishwanath Dutta lived, all were happy. The man earned no small income and spent it lavishly. Yet, upon his death, Narendranath's uncle Taraknath's widow, Gyanadasundari Devi, Swamiji's great-aunt, filed a lawsuit against Bhubaneshwari Devi. She claimed that all the property in Bhubaneshwari's name was bought with Taraknath's earnings since Vishwanath owned no property. Even the maintenance of Vishwanath's wife and sons was said to be from Taraknath's funds. But in his life, Vishwanath Dutta never begged from anyone; he only gave with open hands. In truth, he never understood the naked greed of people. Everything was exhausted to cover the costs of the lawsuit. Today, the whole family's situation was unbearable.

Swamiji felt deeply helpless. But what pained him more was the plight of his mother. How much suffering she endured—silent and concealed. As a son, he could do nothing for her. She had wished that as the eldest son, Naren would marry well and get a good job, so the family could revive. But he had failed to fulfil her wish. If not that, then whose wishes could he fulfil? The call of the universal world echoed louder than his own household—the call to serve humanity's welfare. What greater purpose could there be?

16 Grandfather

Swamiji had become absent-minded. A horse-drawn phaeton rushed past him. The rhythmic clatter of hooves echoed across the open fields. The coachman's shouts brought Swamiji back to consciousness.

He stepped aside and slowly walked forward. Passing through the gate and the veranda, a few steps inside, he saw a figure emerging from within—it was his great-aunt, Gyanadasundari, the very woman against whom multiple lawsuits were ongoing. For a moment, irritation filled his heart. Though family, she had become a fierce enemy, consumed by a thirst to destroy. He turned to look away, but stopped. He had forgotten he was a monk. To a monk, there is no enemy or friend; in all things shines the supreme Brahman. The Gita's words came to his mind:

> Untroubled by sorrow, unperturbed by joy, Free from longing,
> fear, and anger—Steadfast, the sage is called truly wise.

Calming his mind, he stepped forward and bowed low.

Great-aunt, perhaps unprepared for this, met his greeting quietly. 'How are you?' she asked.

'Good. And you?'

'At this age, what can one expect? A thousand ailments. But enough about me. These days, I hear much about you. People say many things.'

Swamiji smiled softly, 'More bad than good, I imagine.'

'People say what they will,' she said. 'You've come to your mother's house! Go see her. I must leave; I am off to the temple. I want to spend these few days with some merit.'

She did not linger. Her waist was bent with age, and she walked slowly. Swamiji thought, how strange it was that at the end of life, some people still ran madly after small gains. Who knows when this endless human greed will end?

Passing the veranda, a narrow alley lay ahead—damp, dim, and deserted. Memories flooded Swamiji's mind. How many people had lived here in his childhood? The house used to bustle during festivals; fifty or sixty meals were served daily. Now, it was empty, silent.

At the alley's end stood a large room with its open door. Through it, Swamiji saw his mother sitting on the cool floor mat, sewing quietly. From outside, he called softly, 'Mother.'

Hearing her son's voice, Bhubaneshwari Devi turned. An indescribable joy blossomed across her face.

'Bilu, you've come!'

Swamiji bowed and sat beside her, his face bright with happiness. With her, all sorrows melted away.

'How are you, Mother?' he asked, knowing well that however much pain she bore, she would never speak it aloud.

Their joint family's guardians had been the great-uncle and great-aunt, who tormented her in many ways for their own gain. As a daughter-in-law, Bhubaneshwari Devi had silently endured it all, never uttering a word. When Vishwanath Dutta learned the truth, he had lamented bitterly, 'It's strange. I earn so much, yet my wife cannot eat her fill.' That day, Bhubaneshwari Devi said nothing. Even now, she remained silent to her son's questions, only saying gently, 'Enough about me. How are you?'

Swamiji spoke with enthusiasm, 'Today I feel free, Mother. I have entrusted all the duties of Ramakrishna Math to Rakhal and Sharat. From now on, they will manage everything.'

'What will you do?' she asked. 'I know you cannot sit still quietly.'

A faint smile touched Swamiji's lips. 'Who knows me better than you, Mother? For years, I have not thought of myself even for a moment. I have worked like a madman. Many days I did not eat properly, sometimes nothing but water. On cold, bitter nights, I earned Rs 200-400 by walking the streets and lecturing. I have done nothing for myself. Now I am very tired. Sometimes I wonder if I have done all I can. What lies ahead, I do not know. Perhaps many things: a grand mansion, comfort, luxury, all arranged so no one will suffer—a life of complete happiness.'

His mother's chest swelled with love. Gently, she stroked his head. 'Your health is not good. I say, take rest for a while. Or come, let us travel somewhere. Somewhere that will heal your body.'

A childlike joy welled in Swamiji's heart as he took her hand. 'Where shall we go?'

Bhubaneshwari Devi thought for a moment. She had travelled here and there with her husband a couple of times, but since he passed, she had clung to the household. For some time, she said nothing. Finally, breaking the silence, she said, 'I long to go to Kashi, the sacred *Shivakshetra*. Mother Ganga dwells there. Your Thakurda[17] was there too.'

Kashi! Swamiji's heart stirred deeply. Thakur Sri Ramakrishna had gone there. Mother Thakurani[18], too. An eternal pilgrimage site, every speck of its dust is holy.

'I will go to Kashi. I will take you there. But first, we must visit East Bengal once more.'

Bhubaneshwari Devi's surprise was evident. East Bengal had rivers, canals, and marshes. Except for a few towns, it had mostly villages and simple folk. After travelling abroad so long, what would Naren do in such a remote village?

Swamiji understood his mother's unspoken thoughts. She

---

17 Grandfather

18 Shri Sarada Devi

had no particular interest in the purpose of his East Bengal visit. Long ago, he had planned to go there, but time had slipped away. Before his second foreign journey, two disciples, Virajananda and Prakashananda, had gone to Dhaka to spread the teachings of Sri Ramakrishna, to establish a branch of the Ramakrishna Mission there. Their mission had been fulfilled.

Subsequently, many others held meetings and societies in Dhaka and various places in East Bengal. Through these, people became increasingly enthusiastic about the teachings of Ramakrishna. Since the unprecedented success at the American Religious Conference, Swamiji had become well-known among the people of East Bengal. From then on, many expressed the desire for Swamiji to visit East Bengal. Repeated petitions and requests reached him. At last, responding to their wishes, Swamiji resolved to go to East Bengal.

Looking towards his mother, he said, 'You come with me to East Bengal. It's not what you might think. You will feel very happy there.'

For a long moment, Bhubaneshwari Devi remained silent.

Then, as if weighing his words, she said, 'If you say so.... I will think it over. If anyone else wishes to go, I will let you know later.'

Suddenly, something came to her mind, and she said, 'Today, I ate a little *payasa*, Gopal's[19] offering. It's good you've come.'

Swamiji's face softened with sadness. He quietly replied, 'I am not allowed to eat sweets.'

'Won't you eat even a little?' His mother's eyes filled with tears.

Unable to bear her pain, Swamiji smiled and said, 'Bring it to me. I will eat.'

19 Krishna

Shivaratri

Late winter noon—there is a hush over the tranquil monastery, this is the hour when all find respite. The mellow sun of *Phagun* still holds a sweet, lingering warmth. Around, the trees begin to shed their leaves, bidding a quiet autumnal farewell. The earth wears a sun-baked austerity; there is a touch of roughness in the air. Clusters of cicadas rest upon the palmyra trees, their wings fluttering softly in the gentle breeze. Soon, new leaves will unfurl on every branch, carpeting the ground with the fallen foliage, and at dusk, a bonfire will be kindled, crackling dry leaves casting flickering shadows. The fire dances in myriad hues as *Chaitra* days draw to a close. The sal and teak trees burst forth with tender green shoots, their young leaves shimmering in the morning light like threads of pure gold. Nature, in her eternal cycle, reveals herself anew.

Seated on the upper-floor veranda, Swamiji gazed across the vast expanse of the monastery grounds. The river meandered through lush green fields and golden paddy. To the south, Neelambar Mukherjee's house stood in quiet repose. In the thick cold of Paush, the world had glowed in vibrant colours; now, the hues had softened into gentle pastels. From sunrise to sunset, the sky over the Ganga displayed its own kaleidoscope of colours. Along the monastery wall crept a vine, blossoming clusters of red flowers like scarlet flames. It seemed as if God Himself revealed His presence in these quiet details, in the play of light, in the breath of the wind.

Within the monastery, new brahmacharis had arrived. To them, Swamiji poured forth the innermost stirrings of his soul. Sometimes, he wondered if they truly understood his words, whether the colours of his consciousness might brighten their hearts, or if everything passed by like routine, like mere habit of bathing, eating, sleeping. They came, they went, sometimes like clockwork machines. Unlike his Guru, Sri Ramakrishna, who was a divine incarnation, the very touch of whom could transmute iron into gold, Swamiji was but a humble seeker. Yet, even so, a few among them....

His thought was interrupted as Nirbhayananda entered.

'Will they come soon?' Swamiji asked.

Nirbhayananda bowed his head softly and said, 'Miss MacLeod and Mr Jules Bois are arriving.'

Miss Josephine MacLeod, was an American woman, a devoted admirer of Swamiji, and a close friend. Swamiji called her Jo, sometimes Jaya. She had come to India only recently, and from here would proceed to Japan. Swamiji had invited them to Belur.

Turning back to Nirbhayananda, he asked, 'Have they arrived yet?'

'Not yet. Someone came from across the river and said a *memsahib* and a gentleman wait at the ghat. I suppose they will arrive on the next boat.'

Swamiji rose, draped a shawl from the table over his shoulders, and placed a gentle hand on Nirbhayananda's. 'Come, let us go to greet them.'

After a few steps, he stopped, recalling something.

'What is it, Gurudev?' Nirbhayananda asked eagerly.

'This morning, the gardener brought me some lotus flowers, and kept in a basket by my bed.'

Understanding his silent wish, Nirbhayananda went and returned with four drops of lotus petals. Swamiji smiled softly. Together, they stood at the riverbank; the tide was full, the water flowed ceaselessly. A few brahmacharis came and went quietly. Then, a boat appeared, cutting through the river's waves, the boatman guiding it ashore. Josephine MacLeod and Jules Bois stepped onto a wooden plank laid from the boat to the ghat.

First came Miss MacLeod, clad in a deep maroon gown, a hat perched upon her head, her features strong and assured, her bright, fearless gaze sharp and commanding. She was five years older than Swamiji.

Behind her came Jules Bois—a famed French philosopher, journalist, and writer—his appearance offered a contrast: a soft, feminine grace illuminated his smiling, radiant face.

Swamiji advanced, inclining his head slightly. 'Welcome, Jo. Welcome, Mr Bois.' He placed two flowers each into their hands.

Bois' face broke into a broad smile. Taking Swamiji's hand, his voice softened, 'I am overwhelmed. From the boat, I saw the most extraordinary sight: a line of palm and coconut trees, the temple in the midst, crowned with a trident pointing skyward. I felt as if the very precincts of the monastery, these steps, this temple, were beckoning me.'

'And Swamiji! Did you see Him?' MacLeod teased, tossing a playful question to Nirbhayananda at his side.

Bois' expression flickered with complex emotion. In a

voice thick with feeling, he said, 'I saw Swamiji standing by the riverbank, at the ghat. His robe, his countenance, all was encompassed by those deep, profound eyes.'

Swamiji chuckled, pleased by the earnestness of this straightforward man. 'Do you know what your heart tells me?' he said, pausing between words. 'How could I know the secrets of your mind?'

Bois continued, 'You are like an Aryan sage of six thousand years past, born far from my country, speaking a language entirely different, worshipping gods unknown to us, living in a realm of thought utterly foreign. Yet, somehow, you have become my dearest friend. Travelling Constantinople, Greece, Egypt with you in my mind's eye, I often felt as if you came here from India just for me.'

Swamiji felt the warmth of Bois' emotions and, holding his hand, said, 'That such a person as you should come to the monastery fills me with immense joy. Come, Jo, you too.'

As they walked, Swamiji spoke softly, 'Everything in this monastery is for Jo and her friends. Without them, I could do nothing.'

They gathered at Swamiji's door, the young monks and brahmacharis assembled on the veranda, smiling, their foreheads marked with sacred ash, their faces shining with genuine simplicity. All greeted the visitors with folded hands.

Bois was enraptured. He bowed his head in reverence. The three entered the upper chamber, where seats had already been arranged, and everyone settled quietly.

Jo said, 'Swamiji, after this, we are going to Japan. We shall stay there for some time. Okakura is there, a specialist in art. You must come to Japan.'

Swamiji's face grew serious. His heart yearned to see and

learn much beyond this land and abroad. Yet his body, worn by years of toil, could no longer bear such exertion. He quickly grew weary and could not endure hardship as before. Still, unwilling to say so, he replied, 'I must first visit East Bengal. I have long been invited there but never had the chance. Perhaps now it will be possible.'

A brahmachari entered.

'Is the tiffin ready?' Swamiji asked.

'It will be shortly.'

'Good. Bring it when it is ready. We shall go sit on the roof.'

The sun was hidden by drifting fragments of cloud. Carpets were spread on the terrace, and open nature stretched all around. Bois moved to the edge, gazing eastward towards the ripening fields. Through breaks in the clouds, shimmering light flickered over the paddies like twin mirrors, reflecting the rows of palm and coconut trees. To the west, the Ganga, strong and steady as a noble guardian, embraced the monastery and temple in its vast arms.

Vivekananda came and stood beside Bois, gently resting a hand on his shoulder with a tender touch. For a long moment, silence reigned.

Then Swamiji extended his hand towards the far shore of the river. 'Look, across the Ganga,' he said. 'See that massive banyan tree?'

Though distant, it stood clear in the eye's gaze.

'What lies there?' Bois asked.

'Beneath it is the first *samadhi* of my Guru, Sri Ramakrishna. It is a place as sacred as Bodh Gaya with its holy Bodhi tree.'

'I have read of him,' said Bois in a tone steeped in reverence. 'A great soul, as holy as the Buddha.'

Swamiji's emotions surged. Sri Ramakrishna was more than a Guru to him—he was meditation itself, the very essence of contemplation. Turning to all present, he said, 'My Acharya was a wondrous man. He never uttered a harsh word to anyone. He did not curse, nor did he criticise. His vision had lost the power to see anything in this world as evil. He had no capacity for malice or grudges. He saw nothing but goodness. That supreme sanctity and self-sacrifice alone was his path to the divine. The Vedas say, "Not through wealth or progeny, but through sacrifice alone does one attain immortality." Jesus said, "Sell all you have, give to the poor, and follow me." Great teachers and saints have all taught this and lived it. Without sacrifice, where lies the possibility of spirituality? Behind every religious ideal is sacrifice.

'Sri Ramakrishna was the living embodiment of sacrifice. In our land, those who take up renunciation must give up all wealth, all honour, all respect. My Gurudev lived this ideal in every letter and deed. He did not even touch gold. That sacrifice was so united with his being that even in sleep, the touch of any sensual pleasure would break his rest, causing him to cry out in pain. He was a living example of conquering desire and gold, a man much needed in this present century.'

For a brief moment, Swamiji fell silent. One by one, the brahmacharis gathered near.

'Do you need anything?' he asked.

'Yes, Swamiji. The tiffin is ready. Please come inside, everyone.'

On the table, the food was arranged neatly on a new plate, perfectly tidy. All this was the teaching of Swamiji himself. He arranged the food with his own hands: eggs, milk, rice, mango. MacLeod asked, 'Swamiji, aren't you taking anything?'

'Today is Shivaratri. We fast on this day. After performing the worship of Shiva at night, we will break our fast. You all eat,' Swamiji said.

While eating, Bois spoke in a simple, straightforward manner.

Suddenly, turning towards Miss MacLeod, he asked, 'How did you come to know Swamiji?'

MacLeod instantly became somewhat pensive. Such a sweet memory, a world of dreams. In a soft voice, she said, 'The day was 29 January 1895. The day I was born.'

Bois burst out laughing. 'That's funny! So, you're just a six-year-old kid now!'

MacLeod didn't laugh. Speaking simply as before, she said, 'That day, I saw Swamiji for the first time. It was like a rebirth for me, though I was thirty-seven then. A friend of mine had written that an extraordinary man had arrived from India. "Go see him," she said. Out of curiosity, I went. It was a rented house's meeting room, with about ten or twenty people gathered. All the chairs were full; I sat on the floor. After a short while, Swamiji entered the room. He stood in the corner. Someone introduced him: this was Swami Vivekananda, from India. In the soft light of the fireplace, he seemed like a man sent by God. His saffron robe looked like a flame of fire. His bright eyes had turned red. He spoke, and listening to him, it felt as though I was hearing the words of a great soul, the Supreme Truth. He filled life with a new enthusiasm. Since then, every time I have heard him, it has felt like Absolute Truth. He is like a shining sun. Once seen, never forgotten.' Miss MacLeod was trembling with excitement.

Swamiji said gently, 'Calm down, Jo. I know you all respect me, love me. You have come to love my India as well. In truth, the few moments I have spent in your company have given me so much peace, something I have found from very few foreigners.'

MacLeod returned from her world of thoughts to reality. So many old memories! She said, 'I remember that day, Swamiji, the Parsy estate in Hampshire, Mr Leggett's house. Oh, what a wonderful time I had there!'

Swamiji seemed to return to his own past. 'Mr Leggett's house,' he said. 'Ah! Among all the beautiful places I saw in Europe and America, there was nothing like that. Deep forest, mountains, a lake in between.' Jo MacLeod added, 'Only a few of us were there, no one else. It was so beautiful that it felt as though my life span had increased manifold. And when you walked through the garden—oh, what can I say? It felt as if you were striding over the world on two feet, ignoring everything around. I have never seen anyone walk like that.'

Swamiji showed no change in expression at MacLeod's praise. Calm, with contentment in his eyes, he said, 'There I meditated for hours. Those days were so joyful.'

There was a suppressed excitement on MacLeod's face. 'One day, when we saw Swamiji meditating, we were really scared.'

Bois immediately asked, 'What happened?'

MacLeod finished her tiffin, put her spoon aside, and said, 'Swamiji often went out alone. For hours, he meditated under a white birch tree. One morning before breakfast, Swamiji left his room with the Bhagavad Gita in hand. I followed him. Pointing to a distant pine tree, he said, "Jo, I'm going to that pine to read the Bhagavad Gita. Make sure today's breakfast is tofu." We didn't disturb him. Half an hour later, when I went near the pine, I saw Swamiji sitting motionless. The Gita had fallen from his hands. The front of his saffron robe was wet with tears. As I came closer, I saw his breathing had stopped completely. I was trembling with fear, thinking Swamiji had died. Without shouting, I ran to Leggett and said, "Come, quickly, Swami Vivekananda has left us." My sister started crying, holding her chest, and ran. Everyone else there gathered. Tears filled their eyes. Seven or eight minutes passed like this. Swamiji remained in the same posture, motionless. Someone said, "He is in samadhi. I'll try to shake him out of it."

'Hearing that, I shouted, "No! Never do that!" I remembered Swamiji once said that when he is in deep meditation, no one should touch him. After a while, faint signs of breathing returned. His eyes that had been half-closed, now slowly opened. Swamiji seemed to speak as if to himself, "Who am I? Where am I?" Saying that thrice, he stood up. Seeing us, understanding everything, he said, "I am very sorry for frightening you all. But this happens to me sometimes. Don't worry, I will not leave this body in your country. Jo, you must be hungry. Let's eat quickly. Let's see what good food there is."'

MacLeod was talking, while Swamiji smiled softly, clearly amused. Bois was silent, realising that Swamiji had reached the depths of meditation. He asked, 'Has this ever happened before, Swamiji?'

Swamiji slowly nodded. 'Many years ago, the first time I went to my guru, Sri Ramakrishna, in Dakshineswar. One day, as Sri Ramakrishna touched my chest, I saw the house, doors, windows, veranda, trees, sun, moon—all spinning wildly, breaking down into atoms, and finally merging into the sky. Then gradually even the sky disappeared; along with it, my sense of self vanished. What happened after that, I don't remember. The first time, I was very scared. After coming down from that state, I could see the house, doors, windows, veranda, and everything as before. Then a similar experience happened at Mr Leggett's house in America.' Boehmer added, 'Our scriptures offer no explanation for this.' Swamiji nodded in agreement with Boehmer's words.

'You are quite right. This experience of oneness, the very realisation of Brahman, is what our Upanishads call *Brahmoplabdhi*. To truly know this is to be forever freed from fear and the chains of birth and death.' And then Swamiji fell silent, his words trailing off.

At the door stood the disciple Nirbhayananda, as if waiting to speak. 'The *puja* is ready.'

'Yes, yes, I am coming.'

All had finished their meal, hands cleansed. Boehmer asked, 'Where shall we go now, Swamiji?'

'Let us go. The worship of Shiva is underway. Shiva, the symbol of truth, beauty, and benevolence. Within Him resides sacrifice and renunciation. In every Hindu home, Shiva is revered.'

Excitement gleamed in their eyes with the eager anticipation of witnessing something new. They walked over the grass, the soft earth beneath their feet. Boehmer turned to Swamiji. 'Your ashram is truly beautiful. I have visited many churches and mission sites across Europe and America, but nowhere amidst nature have I found such sanctity. I have read in your ancient histories that sages of old left the cities and towns to dwell deep in forests by riverbanks. There, they meditated and chanted.'

Swamiji gently nodded. 'You speak truly. This monastery is indeed a place of penance and meditation. All who dwell here are ascetics.'

MacLeod spoke, 'Do you think, Swamiji, that there will come a day when people from all over the world will flock here? Thousands of devotees, countless monks and celibates? Will it remain as it is now, then?'

Swamiji perceived the thoughts behind MacLeod's words. As they walked, he replied, 'Time changes all. New ages dawn, new people come, and with fresh thoughts, all must be rebuilt anew. One must learn to embrace change.'

The clang of a brass bell echoed softly in the breeze. A brahmachari stepped forward. 'Swamiji, the *puja* has begun.'

Beyond the monastery and gardens, in a broad open space, stood a large fig tree. Beneath it, gathered a group of monks and brahmacharis. The sun hung low on the western horizon. Against the monastery's green backdrop and the saffron robes of the ascetics, a radiant glow played. Beneath the fig tree lay an earthen altar, upon which a trident stood, adorned with flowers. A sacred fire burned nearby, its fragrant smoke swirling, perfuming the air with incense.

The ascetics sat in a circle. Shashi Maharaj chanted the *Shiva Stotra* with a deep, sonorous, and melodic voice. As he intoned the mantras, flowers were offered on the altar.

Swamiji removed his shoes and stood quietly. MacLeod and Bois followed suit, barefoot and reverent. All were still, immersed.

Bois felt as though the majestic chanting stirred a dormant spirit deep within his soul, a flash of light illuminating the darkness inside.

The *puja* concluded. Shashi Maharaj spoke softly, 'Is everything prepared for the *yajna*?'

Two brahmacharis nearby murmured, 'Yes, Maharaj.'

In a large vessel, wood was arranged for the *yajna kund.* Beside it, another container held various offerings. The fire was kindled. Soon, tongues of flame spread and danced with the breeze. The smoke spiralled upward, as if ascending to the feet of the Divine.

At last, the *yajna* was complete. Each received the sacred mark upon their forehead.

One ascetic rose and began to sway, moving rhythmically as though possessed by a divine spirit. His hands grasped a trident. It was as if Nataraja himself had descended to earth, dancing the cosmic dance. His companions joined in song, their voices united in sacred chant:

Tathaīyā tathaīyā nāce bhola, bam bab baje gāla.
Dimi dimi dimi damaru baje, duliche kapalmal.
Goraje ganga jaṭāmājhe, ugare onala triśūl raje.
Dhak dhak dhak maulibandha jāle śaśāṅkabhāla.

Mṛityunjaya Shiva is the Conqueror of Death. Once, the world trembled to the rhythm of His dance. Swamiji seemed to find himself within Shiva's very essence, and his song poured forth from that place.

Silent, spellbound, Bois felt the flames of the *yajna* and the sounds of the music unfurl wings and become the very mantras of the Vedas. Enraptured, he stood still.

MacLeod turned, watching Swamiji, motionless and serene, hands folded before his heart, whispering softly to himself, 'Shiva, Shiva, Shiva.'

Unconsciously, the two spoke in unison, their voices rising, 'Shiva, Shiva, Shiva.'

On the Way to East Bengal

By the time the *Dhaka Mail* reached Goalanda, the sun had risen well into the sky. The evening before, Swamiji had boarded the train from Sealdah, accompanied by six of his disciples: Nityananda, Nirbhayananda, Shuddhananda, Manmatha Ganguly, and two others. All bore tin suitcases in their hands, coarse cloth satchels slung over their shoulders—except Swamiji, who walked ahead as they disembarked onto the modest platform, teeming with a human tide.

This was Goalanda, in the Faridpur district, a great mart, the easiest artery linking East Bengal with the rest of the land. Nearby flowed the hallowed Padma, here called Kirtinasha, the Destroyer of Merit. The river lay but a short walk from the station, down a path strewn with coal cinders. Swamiji turned to Nirbhayananda and asked with a gentle smile, 'Kanai'—for that was his householder name— 'did you sleep well last night?'

A flicker of restrained irritation crossed Nirbhayananda's face. 'Not a wink, Maharaj. The jolt of the train robs me of all sleep.'

Swamiji laughed softly. 'Then what will you do aboard the steamer? It sways as a cradle does, without rest, without respite.'

Shuddhananda interjected cheerfully, 'I slept well.'

Swamiji tapped him lightly on the back. 'That's the spirit! Wherever one finds oneself, one must learn to dwell in harmony. Our Master has shed his earthly frame. We have taken to the road. As wandering monks, we have roamed the far corners of *Bharatvarsha*, and slept beneath trees, and at times, under palace roofs. No difference have I felt. I have learned to abide in all things.'

None responded. To them, Swamiji stood apart, cut from another cloth. They pressed forward through the crowd. Behind them, the train stood idling on the tracks, its cargo being unloaded. By evening, it would depart again, bound for Sealdah by dawn. Those who would go were already claiming their seats.

Outside the station, bullock carts stood in a line—heavy-hoofed and laden with goods. Then came the shops, hawkers of trinkets, tea-sellers, sweetmeat vendors, and rice-houses. People bustled everywhere. Goalanda was a great junction; from near and far, travellers gathered here to catch the train.

East of the ghat, the air thickened with the tang of fish. The night-long labour of breaking ice and packing silver *hilsa* into crates continued without pause. The fish would soon journey onward to Calcutta. Porters with bundles on their heads dashed about with urgency. The whole terrain was sandy loam—treacherous in monsoon, yielding dust in summer and winter alike. The earth sloped gently until it met the vast Padma, now in lean season, though many times wider than the Ganga at Calcutta—so wide that if one stood on the shore, one could not glimpse the other.

Boats were moored in long lines. Some were setting off, freighted with goods and men, bound for distant banks. Midstream, floated a grand steamer, majestic, anchored like a sentinel. One must first cross by boat to reach it. A ticket counter was nearby. It was here that Manmatha Babu said, 'You wait here; I'll go and fetch the tickets.'

'I'll come with you,' offered Shuddhananda.

They joined a long, unruly queue comprising mostly villagers, pushing and shoving to reach the front. A stout guard with a stick struggled to contain the throng. Seeing the saffron-clad monks, the guard approached.

'Where are you headed, Maharaj?'

'Narayanganj.'

'How many of you?'

'Seven.'

'Come with me.'

With quiet deference, they followed. At the counter's narrow window, tickets were being tossed out amid jostling hands. But the guard cleared the crowd himself and returned with seven tickets.

'You'll take the *Ostrich* steamer,' he said. 'It's the best of the lot. You'll be well cared for.'

Shuddhananda folded his palms. 'May Sri Ramakrishna bless you.'

One by one, they made their way past the platform, down to the ghat. In the rains, the river rises to kiss the platform's edge, but now the water lies far below. Boats were moored to poles plunged into the muddy bank as far as the eye could see. Men bathed in its sacred flow. The pulse of human life beat unceasingly, on water and land alike.

At a distance, fishing boats lay anchored, having returned from the night's catch. Loud cries filled the air as haggling and hawking began in earnest. In the middle of the Padma floated the steamer *Ostrich*, its name scrawled across its hull.

'There,' said Shuddhananda, pointing. 'That's our vessel.'

A boatman came forward. 'Are you sadhus bound for that steamer?'

'Yes,' Swamiji replied. 'Will you take us there?'

'How many?'

'Seven.'

'Seven paisa.'

Manmatha Babu handed him the fare. 'What is your name, brother?'

'Azgar.'

'Very good. Brother Azgar, let our journey to East Bengal begin with your boat.'

They stepped in, one by one, the craft brushing against countless others in the throng. With a thrust of his pole, Azgar dislodged his vessel from the tangle. Near the steamer, a small boat was moored to its side. A thick gangplank connected the two. A coarse mat had been spread on its wooden surface.

They crossed and stepped aboard.

It was a two-tiered steamer, almost a small ship. On the right was the engine room, humming with mysterious machinery. A narrow corridor ran through the middle, with stairs rising to the upper deck. Forward lay small cabins, cushioned and curtained, with their high-priced luxury berths. To the rear was the second class section. In the centre was the third class, the lot of the humble.

Swamiji asked, 'Kanai, where are our seats?'

A crewman glanced at their tickets. 'Back there,' he said. 'Go on through.'

There, they found cushioned benches. A few others were already seated. Along the railing, the monks settled in. Third class swelled with crowds, voices rising in cacophony. There was no room for bundles, people shoved theirs beneath each other's seats, sparking arguments and curses.

From the deck, they could still see the ghat, the station, the shops, and beyond. Nityananda, who had never before ventured this way, said, 'Guruji, have you noticed? There's not a single brick building here, just huts of mud and bamboo.'

Opposite sat an old man, who spoke before Swamiji could reply. 'The Padma is a fickle river, *sadhu baba*. I remember when I was a boy, where we now sit was ten minutes from the water's edge. Now the river has swallowed all. In ten years, it might return to its old bed. There's no count of the villages that vanish each year beneath its waves.'

'Life must be hard along these shifting banks,' someone said.

'Yes, *Baba*. People build their homes with such toil, only to see them destroyed by the Padma's fury. Their sorrow has no end.'

Swamiji said nothing. Human suffering was a weight he felt too deeply to express easily.

More passengers trickled aboard. Soon, the steamer was filled to the brim. Not a single seat remained. Those without benches squatted by the railing. At ten, the bell rang, *dong, dong*. A few latecomers dashed in, clambering from boat to steamer. When they were aboard, the gangplank was withdrawn. A metal railing was drawn across.

Then came the whistle, like a piercing cry that rent the sky. The steamer lurched, then moved forward. The water churned in great waves, and the boats at the shore bobbed like hollowed gourds. For a moment, there was noise and flurry. Then, slowly, quiet returned.

The steamer hugged the river's right bank, gliding past sloping shores where, in places, the water lapped up to beds of grass and trembling foliage....

Now the far bank came into view with its trees and groves, gardens and hamlets, and sprawling fields. Beyond the wide expanse of water, the opposite shore fades into a haze, resembling just a trembling line on the horizon. As far as the eye can see, there is water, only water. Great waves roll and tumble, shimmering in a thousand hues beneath the sun's caress. Most delightful are the flocks of whistling ducks. Wings outstretched, they wheel on both sides of the steamer, catching scraps of food mid-air before they even touch the water. Their chirping fills the air around the vessel, a ceaseless murmur of joy. Here and there, mustard fields bloom golden. There is an entire plain bathed in yellow, as if some unseen hand had brushed the earth with light. It pleases the eye and soothes the soul. Villages emerge now and then, mud houses, tin roofs glinting like ripples, nestled among mango, coconut, *jamun*, and banana trees. A riverside market bustles with life in tin-roofed stalls and merchant godowns. Boats ply the river's flow; their sails full, oars slicing, and poles pushing. Sometimes, a fisherman's skiff floats close, rocked like a banana sheath in the steamer's wake.

Swamiji sits enthralled. Nature here seems lost in meditation upon the Infinite. He glances at his disciples beside him and says, 'Have you seen such beauty? Nowhere else on earth will you find such a sight!'

Nityananda nods with a smile. Slightly older than Swamiji, he is fond of jest and stories. He hesitates a little, then chuckles, 'All's well, Gurudev… except that my stomach's been empty too long to enjoy it fully.'

Nityananda loves to eat, and even more, to feed others. Shuddhananda turns to him, 'Dada, do you have anything with you?'

'Wait a bit,' he says, opening his satchel. Out come two mid-sized tiffin tins, packed with *luchis* and vegetable curry. They divide the food among themselves. Manmatha Babu stuffs an entire *luchi* into his mouth and, swallowing with effort, asks, 'When did you manage to arrange all this?'

'I told the Brahmin cook before we left Belur. Everything was packed and ready before we set off.'

Swamiji laughs, 'When we return to Belur, I'll appoint you Royal Keeper of the Kitchen. Then no one shall ever go hungry!'

The steamer moves again. Below deck, Swamiji heads to the restroom, but pauses. He sees a small chamber ablaze with fire. In the next room, there are heaps of coal. Two men in robes, long-handled shovels in hand, throw coal into the fire. Sweat trickles down their bodies; the heat reddens their faces. A few others work in a small kitchen nearby. A pang of sorrow grips Swamiji. How much hardship people endure just to stay alive.

Ahead lies a pier. The steamer halts. Some disembark, others board. Swamiji stands by the railing. Around the dock, float several fishing boats, their nets cast. On the boats, heaps of silver hilsa shimmers as sunlight dances on their scales. A middle-aged boatmaster supervises the crowd. Swamiji approaches. He's never seen hilsa caught before but ventures a guess, asking, 'Brother, is that hilsa they're catching?'

'Yes, master. Fresh Padma hilsa. What taste, what aroma! Haven't had it in so long.'

Swamiji's eyes gleam with delight.

Nirbhayananda asks, 'Would you like some, Gurudev?'

'I could have some. How much do they cost? Go find out.'

At Swamiji's word, the boatmaster calls out to a fisherman, 'How much for the hilsa?'

'One anna each, Babu.'

'Three should be plenty for us,' Nirbhayananda suggests.

Swamiji thinks for a moment. 'Buy a full rupee's worth.'

Nirbhayananda's eyes widen. 'That's fifteen or sixteen fish! What will we do with so many? We're just seven!'

Swamiji smiles, 'Are we the only ones to eat? Those who work on this steamer will eat too. They are poor souls. But hilsa alone won't do, if only we had some Malabar spinach to go with it....'

'How long will the launch stop here?' asks Nirbhayananda.

'Half an hour,' replies the boatmaster.

'Then I'll go to the shore and see. Perhaps we can find some.'

'Don't be late,' Swamiji warns. He worries over his disciples more than he lets on.

Down the gangplank leaps Shuddhananda. No shops in sight near the dock. A few people gathered nearby. He paused. 'Brothers, can I find Malabar spinach here?'

'Malabar spinach? Go to the market, you'll find it there.'

'Where is the market?'

'About two krosh (6 kms) away.'

Too far. The launch will depart soon. Still, Shuddhananda lingers. Swamiji had *spoken* of the wish to eat spinach. Nearby, two men stand watching. On impulse, he approaches. Seeing a monk, they fold their hands, '*Pranam, Sadhu Baba.*'

'Bless you,' he replies. 'Do you know where I might find Malabar spinach?'

One man looks startled. 'Of all things, a sadhu seeking spinach?' Then, softening, 'Yes, it can be found. Where are you all coming from?'

'Belur Math, heading to Dhaka.'

'Belur Math! I've heard of it. Who else is with you?'

A villager's idle curiosity. Reluctantly, Nirbhayananda replies, 'Swami Vivekananda is travelling with us. Do you know of him?'

The man's face transforms. Hands folded tight, he whispers, 'He went to America, didn't he? I know his name.'

'You are right. Swamiji went to speak at the World's Parliament of Religions in America. He's the one who wished for spinach.'

The man trembles, overwhelmed. 'Did you say—Swamiji wishes to eat spinach? Come! My house is nearby. We have a garden full of it. As much as you want. But, just one request.'

'Don't worry,' says Shuddhananda quickly, 'We'll pay whatever price you ask.'

The man's face is flushed. 'No, no, I ask no price.'

Shuddhananda is puzzled. 'Then tell me, what do you ask? If it's within our means, we shall give it.'

The man lowers his head, voice trembling. 'Let me see Swamiji. Just once. In this life, I will never be so blessed again.'

Shuddhananda's eyes brim with tears. He hadn't expected this from a simple village soul. He places a hand on the man's back, 'So be it.'

'Come,' the man calls. Not far stands his house. In the garden, spinach vines twine up the fence, their tender leaves glistening. He gathers a basketful and carries it on his head.

Swamiji paces in anxious wait. The launch is ready to depart. Then Shuddhananda returns, and before Swamiji can speak, the man lays the basket at his feet and collapses, prostrate before him.

'Never did I dream I would see one such as you,' he chokes. 'How boundless is Thakur's grace, that you would think of eating my humble greens! If you truly have such grace for me, give me initiation, let me walk the path.'

Swamiji stretches out both arms and draws him into his chest. The launch bell tolls. Swamiji says gently, 'Fear not. Your devotion, your love for God, is true. On my way back, I shall return and give you initiation myself.'

Tears stream down the villager's cheeks, silent and shining.

The Sacred Pilgrimage to Langalbandh

After travelling through Deobhog in Narayanganj, Swamiji finally arrived in Dhaka. Arrangements for his stay had been made at the residence of Zamindar Mohini Mohan Das. It was a grand house, befitting such a guest. The host had left no stone unturned in hospitality. A place was prepared in the drawing room where visitors could gather, and it didn't take long for word of Swamiji's arrival to spread. Devotees began pouring in throughout the day, each eager to hear him speak, to ask questions, and to make heartfelt requests. Swamiji, ever patient, showed not the slightest sign of weariness. He understood that life, bound within the same relentless cycles, often leaves the human spirit deeply tired, and when it glimpses a path beyond, it rushes towards it with desperate longing.

Someone asked, 'Are knowledge and devotion separate paths?'

Swamiji replied, 'There is no difference. Devotion is offering all your love at the feet of the Divine. And when you can truly do that, you begin to see the divine form of love in everything around you. This love is without desire, without attachment, and even without identification with the body. Knowledge, on the other hand, is knowing the true nature of God, free from ego. Yet, foolish people waste their lives arguing which is greater—knowledge or devotion. It's like the tale of Shiva and Rama. Once, they were said to have battled for two days, and in the end, neither was greater nor lesser. But Shiva's ghostly attendants and Rama's monkey allies began to quarrel, and that quarrel, full of bickering and noise, has yet to end.'

Everyone laughed. Just then, a man arrived, his face etched with sorrow. 'I couldn't come earlier,' he said. 'My son is very ill.'

Swamiji sensed the man's helplessness. Taking his hand, he said gently, 'There's no need for hesitation. If I were a householder and my child were sick, and a monk came to see me, I would ask him to return another time. The monk I could see again, but if my child were to leave, I could never bring him back. I would give all my heart to my child and pay no attention to anything else.'

The man, overcome by such compassion, began to weep. 'You are God to me,' he cried. 'Please bless my son, just once. He will surely be healed.'

Swamiji could feel the father's desperate yearning. 'I am no God,' he said quietly. 'I don't even know if I possess any such power. Still, I will go.'

The next morning, Swamiji visited the man's home. The child lay pale and lifeless, nearly sunken into the bed. His mother, tearful, collapsed at Swamiji's feet. 'He is my only son. What will become of him?'

Swamiji understood the mother's pain. Placing a gentle hand on the child's head, he chanted softly for a while. 'All will be well,' he said at last. 'By the grace of the Lord, everything will be alright.'

Returning to the Zamindar's house, one of Swamiji's companions who had witnessed everything asked, 'Swamiji, you are a monk. It is said that monks are to remain detached from worldly concerns. Yet you show such deep love for people?'

Swamiji grew still, his voice tinged with emotion. 'I received this love from my Guru, Sri Ramakrishna. He was made of love. When one sees the presence of the Divine in all beings, one begins to feel a profound kinship with every soul. There remains no division.'

He told a story. 'Once, Sri Ramakrishna stood at the ghat by the Ganga in Dakshineswar, absorbed in a divine mood, his gaze lost in the river. Nearby, two boatmen began to quarrel. First, heated words flew, then fists. One struck the other sharply on the back. In that moment, Sri Ramakrishna screamed in pain. His nephew, Hriday, ran from the Kali temple. "What happened, uncle?" he cried. Lifting Ramakrishna's shirt, he saw his back was red and swollen, as though struck. Ramakrishna whispered, "No one hit me, Hriday. But when one boatman struck the other, I felt it as though it landed on me."' As Swamiji spoke, he seemed to drift into a higher state. Devotees—residents of Dhaka, people of learning and stature—sat around him in silence. Each day they came to hear him, listen to his words, and ask him their questions. Be it Shruti, Smriti, Puranas, Gita, Upanishads, poetry, or epics—no matter the question, Swamiji's answers came effortlessly, as if he carried all the scriptures within. There was never a moment's delay in a response, as if Saraswati, herself, resided within him. Every doubt dissolved in his light.

One day, someone asked, 'Tell us about religion, Swamiji. Do you accept all faiths?'

With a serene smile, Swamiji replied, 'I accept all religions of the past as true. I have joined in their worship. In every way they worship the Divine. I, too, worship that same Divine. I have gone to mosques with Muslims. I have knelt before Christ in churches. In Buddhist *viharas*, I have taken refuge in the *Dharma*. In solitude, I have meditated beside Hindu yogis. My heart has thrown open all its doors. I bow to the sages of the past, the great souls of the present, and all those who are yet to come.'

The audience sat in stillness. They knew that not everyone could fully grasp the depth of his words. Only one who had ascended to the highest realm of spiritual understanding could truly comprehend a soul like Swamiji's. Yet even a drop from that vast ocean was enough to nourish their hearts.

Just then, the father of the ailing child returned. He fell at Swamiji's feet. 'By your grace, my child has recovered. You are God incarnate.'

Swamiji lifted him up with both hands. 'I am not God,' he said. 'Whatever happened was due to the blessings of my Guru. It is his boundless compassion.'

Two days passed. The Zamindar suggested a pilgrimage to Langalbandh. Swamiji was delighted. His mother had come; he would take her with him to this sacred site.

In a letter to his disciple Ole Bull, he had written:

'I am taking Mother on pilgrimage. It will take a few months to complete. For Hindu widows, pilgrimage is the deepest yearning of the soul. All my life, I have caused sorrow to my family. Now I am trying to fulfil at least this one wish.'

Swamiji had always wished to bring his mother to Dhaka, but it had not been possible earlier. His mother, too, had shown little interest then. But once he renounced the world, she felt she should have gone. His elder sister, Swarnamoyee, also expressed a desire to go, along with a few other women of the household who had never travelled beyond their four walls. Now, the idea of stepping outside—into liberation, into the realm of merit and sacred vision—filled them with longing.

Bhubaneshwari Devi was torn. Naren had asked her to come earlier. She hadn't. Now he was not with them. She was unsure of what to do. Then she thought, perhaps Sharat or Rakhal could help. They, too, regarded her as a mother and loved her deeply.

Swarnamoyee said, 'Yes, Ma, I feel the same.'

So Bhubaneshwari Devi went to Belur to see Rakhal (Swami Brahmananda). He immediately became attentive. 'Yes, Ma,' he said. 'I'll send a telegram to Naren and see what he says.'

Swamiji was overjoyed to receive it. He had longed to bring his mother. He replied, 'Rakhal, arrange for Ma's journey. Send Sadananda along to accompany her. Let me know when she will arrive.'

Swamiji had arrived in Dhaka on 19 March. Bhubaneshwari Devi arrived on 25 March. After a day of rest, they began their journey to the sacred pilgrimage site of Langalbandh.

The scriptures proclaim the waters of the Ganga to be eternally pure, and ablutions in her flow, whether daily, monthly, or yearly, wash away sin. Yet the Brahmaputra, mighty and vast, bears a different decree. Her waters are impure, save for one sacred day. When the eighth lunar day of the month of *Chaitra* aligns with the propitious *Budha Nakshatra*, the heavens call it *Budhashtami*. Only then, once a year, does Langalbandh awaken as a supreme pilgrimage site, the veil of time parting to reveal a tale of sorrow and sacrifice on its banks.

In an age long vanished, there lived a sage named Jamadagni. His wife was Renuka, a woman of virtue, and together they had five sons—the youngest of whom was Parashurama. One day, Renuka went to the Ganga to fetch water. There, on the river's edge, King Shatabahu was sporting with his queens in playful abandon. The sight stirred something dormant in Renuka. Her body trembled, her soul quickened; how long had it been since she had known union with her ascetic husband. Transfixed, she lingered, seized by an invisible longing. When at last she returned, the thirsty Jamadagni asked, 'What caused your delay?'

Renuka said nothing. How could she speak of her heart's turmoil? But the sage, with his yogic vision, perceived all. His fury ignited like dry tinder. 'She has strayed from the path of *dharma*,' he roared to his sons. 'She must be punished.'

The sons stood frozen, aghast. Questioning the father was not their right, yet they pleaded, 'Forgive her, Father.'

But Jamadagni's wrath would not be quelled. 'There is no pardon for such impurity. I condemn her to death. Who among you will carry out my sentence?'

One by one, the elder sons lowered their heads in silent refusal. None dared stain their soul with the sin of matricide.

The sage's fury knew no bounds. 'You have defied your father's command! Be cursed. May you fall into the dullness of stone!'

Then Parashurama stepped forward. His face was like iron. With his axe, he struck down his own mother.

The sage, now pleased, asked, 'What boon do you seek, my son?'

Parashurama bowed. 'Let my mother live again. Let her memory be free of this dark act. Let my brothers be freed from your curse. And let no taint of this sin cling to me.'

But even as he uttered the words, the sin had already taken root. The moment his axe fell, the curse of slaying a woman—his own mother—wrapped itself around him. Not even Jamadagni's ascetic might could lift it. The axe clung to Parashurama's hand, fused with his flesh, immovable and damning.

Tormented and lost, he turned to his father. 'How shall I be freed from this evil?'

'Go forth on a pilgrimage,' said Jamadagni. 'Bathe in every

sacred water. When you find the *tirtha* where the axe falls from your hand, know that place to be holier than all others.'

So Parashurama wandered until at last he came to Manasarovar, nestled in the Himalayas. There he bathed in the divine *Brahma-kunda*, and in that instant, the axe fell from his hand. The burden lifted.

Gratitude surged in his heart. If only this sacred water could be brought to the mortal world, it would bless all humankind. Remembering his plough, his constant companion in tilling his father's land, he cleaved the earth and brought the celestial stream down from the mountains. Thus was born the Brahmaputra, the 'Son of Brahma.'

He led the sacred flow across the plains until he reached a place that would come to be known as Langalbandh, the Place of the Plough. There he paused, remembering that his pilgrimage was not yet over.

He turned to the river and said, 'Wait here. I shall return once my journey is complete.'

But when he returned, the Brahmaputra had defied him, flowing far ahead to merge with the Lakshya River.

Parashurama's heart blazed with fury. 'You disobeyed me,' he cried, 'and so, I curse you, your waters shall lose all sanctity, and be deemed impure!'

The Brahmaputra pleaded for forgiveness. Moved, Parashurama relented—'On the eighth day of the bright fortnight in *Chaitra*, the day of *Ashoka Ashtami*, your waters shall once again be pure. Whoever bathes in you on that day shall be freed of all sin.'

Since then, Langalbandh has stood as a holy place of pilgrimage.

Now, from Dhaka, Swamiji and his companions journeyed towards Langalbandh—a distance of 21 km in two boats. In one, sat Swamiji and his devotees; and in the other, his mother,

Bhubaneshwari Devi, his aunt, and elder sister, along with Sadananda and Nirbhayananda. They had set off at night's end. Mohini Mohan Babu, the local zamindar, had arranged everything.

The boats glided silently while the pale veil of night clung to the sky. The riverbanks were shrouded in shadow, and nothing was clear, but one could glimpse erosion, and distant sandbars where shrubs grew wild. Villages flickered past, along with groves of mango, bamboo, and jackfruit trees. Gradually, darkness lifted. The boats sailed on, and with every mile, the gathering of pilgrims swelled.

At dawn, Swamiji's eyes grew tender. This threshold between night and day, stirred him. He gazed at the sky, humming softly to himself.

Beside him was Shuddhananda, silently moved. Whenever he was near Swamiji, some rare current passed through him, a radiant stillness of body and soul. Swamiji drew people in as if by divine magnetism, as if Sri Ramakrishna's own power flowed through his being into his disciples.

He remembered a day from some months ago at Belur Math. Swamiji had declared, 'Today I shall worship Sri Ramakrishna.' Excitement rippled through the ashram. All gathered to witness how he would perform the rites.

The upper-floor shrine was adorned with flowers, fruits, and offerings. Swamiji sat in silence. He touched nothing, but closed his eyes and entered deep meditation. His disciples, seated around him, followed suit.

After some time, they felt a presence moving among them. Curious, someone opened his eyes and was astonished. Swamiji had risen. In his hands was a tray of flowers. He dipped each blossom in sandal paste and touched it to their foreheads, one by one.

A wave of wonder swept through them. These were the

flowers meant for the Master's feet, so why was Swamiji offering them to the disciples? Was he worshipping his disciples just as Sri Ramakrishna once worshipped the Divine Mother?

Later, someone asked. Swamiji smiled gently and replied, 'I want my Guru's power to flow through you. He lives within each of you. These flowers, though placed upon your heads, were offered to His lotus feet.'

Shuddhananda reflected quietly. Swami Vivekananda poured himself into others like a mother bird shielding her chicks with her wings. Perhaps that is why he once declared, 'Fear not, those upon whom I have laid my hand shall have no cause to worry. Even if my disciples fall into hell a thousand times, I shall raise them up a thousand more. If this is false, then let my Master and Mother be false too.'

A gentle touch brought Shuddhananda back from his thoughts. The boat moved steadily beneath a sky streaked with rose. Along the eastern horizon, crimson light bled into the dawn. The colours shimmered like the trembling curtain of some cosmic play when they were reflected in the Brahmaputra's waters.

Strange boats floated past, lining both sides of Swamiji's vessel. Judging by their passengers, all were pilgrims bound for Langalbandh. Hymns, *kirtan*, and the chanting of the Lord's name filled the air.

The river here stretched more than a mile wide. But the water was shallow, dotted with sandbars. Long ago, the Brahmaputra flowed here majestically, its wild waves thundering past. Not far away ran the Yamuna, a branch of the Brahmaputra. But in nature's strange will, the Brahmaputra changed course, forsaking its path to pour into the Yamuna's bed. Now, its old channel was almost dry. And yet it was along this very path that the pilgrims made their way to Langalbandh.

A kilometre before the bathing ghat, the banks were already full. Boats were packed tightly along the shore.

The boatman called out, 'Holy Baba, we can go no further. Since midnight, boats have been arriving here. There's no space left to moor.'

Nirbhayananda looked around, astonished. 'I never imagined so many people would come here,' he murmured.

All wished to partake in the pilgrimage. Swamiji rose to his feet, his eyes scanning the horizon. Mother's boat was nowhere in sight. A quiet anxiety stirred within him. Manmatha Babu, sensing this unease, gently said, 'I saw her boat not long ago.' Just then, Shuddhananda cried out, 'There it is, Didima's boat!'

The boatman ferrying Mother had spotted them too and rowed swiftly towards them. A small gap of water separated the two boats. The boatman of Swamiji's craft called out, 'Anchor here.'

Two large mango trees stood on the shore, side by side. Swamiji pointed towards them and said, 'If anyone is lost in the crowd, they should return, keeping these trees in sight.'

The boats were moored. Swamiji stepped forward himself, took his mother by the hand, and helped her ashore. Mohini Babu's servant, a local man, had been entrusted with everyone's care. He carried two small bundles on his shoulder and led the way. The others followed close behind. As they walked, the crowd around them swelled—children, the aged, boys, girls, young women, housewives—everyone was there.

The servant spoke as they moved, 'Only once a year does such a crowd gather here. At other times, people come, but very few.'

Halfway along the path, the bathing ghats began—thirteen in total. Manmatha Babu asked, 'Brother, at which ghat shall we bathe?'

The servant replied as he walked, 'Rajghat. The King of Nepal bathed there.'

Swamiji smiled faintly. 'If one must bathe, better to do so at a king's ghat.'

The ghat was broad, paved, and bound by stone, yet not an inch was free. They halted at one side. By then, the sun had risen, and both bathing water and land were bathed in a crimson glow. Far across the river, men and women stood shoulder to shoulder, immersed in their sacred bath. The water was waist-deep—muddy, thick, and tinged with green. Some squatted, some knelt, some bent low trying to submerge. Many women's garments had come undone, but no one seemed to mind. All sought the joy of pilgrimage.

Swamiji bent low and touched the water, as he paused in thought. Then, turning to his companions, he said: 'You may enter the river and bathe, but do not drink even a drop. It may sicken you.'

Bhubaneshwari Devi asked, 'And if some water accidentally enters the mouth?'

'Don't swallow it. Rinse your mouth with clean water after you return to shore.'

All stepped into the river. The other pilgrims made space, honouring the sadhus. The riverbed, firm with sand and stone, lay beneath. Swamiji's sister held their mother's hand. They went a little farther into the stream. The water was too shallow for a full immersion. So they poured water over one another's heads, thus completing their ritual.

Gathering around Swamiji, they waited. He looked at them briefly and asked, 'Have any of you drunk the river water?'

'No, no,' came the chorus of replies.

Smiling, Swamiji said, 'Once, with great effort, I managed to take a dip. A drop of water entered my mouth, and I drank it. Who knows from where grace may flow?'

They changed their clothes. It was time for temple visits. On both riverbanks rose countless monasteries, temples, and ashrams, teeming with devotees. Bhubaneshwari Devi wished to visit the main temples. Swamiji, unwilling to deny his mother anything, said, 'Come, Mother. Wherever you wish to go, we shall go.'

Ahead stood an ancient temple, its spire broken. Peepal and banyan trees clung to its cracked walls. Around it lay a garden, though wild growth outnumbered the flowers. A few people wandered there. Bhubaneshwari Devi said, 'I will go inside.'

Swamiji agreed. 'Let us enter.'

The doorway was low and there were no windows. Inside, darkness prevailed. A lone lamp flickered faintly, casting a dim glow. In that wavering light, a pedestal and an indistinct deity, thickly smeared with vermilion, came into view. Swamiji guessed it might be Shitala or Kali. Bhubaneshwari Devi offered her *pranam*, then touched the deity and gently placed that hand on Swamiji's head.

Beside it stood another temple. People entered with vessels of water, Swamiji knew it was a Shiva temple. He filled a vessel himself and placed it in his mother's hands. Inside was darkness again. At the centre stood a sacred pit, surrounded by devotees who reached within, touched the Shiva *linga*, and poured their water.

Shuddhananda came forward, parting the crowd to lead Bhubaneshwari Devi to the front. The linga lay deep below; she had to lean in to touch it. Swamiji stood quietly in a corner. Shuddhananda supported her as she made her offering. Then the priest called out, 'Come, *Maharaj*, please step forward.'

Swamiji moved ahead, bent low, and touched the linga. In

that instant, a tremor coursed through his body. All around, voices rose in triumphant exclamation:

'Victory to Bhairavanath Baba! Jai Baba Bhairavanath!'

Swamiji joined the chant, his voice in harmony with the crowd:

'Victory to Bhairavanath Baba! Jai Baba Bhairavanath!'

Mahananda Kaviraj

Swamiji had returned to Belur. He sat quietly in his room, resting on an armchair, though no comfort truly touched his ailing body. His feet were swollen; his breath came in shallow drafts, and a loose tooth had ached since morning. He had closed his eyes, seeking a moment's quietude. A gentle touch stirred him. Opening his eyes, he saw his disciple Sharatchandra, who bowed and sat at his feet.

'How are you, Gurudev?' he asked softly.

A melancholy, wistful smile played on Swamiji's face, but he remained silent for a long while. Sharatchandra, anxious, leaned in: 'Shall I send for a physician?'

Swamiji tried to appear composed. 'What use would that serve?' he said, gently. 'If the others in the monastery hear, they will come running. I cannot bear to trouble anyone on my account. No, there's no need to inform anyone. I've travelled far and wide; this body is worn. A bit of illness is only to be expected. I've grown used to it. The days I have left, I must live with thirty ailments beside me. Tell me, how are things here?'

Sharatchandra nodded. 'All is well.'

Swamiji sat upright. A fine sheen of sweat glistened on his brow. Seeing this, Sharatchandra at once took up a fan and began to wave it gently. Swamiji felt some relief and said, 'This last journey to East Bengal, how sweet it was. Most of all, I loved visiting the home of Nag Mahashay at Deobhog. A soul like his is rare. Having come so far, how could I not pay homage to his birthplace? His wife was there. She cooked for me with such affection. It was their village home, serene, like an ashram. I swam in the pond, then fell into a deep sleep. Slept straight through till half-past two—one of the few truly restful sleeps of my life. Later, she gave me a piece of cloth, and tying it about my head, I set out once more for Dhaka. The land is beautiful, with rivers and water everywhere. Where we have carriages, there they have boats. Fields stretched out in between, heavy with grain. Hills rose to the north, such lovely sights. But most magnificent was the Brahmaputra Valley.'

He paused, his eyes distant with memory. 'One thing I noticed—the people there are strong, healthy, and hardworking. Perhaps because they eat more fish and meat. But too much oil and fat is not good. It breeds excess in the body.'

Sharatchandra listened intently, always a devoted listener. He knew that Swamiji's eyes saw deeper than most; what others passed over, he perceived in full. 'Did you go to Kamakhya?' he asked.

'Yes,' Swamiji nodded. 'First to the hill shrine of Chandranath. After paying respects to Baba Chandranath, I made my way to Assam, to the temple of Goddess Kamakhya. There, people have deep faith in their hearts. Devotees come from all across the land. I spent several days in Guwahati. But my health worsened; everyone was deeply concerned. Sir Henry Cotton, the Chief Commissioner of Assam, holds me in great esteem. He arranged for me to stay in Shillong. The civil surgeon there attended to me, but even so, there was no improvement.'

Speaking grew more difficult. His breathing was laboured. Three other disciples arrived and, one by one, bowed before him. Swamiji, through his discomfort, smiled and placed his hand gently upon each of their heads in blessing. Sharatchandra, not wishing his master to exert himself further, said, 'Come, let us go. Guru Maharaj will rest now.'

They descended quietly. Shuddhananda was seated on the veranda, occupied with some task. Looking up, he asked, 'You spoke with him?'

Sharatchandra's face was drawn with sorrow. Even the slightest pain of the Guru struck deep into his heart. 'He was short of breath,' he murmured.

Shuddhananda sighed. 'That is nothing. The suffering he endured in Shillong, indescribable. Fever, asthma, and his entire body was swollen. When the asthma worsened, he would stack pillows upon his chest, lean forward, and sit like that for hours, enduring agony beyond words.'

A shadow of a smile flickered as he continued, 'And yet, amidst all that, something curious happened. We were in Dhaka at the time. One day, a courtesan, perhaps having heard of Swamiji's name, arrived. Folding her hands, she pleaded, "Holy Father, I suffer terribly from asthma. When the attacks come, I cannot bear it. Please, if you have any medicine...."'

He paused, emotion welling up. 'Swamiji's face grew more sorrowful. He bore his own suffering without complaint, but the pain of another moved him deeply. With infinite tenderness, he said, "My child, you've come from far. Who could understand the torment of asthma better than I? There are times I feel my soul will depart from this body. I can do nothing. I do not know what might cure it. If I did, would I be in such a state myself?

Still, whatever my condition, I bless you. May you find relief." The woman left, her hope dimmed, but touched.'

Sharatchandra fell silent, sensing someone approaching. It was Niranjanananda. This disciple of Sri Ramakrishna was unlike the others—stern in manner, unyielding in will. Once he resolved to act, nothing could sway him. When Sri Ramakrishna was bedridden at the garden house in Kashipur, Niranjanananda stood guard like a sentinel with a staff in hand, lest visitors disturb the Master. Unless truly necessary, none could pass.

The Master's health had been precarious. Just the night before, blood had poured from his throat. The disciples were distraught and not one slept that night. By morning, Sri Ramakrishna had fallen into a deep sleep. Just then, Master Mahashay[20] arrived, uncertain whether to disturb him. As he moved towards the door, Niranjanananda appeared and, even knowing the deep reverence all held for Master Mahashay, said firmly, 'Do not go up. The Master is asleep. Let him rest.'

No one had imagined that anyone could stop Master Mahashay from seeing Sri Ramakrishna. He stood frozen, as if thunderstruck, then slowly walked out of the room and sat beneath a tree in the garden, quiet and wounded.

The moment he left, a wave of bitter remorse surged through Niranjan's heart. He had wounded, in his blindness, a devotee whom all revered—one unlike any other, wholly consecrated to the Master. He could wait no longer. With quick steps, he went to Master Mahashay, unhesitatingly admitted his mistake, and asked for forgiveness. Then, like a steadfast sentinel, he resumed his place at the door. He knew he had been given the most

20 Mahendra Nath Gupta recorder of *The Gospel of Sri Ramakrishna*

thankless task, but for his Guru, he could endure anything. Let all be displeased with him; he had chosen his path.

As Niranjanananda approached, Sharatchandra bowed to him. Seeing his sorrowful face, Niranjanananda asked, 'What news, Bengali? How is Naren's health?'

Before Sharatchandra could answer, Shuddhananda spoke: 'Since Dhaka, Guru Maharaj has been unwell. In Shillong, his condition worsened.'

Niranjanananda was silent for a moment. Placing a hand on Shuddhananda's shoulder, he said, 'Come, let us go see your stubborn, headstrong guru. He listens to no one, and only follows his own will.'

Shuddhananda said nothing. He knew it was precisely this fierce independence that had turned Narendra into Swami Vivekananda. Together they ascended to his room, with Sharatchandra following them. Swamiji lay with his eyes closed. At the sound of footsteps, he looked up. Seeing Niranjanananda, he said with a faint smile, 'Ah, come. One night in Dhaka, I suddenly thought of you.'

'You must have been very ill that day. And people were troubling you.'

Swamiji laughed heartily. 'You guessed right.'

Niranjanananda's face was grave. 'I haven't seen you in days. From now on, wherever you go, I'll go with you.'

'Good. And bring a heavy stick along!'

Shuddhananda suppressed a smile. Such was the sweetness between the two brother-disciples.

Niranjanananda brought a wooden stool and sat beside Swamiji. Taking his hand in his own, he said, 'You must grant me one request.'

Swamiji smiled through his pain and said, 'How can I say

"yes" without hearing it first?'

Frowning slightly, Niranjanananda said, 'You know I would never ask anything wrong of you.'

Swamiji understood Niranjan would not relent. 'Very well, I'll agree. Now tell me.'

A smile lit up Niranjanananda's face. 'I know a Kaviraj, a true healer. People call him a Dhanvantari.'

'What's his name?'

'Mahananda Sengupta. He comes from a long line of physicians. If you agree, I'll send for him tomorrow.'

Swamiji thought for a moment. He had no real choice. 'All right. Send for him.'

Clasping Swamiji's hand more tightly, Niranjanananda said, 'I promise, you'll recover this time.'

'If so, I'll be glad. Are you going anywhere now?'

'I'm going to Mother's house in Baghbazar. Sharatchandra asked me to see how she's doing. It's been a long time since I offered my *pranam*.'

Swamiji's gaze turned distant. Since his return from East Bengal, he hadn't heard how his mother, Bhubaneshwari Devi, was. She was old now and burdened with many worries. 'Niranjan, can you do one thing for me?'

'Tell me, tell me! What is it?' Niranjanananda asked, eagerly.

'If you can, go to Simla and see how my mother is....'

Before he could finish, Niranjanananda interrupted, 'You don't have to worry. I'll find out and bring news.'

As soon as Niranjanananda left, Sharatchandra said anxiously, '*Deshi* medicine can be quite effective. I've seen it help people. What do you think, Guru Maharaj?'

Swamiji remained silent for some time. Shuddhananda and Sharatchandra waited, watching his face. Then, in a calm voice, he said, 'In my opinion, dying under the care of a scientific doctor is better than living under the hands of a quack who knows nothing of modern science—those who blindly follow ancient texts and shoot arrows in the dark. Even if some of their patients recover, true healing can't be expected from them.'

Two days later, Kaviraj Mahananda arrived. He was elderly, fair-skinned, with tufts of hair like *kadamba* blossoms, and a strong frame. Swamiji lay upstairs. Niranjanananda brought the Kaviraj along with two others. Swamiji sat up. They exchanged respectful greetings.

A chair was offered to the Kaviraj, who sat and looked long and deeply at Swamiji. With his trained gaze, he began to assess his condition. A smile appeared on his lips. 'In our Ayurvedic scriptures,' he said, 'it is written *sharīram vyādhimandiram*, the body is the temple of disease. Many goddesses of illness come and go through it. It is the physician who decides which medicine is for which goddess.'

Laughing, Swamiji replied, 'So many goddesses have made permanent residence in this temple, I don't even know who all are staying here!'

The Kaviraj took Swamiji's hand and began to feel his pulse. For a long time, with deep concentration, he examined every subtle vibration of vein and vessel. At last, lifting his hand, he said, '*Pitta, vayu,* and *kapha*—these three forces are all imbalanced. The disease is complex and will take time. One more thing, my method is unique. You must follow my instructions exactly. Only then will I treat you.'

Before Swamiji could speak, Niranjanananda said, 'I give you my word. Everything will be done as you instruct.'

The Kaviraj nodded solemnly. 'Good. Here are a few powders and mixtures. They must be taken regularly. But the chief rule of this treatment is no water for twenty-one days. Not a single drop. You may drink milk instead.'

Everyone looked at each other in disbelief. What kind of instruction was this? To survive without water in this scorching month of Baisakh? Many physicians had come before, but no one had ever said such a thing. All were eager to speak, but Swamiji, sensing this, smiled and said, 'I'll follow your advice, Kaviraj-*moshai*.'

The Kaviraj continued examining him a little more, then said gravely, 'There are many ailments. But don't worry, you will recover. You must rest fully. I will return in a week. Someone must come to my home for more medicine.'

'I'll go,' said Niranjanananda.

As they left, Sharatchandra said worriedly, 'In this intense summer heat, you drink water four or five times every hour. How will you manage this treatment?'

Swamiji showed no concern. Calmly, he replied, 'What are you saying? On the day I begin the medicine, I'll resolve: "I shall not drink water." Then let's see who can make me drink. For twenty-one days, not a drop shall pass my lips. The body is only the shell of the mind. It must obey the mind. Even the thought of water will not arise.'

Sharatchandra knew his guru's mental strength. Mountains might move, but not Swamiji's will. 'Still,' he said, 'it would have been wise to consult one more physician.'

Swamiji sighed deeply. 'It's not what Kaviraj said that matters to me. Nor the medicine. I agreed only because Niranjan insisted. They are my companions in joy and sorrow. I can't turn them away. Don't worry. The days will pass. Let's see if this new treatment brings some relief. It is all the Lord's will. You see, in the few days I have left, I know I must live burdened with illness.

That does not pain me. What pains me is that so much work remains unfinished.'

Sharatchandra understood Swamiji's anguish. 'Can any of us finish all our work, Guruji? What you've done in one life, others couldn't do in many. Acharya Shankara lived only thirty-two years. And yet he awakened a whole civilisation. After him, it is you.'

Swamiji shuddered. Bringing his hands to his chest, he whispered, 'He was Shiva incarnate, divine in human form. Matchless. And what have I done? All is the power of the Lord, of Sri Ramakrishna. He is ever awake. He *is*. And because He is, I am. But now, the time has come. I want to surrender all at His feet. I see His light shining all around. My time is short. I shall soon vanish into that light.'

Sharatchandra started to speak, then fell silent. Swamiji had grown still, peaceful. He was preparing to dive into the realm of meditation.

Rohu Fish

As on every other day, the hours passed in quiet succession. Swamiji sat, abstracted and remote, as though the ebb and flow of days and nights, the cycle of gain and loss, the play of hope and heartbreak, everything, was but a passing current. No sooner did something settle into place than a new wave came to claim its place. In this worldly ocean, nothing endures. Life does not pause; it flows like the ceaseless turning of the seasons.

Swamiji was seated in the veranda of his quarters in Belur. Upon his lap lay an open book, *Narada Samhita,* but it remained unread. His gaze was elsewhere, drifting in the vast realm of meditation, still and luminous like the unwavering flame of a lamp in a windless chamber. Lately, the face of Sri Ramakrishna often rose before him in that inner vision, like the first golden flush of dawn spreading across the eastern sky. That gentle radiance seemed to suffuse his body and soul. Swamiji grew restless. *Show me the way, Thakur. This vessel of life no longer sails. Will your call come now, at last?*

Suddenly, a burst of noise disturbed the still strings of his inner *veena*. He opened his eyes. Before him were the iron railings;

beyond them, the Ganga shimmering under a sun-soaked sky. And further still, the boundless, radiant firmament. Somewhere amidst all this, he had drifted away. A distant voice rang out. Swamiji turned to look. A boat had docked at the ghats. A few people were disembarking. On Sundays and holidays, devotees visited Belur regularly. That pleased him. The more people came, the more Sri Ramakrishna's words would spread from city to village and to every corner of the land.

Looking more closely, he recognised one among the passengers, Sharatchandra. Something hung in his hand. As he approached, it became clear. It was a large fish, dangling from his grip. Amused, Swamiji sensed what was to come; this fish was sure to stir some mischief.

Sharatchandra, upon seeing Swamiji, bowed from afar and said something. But Swamiji couldn't hear. Of late, his hearing had all but failed him; perhaps he would soon be completely deaf. But he felt no sorrow, no regret. He had accepted everything. What power has man to undo destiny?

Sharatchandra veered away and was soon out of sight. Swamiji knew the routine: he would go to the kitchen, place the fish, and then climb to the shrine upstairs for his devotions before returning.

Just then, Swamiji's attendant, Nirbhayananda, arrived with a bowl of milk. On instructions from Mahananda Kaviraj, Swamiji had stopped drinking water. The summer heat was intense. His throat parched, yet he could not consume much milk either—it upset his stomach. He drank just enough to moisten his lips.

Footsteps on the stairs. Swamiji turned to see Baburam Maharaj, approaching in haste, face taut with concern. Behind him was Sharatchandra, and two others. Clearly, something had happened. If it were a dispute with outsiders, Swamiji could resolve it easily. But if it was among their own....

Swamiji's face became serious.

Baburam burst out, 'Do you know what Sharatchandra is saying?'

A faint, knowing smile touched Swamiji's lips. 'Just what I expected. What's the Bengali up to now?'

'The fishermen were casting nets,' Baburam said. 'Sharatchandra bought a large rohu fish from them.'

Feigning surprise, Swamiji said, 'Is that so? Fresh rohu! Then we shall have a feast!'

Baburam's face remained grave. 'I wouldn't have minded. But Sharatchandra says he wants to offer the fish to Thakur as *bhog*!'

Swamiji clapped his hands. 'Splendid! A fine thought. And you're the one objecting?'

Baburam's voice dropped, laced with frustration. 'You call that a fine thought? Today is Sunday. On Sundays, we offer only vegetarian bhog to Thakur.'

'Why not non-veg on Sunday?' Swamiji asked, feigning innocence.

'It is the scriptural rule,' Baburam replied, solemnly.

Sharatchandra, standing to the side, spoke at last, 'I didn't know. The fish looked so fine, I thought I'd offer it to Thakur.'

Swamiji lit up with delight. 'When a devotee brings something with love for the Lord, rejecting it causes sorrow, not just to the devotee, but to the Lord as well.'

But Baburam could not fully agree. He knew that nothing could be said against Naren. Reluctantly, he added, 'But the cook is preparing a vegetarian meal today. He won't cook meat or fish alongside it.'

Swamiji laughed heartily. 'Such fuss over a trifle! You all go to the kitchen, I'll be right there.'

'I'm heading to Belur Bazaar,' said Sharatchandra. 'Someone is waiting to meet me. I'll return after seeing them.'

As everyone dispersed, Swamiji tightened the cloth around his waist and descended with Nirbhayananda straight to the kitchen. The place was a flurry of activity—pots, pans, ingredients strewn about. A small adjacent room was also used for extra cooking. When Swamiji entered, all activity halted. Baburam rushed to him first.

'Naren! You're not well. You've come here in this heat.'

'I will cook today's bhog for Thakur with my own hands.'

Everyone stood stunned. Swamiji's health was poor. It was midday; the heat was searing, and he had not drunk even a drop of water. Shuddhananda said, 'Master, please rest. I'll do the cooking.'

'You worry for nothing,' Swamiji said gently. 'I am capable of everything.'

Two of the helpers, worried, rushed to him. 'Please, Swamiji, let us handle it. We'll prepare everything.'

Swamiji thought for a moment. 'Very well, you set things up. I'll do the cooking. In the meantime, come sit with me under the tree, and we can talk.'

There was a great tree nearby, casting a wide, generous shade. A soft breeze stirred the air. Towards the afternoon, many gathered there. A brick platform served as a bench. As they sat, Swamiji's gaze fell on a group of women descending from the temple—young girls, middle-aged, and the elderly. They had spotted him, too. One of them whispered something to her companions, and suddenly all faces were alight with curiosity, wonder, and reverence. Yet they stood frozen.

Sensing their hesitation, Swamiji called out with tender affection, 'Come, my mothers, why do you stand over there?'

The sweet invitation melted their shyness. Slowly, one by one, they stepped forward and bowed. Swamiji blessed them all and asked, 'Where have you come from?'

The woman standing before him spoke softly, 'Joynagar, Majidpur.'

Swamiji turned his gaze. A disciple stood nearby and said, 'They have come from far away. Arrange for *prasad*.'

The women were spellbound. Swamiji asked gently, 'Did you visit Holy Mother at Baghbazar?'

One answered in a hushed voice, 'We shall go from here. We'll offer our salutations to Ma before returning home.'

Swamiji's manner was simple, yet deeply sincere. An elderly woman, her voice tinged with quiet despair, asked, 'Revered one, we were born as women. Our whole lives passed pushing the pot of household burdens. Wretched as we are, we could neither call upon God, nor do anything of worth.' Another woman, seated beside her, added bitterly, 'Didi speaks the truth. To be born a woman is a curse. No one thinks of us. We lie forgotten at the edge of the world.'

Swamiji's face grew troubled. With great tenderness, he said, 'Who says the birth of a woman is a sin? You are born of the Mother. Who is holier than She? This body, this mind of mine, everything was fashioned by one such mother. At birth, the mother rears the child, bearing untold pain. Sita, Savitri, and Damayanti—these were not just paragons of womanhood; they are ideals for all of India. Thakur Sri Ramakrishna worshipped Holy Mother as the Divine. And your love, your devotion, is that any less? You know the story of Savitri, don't you?' he asked. 'Princess Savitri saw the exiled Satyavan and loved him. Narada warned her that his days are few. Yet she married him. And when Death came, she followed Yama into the shadows. Her unwavering love and devotion conquered even Death, who returned Satyavan's soul to her.'

Tears welled up in the eyes of the women. For a fleeting moment, it was as if a breeze of liberation passed through their hearts. One asked, 'Swamiji, is there nothing we can do for society or the country?'

Swamiji's face grew luminous with passion. He knew how society had pushed women into the shadows. And yet, a few had begun to rise, though mostly from privileged classes. But true progress could not come from a chosen few. It required the participation of all—women and men, side by side.

He declared, 'Until you step forward, no change will come. Look at the women in foreign lands, how far they have advanced, while you are still bound.'

Just then, *prasad* was brought on a plate—fruit, sweets, and fried bread. They shared it among themselves, and their hearts overflowed with contentment. At the ghat, the boatman called out, 'The tide is coming. Time to depart!'

They rose to leave. Another round of humble salutations. Some tied dust from where Swamiji sat into the corners of their saris. 'We take your leave, Baba. Our hearts are full.'

'Come again,' he said with quiet affection.

As the women departed, someone remarked, 'How simple and full of faith our mothers are.'

Sharatchandra turned to him. 'Master, you have seen women in the West. Now you see our own. Are they really so different?'

A strange expression crossed Swamiji's face, like the shadow of a memory. For a moment, he was lost in silence. His mind soared beyond boundaries, and across oceans. Then, breaking his reverie, he said in an impassioned voice, 'How pure those women are! None marry before twenty-five or thirty. They are as free as birds in the sky. They run markets, earn their living, teach, profess—yet remain untouched in spirit. The wealthy among them dedicate their lives to the welfare of the poor. And what of us? We tremble if our daughter is not wed by eleven, fearing she will fall into disgrace. What kind of people are we?'

Swamiji had grown slightly agitated. Then he said, 'My heart yearns to establish an ashram on the far bank of the Ganga, where unmarried maidens and widowed brahmacharinis may dwell. Devout householder women too may come and stay for some time. No men shall reside there. Only aged monks from the male monastery will oversee affairs from a distance.

'There shall be a school in that women's monastery, where the scriptures, literature, Sanskrit, grammar, and a little English shall be taught. Alongside, they will learn the duties of home—cooking, sewing, child-rearing. And of course, meditation, prayer, and worship will be a part of daily life.

'Those who can leave their homes to live there will be provided food and clothing. But after receiving their education, not all will choose the path of renunciation. They must be free to decide for themselves. Without the upliftment of womanhood, no good can come to the world. That is why I speak of founding a women's monastery first.

'Holy Mother has returned to this land to awaken the *Mahashakti*. Through her grace, the Gargis and Maitreyis shall be born again. Without the blessing of that Divine Power, all efforts will be in vain.

'I ask myself one thing—why is there such a chasm between man and woman in our land? Who created this gulf? The Vedanta declares that the same Consciousness dwells in all beings. Yet, you never cease to revile women. Tell me, what have you done for their upliftment? You've made them into mere instruments of reproduction. But these women, these are the very images of Mahamaya Herself. If you do not raise them now, there will be no hope left for you.'

'Your wish will surely come to pass.' None had noticed when Saradananda had arrived and stood quietly behind him. Swamiji smiled gently. Saradananda said, 'Even if the women's monastery is delayed by a few days, it won't matter. But today I heard you were going to cook fish. In this heat, if you wait too long, it will spoil.'

Swamiji sprang up. 'Ah! I had entirely forgotten in the midst of this talk.' The cook had already kindled the fire, cut the fish, and prepared everything. Swamiji joined in the cooking himself. He had not had even a drop of water in over a week; his body had withered. Yet he stood firm, face flushed from the heat of the flame, without the slightest sign of discomfort.

It was a large fish, Swamiji had already seen to that. Glancing once at Baburam behind him, he said, 'Fried fish, fish curry, and a rich *kaliya*. Three preparations. Thakur will be pleased today.'

Baburam, half-irritated, replied, 'And now that you're cooking it yourself, Thakur will surely be even more pleased.'

The cook had arranged bowls on the side. As each dish was finished, Swamiji offered the first portion in a bowl for Thakur's offering. At a signal from Baburam, a brahmachari stepped forward. 'Careful,' Baburam whispered, 'this is for Thakur.'

There was plenty of fish. Swamiji smiled and said, 'You all must eat well.' Everyone present seemed moved beyond words. One asked softly, 'Gurudev, will you not eat?'

A flicker of both humour and sorrow played across Swamiji's face. In a quiet voice, he said, 'Even if the mind longs, the body does not permit. The physician has forbidden it.

For me, this large fish is poison.'

Baburam stood still, overcome with remorse. It was for his sake that Swamiji had laboured in his frail condition, only to abstain from the meal himself. But Swamiji, sensing his pain, said gently, 'Do not grieve, Baburam. Your joy in eating shall be my own.'

The Casket of Atmaram

Dawn had just broken. The temple bells of Belur tolled gently for the morning arati. Swamiji had already risen from bed. With quiet, deliberate steps, he emerged from his quarters. The monastery was still and sparsely populated—only a few devotees were about, already immersed in their daily tasks. A young brahmachari, heading towards the temple, prostrated at Swamiji's feet as soon as he caught sight of him. Swamiji blessed him silently and moved on, his soul steeped in such deep contemplation that the world around seemed not to touch him.

He climbed the stairs to the temple on the upper floor. His fellow disciples were absent. A line of young monks and brahmacharis stood in reverence. They offered him a seat. One of the brahmacharis was performing the brief dawn arati. As the ritual ended, Swamiji softly intoned, '*Jai Ma. Jai Thakur.*' He rose and bowed low, placing his forehead on the sacred sandals of the Master that lay upon the altar. He drank the *charanamrit*—the sanctified water touched by the Master's feet. Beside it stood a small, unassuming casket containing the sacred funeral ash of the Master—*the casket of Atmaram.*

Memories stirred.

It was long ago, just after the passing of Sri Ramakrishna. His sacred ash had been collected in a vessel. But where would it be kept? Narendra was at a loss. The garden house at Kashipur had to be relinquished. Until now, all expenses had been borne for the sake of the Master. But why should anyone continue to give now that he was gone?

Ramakrishna's devotee, Ramchandra Dutta, had offered a solution. He would build a memorial shrine in his Kankurgachi garden, where the sacred relics could be enshrined. But Niranjan, ever forthright, raised a stern objection. He would not bow before anyone. Standing firm, he told Ramchandra: 'We will not give away the urn. We are the children of Thakur. He shall remain with us.' Shashi and a few others sided with Niranjan. Narendra, caught in the middle, did not know what to say. To bring peace, he spoke, 'We should not quarrel over the urn. We have no permanent shelter. We don't even know where we will live next. Ramdada is offering his garden in Thakur's name and proposing a shrine. Perhaps it is best that the ashes be placed there.'

Niranjan said nothing, but inwardly, he could not accept this plan. That night, after Ramchandra had departed, a secret resolution was made. The next few days were to see a public procession for the relics. But that very night, as all slept, Niranjan, Shashi, and the others rose. They would secretly retain a portion of the sacred ash. No one else would know. A small casket was filled with the Master's funeral ash.

When Narendra came to know, he did not protest. Rather, he said, 'Perhaps this is what Thakur himself would have wished.' He proposed hiding the casket at Balaram Bose's house. Ramchandra was not to know. 'One day,' Narendra said, 'if we ever build a temple ourselves, this sacred ash will be installed there.'

Each took a pinch of ash with reverence. Narendra was the first. Niranjan too, with the words 'Jai Ramakrishna,' partook of it. It was Narendra who gave the casket its name: *Atmaramer Kouṭo*—the Casket of Atmaram. He believed that it held not merely ashes, but a living fragment of Ramakrishna's very soul. To him, it was holier than any image on the altar.

Swamiji touched the casket gently and prostrated himself fully before it. It was as though he felt the presence of Sri Ramakrishna again. For a long moment, he remained thus, lost in the tide of devotion. Then, regaining composure, he stood and looked around. All were seated in stillness. But one was missing, Nirbhayananda. It was unlike him to be absent. Swamiji recalled that even yesterday evening, Nirbhaya had not been present.

Turning to one of those seated before him, he asked, 'Where is Nirbhaya?'

'He is unwell,' came the reply.

A flicker of concern crossed Swamiji's face. 'What happened?' he asked, his voice edged with urgency.

'Seems like a fever.'

Swamiji frowned. 'How can you be so unaware of your own companion's health? Come, I'll go see him myself.'

They crossed the temple and approached a nearby house, where the brahmacharis lived on the upper floor. Saradananda was returning from his morning walk and met them on the way.

'Where are you all heading?' he asked.

'To see Nirbhaya. He's sick,' Swamiji replied.

'Come by my quarters afterward,' said Saradananda. 'I need to speak with you.'

The staircase to the upper floor was still made of wood, not yet replaced by stone. A narrow veranda led past several small adjoining rooms. Shraddhananda stood at the far end and opened a door: 'Come in, Gurudev.'

The room was small and bare. A rope hung from the wall to hold a few pieces of clothing. A clay water pot and a glass sat on the floor. A framed portrait of Sri Ramakrishna adorned the wall. A mat was on the floor, and on it, Nirbhayananda lay with eyes closed, his face restless and flushed. Swamiji called his name. No reply. He knelt beside him, and placed a hand on his forehead. The fever burned like fire.

He turned to the anxious disciples behind him, 'He's burning up. Must be at least a hundred and five. Get water and air flowing immediately.'

A young boy named Sureshchandra, who had recently joined the monastery and was full of boundless zeal, cried out, 'I'll bring the water!'

Swamiji waited no more. He knew the others would now act with diligence. No delay could be afforded. No service would go unfulfilled.

He returned to Saradananda's room.

'You were saying something?'

Saradananda had been writing in a small notebook. He closed it and remained silent for a while. Swamiji sensed a weight upon his mind. Though Rakhal was the president, he was not one for broad worldly concern. But Saradananda—he missed nothing, neither small detail nor big.

At last, Saradananda spoke:

'I've heard that British intelligence agents, disguised, are coming here. They suspect we are aiding revolutionaries.'

Swamiji's expression grew grave. The news did not surprise him. He, too, had felt the chains of foreign rule, and had spoken often of its shame. Though he acknowledged the good in the British, he never spared those who trampled on human dignity.

Once, when a Maratha gentleman had told him of British atrocities, he had replied with fire, 'Why do you suffer in silence? Are you not men? Crush their throats and drown them in the sea!' And once, when insulted in a train compartment by two English soldiers, he had seized both by the neck and threatened to throw them out.

Saradananda watched him closely and asked softly, 'What are your thoughts?'

Swamiji tried to shrug it off, 'What is there to think?'

'The British can do anything. They will try to harass us in many ways.'

Swamiji smiled faintly. 'I know that. But we need not fear. MacLeod has good ties with the Viceroy. She will speak on our behalf. But truly, the greater enemy is among our own. There are those in this land who wish us harm, who care not for their own country's well-being. Ever since Thakur left us, I have seen dissent, and division among our own ranks….' His voice trailed off.

A soft sound came from outside. Footsteps. Someone was hesitating at the door.

'Who is it?' Swamiji called.

A young brahmachari stepped in. His face was open, and innocent. Who would say what mysterious call had drawn this boy away from the comforts of worldly life? Swamiji saw the concern on his face.

'What is it?'

'Nirbhaya da's fever isn't going down. We're trying water and air. But it keeps rising. Some fear it may affect his brain.'

Swamiji's heart trembled. These young souls had renounced all for Thakur. How could he not bear responsibility for their well-being?

He rose. 'Come, let me see.'

Saradananda, too, rose beside him. He paused for a moment. Swamiji himself was not well; how would he manage alone?

'I'm coming with you,' said Saradananda. 'If needed, we'll send for a doctor.'

Swamiji said nothing. Without a word, he stepped out of the room. By now, nearly everyone had gathered in Nirbhayananda's chamber. The air inside had grown stifling, and there was no space left for the breeze to flow. With a quick glance, Swamiji had assessed the scene and spoke firmly, 'Everyone, save a few, step outside. Let fresh air enter.'

He placed his hand upon Nirbhayananda's forehead. A searing heat surged from it, like the breath of a furnace at the peak of summer, the kind of heat that scorches the air, itself. It was far worse than what he had observed before. His face tightened with worry. He turned to Saradananda.

'What can be done?' he asked, his voice low with urgency.

Saradananda thought for a moment. Out of necessity, he had learned a bit of medicine. He touched Nirbhayananda's body, took his pulse, and tried to decipher what the silent rhythms of the flesh might reveal. A soft groan escaped from Nirbhaya's lips, a sound as fragile as dry leaves rustling in pain. Saradananda's face darkened with concern.

'This is a grave fever,' he said. 'Something must be done at once. Someone should go to Belur Bazaar. There's a man there, Prasanna Babu. He is not a licensed doctor, but he works in a pharmacy and knows how to treat fevers well. His medicines are always on point. Bring him quickly.'

'I'll go,' said Shraddhananda without hesitation.

Swamiji turned to another and said, 'Fetch a large pot of water and a towel. Use the wet cloth to wipe down his limbs and body.'

Nirbhayananda's face had turned red, his eyes inflamed.

Swamiji bent closer, and called out a gentle command, 'Nirbhaya, look at me!'

But there was no response. No stir of awareness. Swamiji grew deeply unsettled. The helplessness of the moment pierced him. Something must be done. In this peril, only one remained, only One to whom he could turn. Rising swiftly, he said, 'Sharad, stay here. I'm going.'

He gave no time for questions, no room for protest. With determined steps, he left the room. For two days now, it had pained him to walk—his knees ached with every motion. But he thought not of himself. Climbing the stairs with effort, he entered the temple chamber. It stood empty. Before the sacred image of Sri Ramakrishna, he knelt down, resting on his knees, hands folded, eyes unblinking.

A silent tide of supplication welled within him. Before him was the living image of his Master, from whose gaze mercy still poured like a quiet stream. From the depths of his being, a cry rose, 'Bring Nirbhaya back to health. He is your child. They are all your children.'

Tears brimmed in his eyes. Unknowingly, his gaze drifted towards the small casket resting beside the Master's photograph—*the Casket of Atmaram.* A sudden awareness, a light within glowed. How could he have forgotten? How could he forget that within that casket lay the presence, not merely memory, of the Master himself?

He reached for a vessel filled with water from the Ganga. With utmost tenderness, he let the holy water touch the sacred casket. Then, bowing low, he returned it gently to its place. He remained there, chanting the Master's name in hushed repetition. Finally, lifting the Ganga water, he turned to descend.

At the foot of the stairs, he saw Saradananda racing towards him, breathless, wild-eyed.

'What happened?' Swamiji asked.

Panting, Saradananda replied, 'I went to Belur Bazaar. Prasanna Babu's gone to Calcutta. He won't be back till nightfall. I couldn't find any other doctor either.'

Swamiji remained calm. A serene smile touched his lips. 'No matter. There is no cause for fear. The Master is with us. All will be well.'

Saradananda was seated by Nirbhayananda's side. Another was fanning him. Swamiji sat down quietly beside them.

'Lift him a little,' he said.

Two disciples supported Nirbhayananda, helping him sit upright. He was too weak to hold himself. His head lolled to one side. His eyes were blood-red, like crushed hibiscus blooms. Saradananda looked at Swamiji and asked, 'What's that in your hand, Naren?'

'The supreme medicine,' said Swamiji. 'Water sanctified by the Master's touch. It will bring him back.'

Just then, Shashi Maharaj arrived. For him, Ramakrishna was a reservoir of infinite power. Taking the vessel from Swamiji's hands, he said, 'Let me feed him. Someone fetch a spoon.'

Nirbhayananda had been utterly depleted—his strength a thread away from vanishing. It felt as though his life hung by the barest strand, like the last leaf clinging to a tree at winter's end, quivering in the wind, ready to fall.

A spoon was brought. With gentle care, Shashi Maharaj fed him the Ganga water, drop by drop. Swamiji anointed Nirbhayananda's head, chest, and back with it. Slowly, they eased him down onto the mat again.

Everyone sat in anxious silence. Time ticked on, each moment heavy with hope and dread. The men gathered around him were like souls holding vigil at the edge of night. Then, at last, Nirbhayananda's eyes opened. Slowly, they turned and focused. His lips parted slightly.

'How are you feeling now?' Saradananda asked in a hushed voice.

'Better,' came the faint, fragile reply.

Swamiji laid a hand on his body. The fever had eased. Beads of sweat had appeared on his brow and cheeks. A soft smile broke upon everyone's face.

'There is no more danger,' said Saradananda. 'The fever is breaking. By afternoon, someone should go bring Prasanna Babu. He'll give medicines if needed. For now, Nirbhaya must rest. Later, he can have some sago or barley.'

One by one, they stood and quietly left. Swamiji too turned towards his own quarters, but paused. No, not yet. He walked instead towards the temple once more.

He stood before the Master's image, his eyes again filled with tears. In a voice barely above a whisper, he said:

'I knew, You were here. I know, You will always be.'

Bagha

Swamiji was walking along the banks of the Ganga, bare-bodied, clad only in his loincloth, with a staff in his hand. He used to walk early at dawn; he would wake before the sun and rouse the others, and all would sit for prayer. These days, however, his body was no longer cooperating. His limbs remained stiff until late morning. That day, after a light meal, he had set out, walking past Nilambar Babu's house to a row of lychee trees. Further on, he crossed a large tract of land, where there were rows of grafted mango saplings—low-branched with young fruits just budding, but still raw and unripe. On the northern side, enclosed by a fence, lay a flower garden full of bushes of *bel* and jasmine, and beds of foreign blooms mingling with *rajanigandha, kamini*, and golden *kanakchampa*.

Beyond the garden was lush green grass spread like a carpet, with a narrow footpath cutting through the middle. Shepherd boys would often come this way to graze their cattle and sometimes even the monastery's cows would join the herd. By evening, each beast would return to its own shed, never missing its mark. A few dilapidated cottages stood nearby. Once, boats were repaired here and oarsmen, craftsmen, and carpenters lived in those huts. Now the place was overrun with wild bushes and was home to snakes. Swamiji went no further. He stood still. The sun was not harsh and the post-monsoon air was blissful. The world, drenched in green, felt reborn. The water level of the Ganga was low and the muddy banks stretched far. A few sandpipers wandered about, poking through the silt in search of food. In daylight, the opposite bank stood clear and visible. Swamiji lingered there in silence. He felt a profound solitude. Even among many, he remained essentially alone—often not understood. Perhaps that is the fate of one who transcends the human threshold. Those around him neither wished to understand, nor could.

Lost in thought, Swamiji was startled as a calf came and stood close by, brushing against him. It was white-bodied, with a patch of ochre beneath its neck. He recognised it—it was the monastery's calf. Gently, he stroked its neck. The calf stood still, enjoying the touch.

His love for animals had been innate; it was an inheritance. His mother, Bhubaneshwari Devi, adored birds. Their home used to echo with the cooing of pigeons; each morning they would flock to the porch for food, and she would feed them puffed rice and grains. In a cage were a few parakeets, and despite all her daily duties, she never forgot to tend to them. At around ten or twelve years of age, Naren (Swamiji) had fancied having pets of his own. And so he did—a peacock, a goat, and a monkey. How enthusiastic he was! He would train them, and raise them with care. They roamed freely. Some mischievous boys in the neighbourhood had their eyes on the peacock. It used to strut along the parapet of their roof, fanning its feathers. The boys would throw stones at it. One such blow killed the poor creature. The monkey, while it was little, caused no harm. But as it grew, so did its antics. The household was exasperated. In the end, they left it in a distant garden.

Even amidst endless duties, Swamiji's affection for animals endured. For years, he had wandered across the country like a madman. Now, at last, he had settled in Belur. Here, his childhood love for creatures was rekindled. All around lay open fields and a feeling of complete calm. He often felt restless among people, but he found these mute beings closer to his soul. The monastery had set aside a stretch of land for them. There were cows, dogs, ducks, cranes, cats, goats, and even a blackbuck. He had named a nanny goat 'Hansi,' and her milk was used for morning tea. A little kid named 'Motru' was his particular favourite. He had adorned its neck with bells. Motru followed him everywhere, jingling joyfully. Swamiji delighted in playing with it, like a child.

But it was Bagha who remained a problem. Though a pet dog, its behaviour was anything but tame. At the sight of a stranger, Bagha would chase them, though it never bit. Still, people were frightened. Everyone at the monastery was irritated. They said nothing, only out of respect for Swamiji.

The day was wearing on. Swamiji, having stood long in the sun, turned back. The calf followed him. Smiling, he said, 'Not today, dear one. I'll pet you again tomorrow.' The calf seemed to understand. It ran off, straight to its mother, and began to suckle, a beautiful sight. Swamiji walked on, absorbed in his thoughts. In one place, monsoon water had collected in a pond. A flock of ducks splashed about merrily. Swamiji stopped to watch. On one side stood a large crane. Someone had brought it as a chick and now it was full-grown. When it stood on one leg, it looked like a meditating rishi. He had seen such ascetics, deep in penance, at holy places. Yet what was the point of such austerity? What was to be gained? Perhaps if Thakur Sri Ramakrishna had been alive, he could have answered such a question.

Swamiji watched the ducks basking in the water. Not long ago, one of them had fallen ill. It had stopped eating, and struggled to breathe. Consulting a veterinary book, Swamiji had tried giving it some medicine. An elderly monk had said, 'Too much water play; it caught a cold.' Latu Maharaj had joked, 'So ducks, too, get colds now!' Two days later, the duck died. Swamiji had been saddened. He could not bear to see anyone suffering.

He had written to Nivedita:

> A deep trench is being dug for drainage of the monsoon water accumulating in the monastery grounds. I have just returned from lending a hand in the work.... My enormous crane and the geese are all quite merry. One of the geese, alas, died yesterday. It had suffered from breathlessness for a week. The feathers of a royal goose were falling off. With no other remedy at hand, I placed it briefly in a tub of water with some carbolic acid—hoping either it would recover or pass. It is well now.

Suddenly, a cry startled him. Two brahmacharis were running with sticks. At the front, was Bagha. Something hung from his mouth. Swamiji knew at once that Bagha was up to mischief again. 'What happened?' he asked quickly.

The brahmacharis turned. Everyone knew how fond Swamiji was of Bagha. They hesitated, caught off guard. One stammered, 'Bagha took the fish meant for the offering to Thakur.'

So that's what was in Bagha's mouth. Bagha had always been greedy for food and a bit of a thief. Swamiji wasn't unaware of his nature. Trying to shield Bagha, he asked, 'But how did Bagha get into the kitchen?'

'The door was open. The cook had her back turned and didn't notice when he slipped in. We went to fetch the fish for the offering and found it missing.'

With a hand gesture, Swamiji stopped them. 'Poor creature, he doesn't know about offerings to Thakur. It's not his fault. Is there more fish?'

'There is.'

'Then ask the cook to prepare some more. What else can we do? And tell her to keep the kitchen door closed next time.'

'No need to cook again,' came a sharp voice. None had noticed Shashi Maharaj approaching.

He stood before Swamiji, visibly upset. 'It is because of your indulgence that Bagha has grown so unruly. Today, he ate the fish meant for Thakur. Tomorrow he might storm the sanctum itself.'

Swamiji realised Bagha had crossed a line today. Gently he said, 'Forgive him, just for today.'

But Shashi's anger had not cooled. 'You can forgive everything, but the rest of us are tired. This is too much. Just the other day someone entered the gate on some errand, and Bagha chased him so fiercely he fell and injured himself. Thankfully, the gardener saw it. Otherwise, who knows what might have happened! I went to the Belur market, asked someone to deliver supplies to the monastery. He said, "You've got the worst dog on earth. Always attacking people!" Just wait until something worse happens.'

Swamiji knew Bagha was a problem. It hurt him. Still, he said softly, 'I have nothing more to say. Do what you feel is best.'

A brahmachari suggested, 'If someone would adopt Bagha....'

'No one will. If he were calm and gentle, maybe. But like this?'

A few others had gathered. All were fed up with Bagha. Their consensus was to release him far away, where he could roam freely.

'Then do that,' Swamiji said, and walked away. As he did, a sorrow passed through him. Despite renouncing everything, had he truly escaped attachment?

That afternoon, he sat on the veranda, writing a letter. The sun had dipped. A light shower had poured at noon, and the air was pleasant. There was no one nearby. At this time of day, all the young monks and brahmacharis were out playing. Swamiji had instituted this practice for them. First the body, then the spirit. He finished his letter. He had a long habit of reading over what he wrote, so he could correct any error before sending it off.

Beloved Nivedita,
I no longer wish to work. I seek only rest and peace now. The truths of time and space are known to me. Yet my fate, my karma, drags me forward—onward into endless toil. Work, work, and nothing but work! We are like cattle, driven towards the slaughterhouse. Just as those doomed animals snatch at tufts of grass along the path, we too take small bites of life, knowing not how close the end lies. This is our karma, our fear. And fear is the fountainhead of sorrow and sickness.

In our confusion and terror, we wound others. Afraid to strike, we strike all the harder. Fleeing from sin with such obsession, we stumble into its very mouth. Around us rises a heap of useless debris, a chaos of our own making. It brings us no benefit. And in trying to avoid suffering, we are led right towards it.

Ah, if only we could be utterly fearless, bold, and defiant.

Yours,
Vivekananda

After reading, he placed the letter carefully in an envelope. He would send it off tomorrow, perhaps through someone headed to the post office. He sat in silence on the veranda for some time.

The day had ended. Darkness fell softly across the land. One by one, stars bloomed in the western sky.

Beside the veranda stood an oleander tree, its white blossoms clustered like stars risen from the earth. Soon it would be time for the evening worship. Swamiji closed the door behind him and stepped out, he was on his way to the temple.

Shashi Maharaj was already on the path and paused as he saw Swamiji approach.

'Have you heard?' he said. 'Bagha has returned.'

Swamiji was startled. Since morning, he had heard nothing of Bagha. 'What happened?' he asked.

'They had put Bagha on Haricharan's boat. Haricharan had taken him across the Ganga and dropped him off on the far bank. But all afternoon, Bagha lingered by the shore. In the evening, as Haricharan ferried passengers back, Bagha slipped aboard with them. Haricharan tried to push him off, but Bagha barked and resisted so fiercely that, in the end, he had no choice but to bring him back.'

'Truly?' Swamiji brightened. 'Where is he now?'

'No idea. The moment the boat touched the shore, he leapt off and vanished. Probably hiding, lying low.'

Swamiji chuckled. 'Scared of us, no doubt. Hunger will bring him out. Come, the arati will begin soon.'

After the arati, Swamiji returned to his room. Lately, he had been going to bed earlier. In the deep night, he awoke with a pressing need. He glanced out through the open window; darkness still cloaked the sky. The hurricane lamp flickered faintly.

He rose quietly from bed and opened the door. The moment he stepped out, he stopped short, as something soft brushed against his foot. He bent down and gasped.

It was Bagha.

Before he could react, the dog collapsed at his feet.

'What are you doing, Bagha? Move aside.'

But Bagha would not. He rubbed his head against Swamiji's feet, as if to say, I have done wrong. I won't do it again. Only, don't send me away.

Swamiji ran his hand gently down Bagha's back.

'I'll speak to them,' he said softly. 'No one will trouble you again.'

Keshta

The rains had ended. Nature wore a green mantle as fields and meadows grew thick with grass, vines and fresh leaves. Even the narrow footpaths were blanketed in tender blades. In places, wild thickets sprang up; in others, a few small streams were half-covered in mud. The entire landscape had transformed since the monsoons. Leeches and snakes were a menace and movement became difficult. For the past two years, a group of Santhals, ten or twelve men and women, had come and cleared the land. They stayed for a few months in a crumbling house near the Belur market, worked, earned a little, and then returned to their village.

As on most days, Swamiji was walking along the banks of the Ganga. Bagha followed him, like a loyal attendant—quiet, subdued since the incident, and now rarely straying from Swamiji's side. As they neared Nilambar Babu's house, Swamiji noticed a group clearing the undergrowth—Keshta and his people. Swamiji enjoyed talking to Keshta. He was simple, honest, and unburdened by wants—a man grown from the earth, a spirit kindred to the wild.

Swamiji approached. Beneath a mango tree, an altar of bricks formed a circle. He sat down. Keshta had his back turned, as he was working. Swamiji called out, 'Keshta, how are you?'

At once, Keshta turned and smiled, 'I'm well, *Swami Baap*. But you, how are you?'

Swamiji smiled gently. 'I'm well. Come, sit; let's talk for a bit.'

Keshta wiped his dusty hands and came forward. Bare-chested, a small cloth wrapped around his waist, a mane of tangled hair, an amulet around his neck, his skin dark as polished stone, he looked carved from the earth itself.

'What news from your village?'

Keshta's face grew distant. 'Not good, *Swami Baap*[21]. The forest around our village, full of mahua, sal, teak, has all been taken. The city men came and cut them down. We planted a little grain, but wild boars and elephants destroyed it. There is nothing left. We eat what we can find.'

Swamiji's heart ached. 'Life is hard for you.'

Keshta replied simply, 'We don't think of it like that. We are forest folk. Somehow the days pass.'

That strange dispassion. Swamiji said, 'If it's so difficult, why don't you live in the city?'

Lighting a *bidi* (Indian hand-rolled cigarette), Keshta grinned. 'I don't like it here for long. The heart calls us back to the jungle, the hills, our village.'

Swamiji said nothing. His mind drifted, his thoughts floated to a Santhal village nestled in the forested hills, a strange, enchanted world. Scorching sun by day, but a different realm altogether at night. An infinite sky full of stars as the air whispered through the sal trees. Through the rustling leaves, a single star pulsed like

21 Addressing someone with respect.

a secret heartbeat. Around it, countless stars, planets, moons—love, beauty, affection—silent and infinite, scattered across the cosmos. In the city's noise, that world is lost.

There, amid bountiful nature, the voice of the Eternal whispers: Don't waste your life chasing petty gains. In this infinite expanse lies eternal life. One day, this mortal body will burn on the pyre and turn to ash. And yet, nature's vast love will remain.

Lost in that vision, Swamiji didn't hear Keshta's call.

'What are you thinking, *Swami Baap*?'

'I'll take birth in your village in my next life,' Swamiji said.

Keshta chuckled. 'You won't like it there. What's even there?'

Swamiji thought, perhaps he was right. What was there? What had *he* truly found? Then he asked, 'Did you eat anything this morning?'

'There was leftover rice from last night. I ate it with salt. I'll cook in the evening.'

Only salt and rice the whole day? Swamiji was pained. 'Come eat lunch with us today.'

Keshta's eyes widened. 'What are you saying, *Swami Baap*! If we eat salt from your hands, we lose our caste. No one would enter our home again.'

Swamiji thought for a moment. 'Fine. I'll serve food without salt.'

Keshta beamed. 'Then we can eat!'

'Good. Come to the dining hall at noon.'

Just then, one of Keshta's people gestured to him, saying something in their tongue. Keshta became restless. 'You go now, *Swami Baap*. We can't work while you're here. *Buro Baap* (Swami Advaitananda) will scold us.'

Swamiji knew well that they never shirked work. 'Alright, I'll tell *Buro Baap* not to scold you. I heard you're married now, tell me about it.'

Keshta blushed.

At a distance, Sharatchandra approached. Seeing Swamiji, he paused. Strange, this was the same man who had stood at the World Parliament of Religions debating with the greatest scholars of Europe and America. And now, here he was, laughing and chatting with unlettered Santhals. It felt like he was with his own kin.

Still, if he didn't speak, Swamiji would scold him later. So he stepped forward.

Swamiji looked up, smiling broadly. 'Speak, messenger of joy! What tidings do you bring?'

'Some students from a college in Calcutta are coming to the Math. Manmatha Babu just informed us.'

'When will they arrive?'

'In the afternoon.'

'Good. No trouble, then. Go to Belur Bazaar, and buy four or five kinds of sweets, and tell the cook to fry fresh *luchis*. Keshta and his people will lunch with us.'

Turning to Keshta, Swamiji said, 'Now there's no chance to chat. Come for lunch, then we'll talk properly.'

Back in his room, Swamiji rested. His body had felt better these past few days. He wrote several letters, writing never tired him. Once, Shivananda had joked, 'You must've been a royal scribe in a past life.' Swamiji had replied, 'I enjoy it. Who knows, maybe in a hundred years, these letters will be priceless to someone.'

Soon, word came, Keshta and the others had arrived.

In the dining room, mats were spread along one side. Keshta

and his companions sat in a line. Seeing Swamiji, Keshta grinned. 'What will you feed us, *Swami Baap*?'

'Sit a while. It's all coming.'

Brahmacharis brought *luchi*, sweets, *mondas*, and curd. Swamiji sat before them in a chair. 'Serve them with care,' he said.

They had never tasted such food. As they ate, Keshta asked, 'Where did you get all this?'

'For you.'

'We're poor field hands. And you brought us such fine food?'

Tears welled in Swamiji's eyes. 'You are Narayana Himself. This is Narayana's offering. Service to the poor is service to God.'

When the meal was done and they departed, Swamiji turned to the assembled monks and said, 'If you can dedicate your life to serving these humble, destitute people, I'll know your coming to me wasn't in vain. Otherwise, wearing ochre is meaningless.'

Sharatchandra felt Swamiji's emotion and, softening the moment, said, 'Come now, the students will arrive soon. You should rest a while.'

By the riverside, in Swamiji's veranda, arrangements were made to receive the students. A carpet was spread, and chairs placed on it. One by one, twelve young men arrived, their faces bright with expectation. This was a moment beyond any price—to meet Swamiji and speak with him. As they settled in, Swamiji entered. Each one bowed. Like a friend, he placed a hand on one's shoulder, patted another's back, held one's hand, and asked their names, where they lived, and what they did. It was all so warm and easy; their nervousness melted away. They felt like they were visiting a friend's home.

One asked, 'Swamiji, tell us about the Chicago Parliament. We've heard others speak of it, but hearing from you would be special.'

Swamiji was quiet for a moment. Then he began the tales of his first journey abroad, of leaving his motherland behind, facing dreadful hardship, where nothing seemed possible. But with the blessing of his Master, Sri Ramakrishna, all became possible. The banner of India and Hindu *Dharma* flew proud in the courtyard of the world.

The boys listened, entranced, their minds filled with wonder. A brahmachari came with *prasad*. They shared it. Then one asked, 'Swamiji, what can we do for our country?'

The fire in Swamiji's heart for India blazed forth.

'I believe in working for the good of the motherland. To do great work, you need three things—compassion, sincerity, and faith. You can do little with mere logic. Great power comes from the depths of the heart. Millions in our land are dying of hunger. For centuries, they've starved. If your heart beats with love for them, only then can you serve your nation. They've told you for ages that you are weak, lowly, powerless. Hearing this, you began to believe it. But look at me, I am one of you. I had deep faith in myself. That is why the very people who once despised us now place me on a pedestal. They travel from afar just to hear me speak.'

One student said, 'But Swamiji, we're ordinary people.'

Swamiji thundered, 'Who says so? You hold infinite strength, boundless knowledge, and an indomitable spirit. Awaken it, and you will be like me.'

Someone asked, 'Thakur Sri Ramakrishna gave you that strength. Who will give it to us?'

Swamiji's eyes burned bright. '*I* am here for you. I will teach you. With that knowledge, go to towns and villages, awaken others, and cry out: *Arise! Awake! And stop not till the goal is reached!* Within you lies the strength to conquer suffering and erase poverty. Only awaken it. Never think you are weak. The one who thinks so remains so forever.'

Swamiji fell silent. His voice had stirred the air around them, and now its echo lingered like a divine utterance, a celestial resonance, as though a touchstone had brushed against common iron and turned it to gold. The young men sat still, as if rooted to the earth. Never before had they beheld their own souls so clearly. Never had they encountered themselves in such light. It felt like a rebirth.

The day had waned. All around them spread a deep contemplative hush. Dusk crept through the corners of the sky, laying its first veils of shadow. Birds called to one another before settling into their night's rest. At a little distance sat Manmatha Babu. He turned to the students and said softly, 'You must return again.'

Swamiji nodded. 'Yes, do come again from time to time. Through you, the Master's message shall spread far and wide. Will you stay to witness the evening arati?'

The boys glanced at one another. One asked, 'What time is it now?'

Swamiji reached into his pocket and drew out a watch, an elegant timepiece of gold, attached to a fine chain. It had been a gift from a distinguished lady during his stay in the West. He used it sparingly.

A young man standing beside him gazed at the watch with wide-eyed curiosity. 'Swamiji,' he asked shyly, 'may I see your watch for a moment?'

Without hesitation, Swamiji handed it to him, chain and all. The youth's face lit up in wonder and delight. Swamiji observed this, thought for a moment, and then said gently, 'I give it to you.'

The youth was stunned. He had never imagined that such a

treasure, this precious gold watch and chain, would be placed in his hands. Stammering, he said, 'But Swamiji… what will I do with this? How can I accept such a gift?'

'You liked it,' Swamiji replied with a smile, 'so I gave it to you. Wear it, if you wish. Only, never sell it.'

Speechless, the young man folded his hands in reverence. 'I will never forget this day, Swamiji. It will remain with me always. We'll take our leave now, we've come a long way. But we'll return soon, to witness the evening worship.'

As the group departed, Manmatha Babu turned to Swamiji. 'You gave away such a valuable watch, just like that?'

Swamiji's expression did not change. In the same quiet, natural voice he replied, 'He liked it, so I gave it to him. I am a *sannyasi*, what need have I for a gold watch or chain? Come, let's go to the temple. It's time for the evening arati.'

Durga

The autumn sky was strewn with clouds, white and blue flocks, like pilgrims drifting to distant lands. A faint chill brushed the air. Here and there, sudden drizzles fell and soaked the earth. Fields, groves, and trees were all tinged with vibrant green. The seasons of autumn and rain seemed to blend and mingle in nature's embrace. At dawn, a subtle wintry mood lingered, and dewdrops veiled the grass. Sheuli blossoms fell softly to the ground, their light yet heavenly fragrance filling the heart. The midday sun still held its warmth, and marigolds glowed golden in scattered corners. All around, as if in secret whispers, came the sound—*the Mother is coming.*

Swamiji's heart was steeped in a deep wistfulness that morning. He gazed silently into the sky. A little while ago, his attendant Nirbhayananda had brought him tea, but he had forgotten to drink it. He sat immersed in thought. Lately, such trances came upon him more often—as though he was journeying through some unseen realm. A soft touch stirred him, and he turned. Brahmananda had arrived.

Gesturing to an empty chair nearby, Swamiji said, 'You, here in the morning? That must mean something important.'

Brahmananda smiled. 'Do I come to you only when there's a need?'

'That I know,' Swamiji replied. 'In this Math and Mission, who is closer to me than you?'

'That's why I've come,' Brahmananda said. 'Last night, I had a strange dream. I saw the ten-armed Durga drifting down the Ganga, from Dakshineswar towards Belur. Her face was radiant—gracious, fear-dispelling. Before I could look closely, I woke. I sat still for a long time afterwards. It felt as if the Mother was trying to tell me something.'

Swamiji looked at him for a few moments, a quiet radiance lighting up his face. Then, in a low voice, he said, 'For some days now, I've felt a longing to invoke the Mother here in the Math. I've bought a copy of Raghunandan's *Ashtavingshati Tattva*. It contains many details on the rituals of Her worship. Perhaps, through your vision, the Mother has expressed the yearning of all our hearts. Wait, I'll call Sharat.'

Saradananda had been writing the household accounts for the day. On hearing the summons, he hurried over.

Swamiji said, 'Sit, Sharat. We have something to discuss.'

Wiping sweat from his brow, Saradananda replied, 'The two of you together? That must mean something serious.'

Swamiji's voice softened. 'I wish for Durga Puja to be held here in the Math this year. Rakhal has seen in a dream that the Mother is coming here.'

Saradananda thought for a while. Then, hesitantly, he said, 'Only three weeks remain. Can it be done in such little time?'

Swamiji's resolve was of another kind. Once his mind was made up, he would not stop until it was fulfilled. 'If it is the Mother's will, it will be possible. But first, we must seek permission from Mother Thakurani. Nothing can proceed without her blessing. She is our living Durga.'

Brahmananda asked, 'Will the worship be done to an image?'

Swamiji looked straight at him. 'I've heard your ancestral home holds Durga Puja.'

'You heard right,' Brahmananda said. 'In our ancestral village in the district of 24-Parganas, our forefather Debidas Ghosh received a vision in which the goddess Durga asked for worship.

'To fulfil Her wish, in 1700 AD, he built an *atchala,* a simple thatched shrine, and began the Durga Puja. A century later, our descendant Kaliprasad Ghosh constructed a permanent temple.

'Even now, we sculpt a single-frame idol and offer worship there. In my boyhood, I would sit before Her image in meditation.'

Swamiji placed his hand gently over Brahmananda's. In a tender voice, he said, 'Then let it be an image of the Mother.'

'But,' Saradananda interjected, 'is it even possible to find a proper idol in such a short time?'

Swamiji replied calmly, 'Let us see what the Mother's will is. At noon, Baburam, Krishnalal and I shall go out. First, Krishnalal will visit Mother and seek her blessing. Then the three of us will go to Kumartuli. Sharat, arrange for some funds; we'll need to commission the idol.'

By noon, the three set out. They crossed the Ganga by boat to Baghbazar. Krishnalal had already visited the house of Holy Mother and now waited with a bright smile.

'She was very pleased to hear about the Puja,' he said. 'She said she will come during the worship.'

'Mother will come! What joy!' Swamiji's eyes lit up, his whole being shone with gladness.

'Come,' said Baburam, 'let's head to Kumartuli.'

Soon, they reached the neighbourhood of the clay sculptors.

One by one, they passed the thatched studios, each filled with Durga idols. Rows upon rows stood in silence. The claywork was done, and white undercoats had been applied. Soon, the artists would begin painting and adorning the goddesses. Every studio buzzed with activity. The artisans were all at work, hands full. Each idol had to be ready in time.

Baburam looked around and asked, 'So many images, which one do you like?'

Swamiji glanced at him and said, 'All that you see has been commissioned, some four months ago, some six. Each one has already been spoken for.'

'Wait,' he added, 'let me ask someone.'

They entered one of the studios. An elderly sculptor was at work. Baburam asked, 'Brother, we've come to commission a Durga idol.'

The man looked up. 'For next year?'

'No, no, this year.'

The sculptor laughed. 'The Mother will begin her journey to each worshipping household in just a few days, and you've come now to commission Her?'

Swamiji said gently, 'We decided only today. We wish to invoke the Mother in our Math. Everyone desires to offer Her worship.'

'I understand,' the sculptor said. 'But I don't have any spare idols. I doubt you'll find one anywhere. Without a commission, no one makes extra. But still, look around. If it is the Mother's will, you may find one.'

One by one, they visited nearly every workshop. None had a spare idol. Baburam's face grew troubled. Swamiji's expression was grave.

In a voice touched with quiet sorrow, Baburam said, 'It seems the Mother has not chosen to accept our worship this year.'

A boy from the side spoke up, 'Maharaj, I've been watching you wander around for quite some time. What are you looking for?'

As soon as Swamiji explained everything, the boy thought for a moment and said, 'Come with me.'

They walked through a narrow alley, idols arranged on either side. Most of the clay work was done, and only the colouring remained. A little further in, they reached a small clay house. A few idols were seated on the veranda. The boy called out, 'Raghu Kaka, are you home?'

A middle-aged man emerged. 'What is it, Bholanath?'

'Maharaj and the others have suddenly decided to hold Durga Puja. But they can't find a single idol. Can you help?'

A smile lit up Raghu Kaka's face. 'What a strange coincidence! This very morning, someone came and said they wouldn't be able to perform Puja this year; their father passed away. They had already commissioned an idol, and I completed it. I was wondering what to do. And now you've come. There it is, on the right.'

It was a traditional single-structure idol. Around the goddess stood Kartikeya, Ganesha, Lakshmi, and Saraswati. At her feet, the demon lay subdued. The first wash of paint had touched the clay. Everyone admired it. Swamiji said, 'We like it.' He placed Rs 10 as an advance. 'Please note it down in your ledger. We'll come for the idol on *Panchami* morning.'

'What name shall I write it under?'

Swamiji paused. Only one name arose within him. Without hesitation, he said, 'Write, Sri Sarada Devi.'

It was *Shukla Panchami* of *Sharadiya*. The end of *Ashwin*. The sky still bore the brooding weight of the monsoon. Rain fell now and then. The autumn skies had vanished behind the clouds. The night before, there'd been a heavy downpour. Damp winds blew across the monastery grounds. A grand pandal had been erected. Its exterior was complete, and the interior was still abuzz with activity. The Mother was coming. Excitement and joy coursed through the monastery. But the image had not yet arrived.

Swamiji sat in his room. The dampness of the season didn't agree with his health. The moisture in the air worsened his asthma. He glanced at the clock; it was eleven. The sky gave no clue. Two brahmacharis stood on the veranda, whispering. They hadn't seen Swamiji, though he had noticed them. He called out in a loud voice, 'Who's that talking over there?'

Startled, the two hurried over, faces pale with apprehension. They bowed. Swamiji asked, 'Do you know when the idol will arrive?'

'All the brahmacharis have gone to fetch it, Maharaj. Shashi Maharaj is with them too.'

'And why didn't you go?'

'We were preparing for the temple rituals.'

'When you work for the temple, let your heart and soul be in it.' Swamiji paused mid-sentence. From a distance, the sound of the *dhak* (drum) rose through the air. He fell still, listening intently.

One of the brahmacharis standing by the door turned his gaze towards the Ganga. Then, raising both hands in delight, he exclaimed, 'She's here! The idol is coming!'

Joy lit Swamiji's face. He hurried to the veranda. A large boat was crossing the Ganga, approaching Belur. At its centre stood the idol of Mother Durga. The two brahmacharis could wait no longer.

'We're going, Guru Maharaj!'

Swamiji smiled. In the midst of austere vows, even a drop of joy sparkles bright. 'Go,' he said. 'I'm coming too.'

Once the two had gone, Swamiji stood. He wrapped his *kaupin*, threw on his cloak, and, on a sudden impulse, picked up two umbrellas and stepped out.

At the sound of the drum, everyone came pouring out of the monastery. Swamiji called, 'Come, everyone! The Mother has arrived!'

The boat docked at the ghat. Commotion, celebration, and the beat of the drums thundered through the air. A wide plank had been laid down. Together, they lifted the idol onto land. Rakhal Maharaj stood at the edge of the ghat, hands clasped to his chest, repeating, 'Careful… be very careful.'

The drummer danced as he played. Another boy clashed the cymbals. Two young brahmacharis, too, began to dance.

Saradananda asked, 'Shall we carry the image to the pandal?'

The others glanced at each other. One said, 'The altar isn't ready yet. We'll have to place her below.'

Swamiji stepped forward. 'The weather's uncertain. Looks like a heavy shower's coming. Let's take the idol to the temple for now. Once the *pandal's* ready, we'll bring her there.'

Saradananda agreed. 'Naren is right. Let's take the Mother to the temple.'

The brahmacharis lifted the image onto their shoulders. Barely a few steps in, the first drops of rain fell. A murmur went through the crowd, 'It's raining! It's raining!' Swamiji quickly opened an umbrella. A tall brahmachari held it over the Mother's head.

They gathered in the temple's ground-floor veranda. The idol was set down. The drums roared. The cymbals chimed. A small cloth veiled the Mother's face, but it had slipped. Shashi Maharaj brought a clean white *dhoti*. Standing on a stool, one of them gently covered the faces of the Mother and her children.

The music ceased. Silence settled over the courtyard.

Then the rain came—dense and heavy, breaking from the clouds. The trees, the distant horizon, everything blurred into mist. Swamiji said, 'Don't move her to the *pandal* today. The weather is fierce. Tomorrow is *Maha Shashti*[22] morning. She will enter her *pandal* then. By that time, the storm will have passed.'

Rakhal Maharaj nodded. 'If Naren says the skies will clear tomorrow, they will.'

A deep, still emotion passed through the gathering. Swamiji folded his hands at his chest. 'Who am I? She will remove every obstacle herself and receive her worship.'

By noon, the skies had cleared. Golden sunlight poured down. Clouds of deep autumn blue drifted towards the horizon.

Swamiji was resting indoors. Suddenly, someone came running. 'Mother has arrived.'

'Where?'

'The boat has docked at the ghat beside Nilambar Babu's house.'

Swamiji stood. To him, Sarada Devi was none other than another form of Durga. 'Let us go pay our respects to the Mother,' he said.

On the second floor of Nilambar Babu's house, Ma Sarada had taken rest. With her were Yogin Ma, Golap Ma, and several other women devotees. Swamiji and the brahmacharis arrived at the veranda. News of his arrival had already reached inside. Golap Ma descended, her face half-covered with her saree. Swamiji, palms folded, said, 'I've come to offer *pranam* to the Mother.'

With a gesture, Golap Ma invited him upstairs. Swamiji ascended softly. Across the veranda, into the room. Golap Ma murmured, 'Go on in, my child. The Mother awaits.'

There, in the middle of the room, stood Ma Sarada, veiled

22 First day of Durga puja

from head to toe. Swamiji bowed full-length before her. In a gentle voice, she said, 'May you be blessed, my son.'

Before her, Swamiji became a child. 'Mother, the idol has arrived,' he said.

'Very good. What greater worship is there than of She who moves the world and home alike?'

'Ma, I wish to perform a sacrifice this *Puja*.'

The Mother trembled slightly. How could she, the embodiment of love and compassion, bear the shedding of blood? From behind her veil, she said softly, 'No, my son. No blood. The Mother never asks for her children's blood.'

Swamiji's mind wavered. Scripture said one thing, but for him, her words were final. 'Whatever you say, Ma, shall be done. I have another wish. I want to perform the *Kumari Puja*.'

Slightly puzzled, Ma Sarada asked, 'What is Kumari Puja, my son?'

'In the Tantras, during Durga Puja, there is provision for worshipping the maiden. The goddess Chandika appeared as a young girl when she came to destroy the demon. Thus, every young girl holds within her a spark of the Divine. Without *Kumari Puja*, all sacrifices and rites are incomplete. Thakur too saw the Kumari as an aspect of the Divine Mother. It is a pure sentiment.'

Ma Sarada smiled. 'Your Thakur worshipped me too as a maiden goddess. It is a pure sentiment. Have you found girls for the worship?'

'Yes, Mother. All of them are five or six years old. I've performed *Kumari Puja* four times before.'

Ma Sarada was surprised. 'I never heard anyone speak of this.'

Swamiji looked abashed. He never hid anything from the Mother. Even if he hadn't had the chance to speak, others surely had. He bowed his head. 'Ma, I thought you already knew. When

I went to Kashmir with Nivedita, Miss MacLeod, and others, we stayed on a boat in the Jhelum. There, the Muslim boatman's four-year-old daughter stirred a strange maternal feeling in me. I worshipped her. Later, at Kshir Bhavani, a Brahmin girl appeared before me as Uma. I worshipped her, too. In Gazipur, I saw the five-year-old daughter of Gagan Chandra Roy Mahashay as a divine form, and found great joy in her worship.'

'What arrangements have you made here?'

'I've given all responsibility to Gauri Ma, Thakur's disciple. She will prepare everything. The *Puja* will take place on *Ashtami*.'

From behind her veil, the Mother said softly, 'Do not worry. Place your faith in Durga Maa whom you worship. She will accomplish everything.'

On *Maha Shashti* morning, every preparation for the *Puja* was complete. Brahmananda had gathered all that was needed. As monks had no right to perform the ritual, the priest's duties were entrusted to Brahmachari Krishnalal. The Tantra guide was Shashi Maharaj's father, Ishwar Chandra Chakravarty, a scholar and adept tantric.

At the moment of the goddess's awakening, Swamiji began to sing:

'Beneath the bilva tree the invocation begins,
with Ganesh's grace, Gauri arrives.'

What sweetness lies in the song, it felt as if the Mother of the Universe herself was arriving.

Thus followed the *Saptami Puja*. On the altar stood the ten-armed goddess, lion-mounted, destroyer of demons, her radiance illuminating all four corners. Before her, in mortal form, stood the Divine Mother, Sri Sarada Devi. Devotees thronged in joy, and the grounds of worship turned vibrant with delight.

Ishwar Chandra asked, 'In whose name shall the *Puja* be offered?'

Everyone fell silent. No one had thought of that.

Standing quietly nearby was Swamiji. Shuddhananda came forward. 'The priest asks, in whose name shall the Puja be dedicated?'

Swamiji didn't hesitate even for a moment. With unwavering resolve, he said, 'In the name of Mother Sarada. As long as this Math and Mission endure, the Puja shall continue, and she shall remain the very centre of it all.'

The vow for the Mother's worship was taken. It was *Mahashtami*. The brahmacharis were all busy with their duties. Every now and then, Swamiji reminded them that nothing should fall short of perfection. But suddenly, he noticed how anxious the young monks looked. Just the sight of him seemed to make them nervous; they were fumbling at even the simplest tasks. Swamiji pondered silently. Beside him sat Holy Mother Sarada. In a low, quiet voice, he said, 'Mother, please bring fever upon me.'

Sarada Devi was puzzled. 'My child, I don't quite understand what you mean,' she said gently.

Before Swamiji could explain, his body began to tremble, and he was struck with a sudden fever. Alarmed, Holy Mother sprang up. In the midst of the sacred rites, this sudden illness, how could it be? 'Wait, let me call Sharatchandra,' she said.

Quickly, Swamiji interjected, 'Mother, please, do not trouble yourself. I have taken this fever upon myself willingly.'

'But my child,' she said, 'how can you lie ill on the day of worship?'

'Don't worry, Mother. I've taken the fever so that the boys can carry on their work unhindered. They are striving with all their might, and, these days, I find it harder to be patient. I'm no longer the same. I don't know when I might lose my temper, scold them, or even slap them in a moment's flareup. That would hurt them. And it would wound me more deeply still. So I thought, what use am I like this? Better I lie quiet for a while, with a fever.'

Swamiji withdrew to his room and lay down. Everyone around grew anxious about what had suddenly befallen him? But Holy Mother reassured them, 'There is nothing to worry about. All will be well. Why fret, then?'

Devotees came and went, their hearts heavy. In the worship hall, Swamiji's absence was keenly felt. The morning rituals ended. Then Holy Mother called out gently, 'Naren, it is time to rise.'

'Yes, Mother,' came the calm reply. Swamiji sat up. There was no trace of illness left in his body. Now he was to attend the *Kumari Puja*.

In front of the image of the Divine Mother, the sacred ceremony of *Kumari Puja* was arranged. On the carpet sat nine little girls, none older than seven. Each wore a bright sari, a crown, and a golden dot on her forehead. Before each of them lay a tray of offerings. They were worshipped with traditional rites—*padya*, *arghya*—as living embodiments of the Goddess. All bowed to them in reverence.

Then Swamiji stepped forward. One by one, he lay prostrate before each child in devout salutation. The last *kumari* was the youngest. There was a depth in her gaze, a stillness in her face, as though she had wandered into the realm of divine ecstasy. Swamiji stood transfixed before her. To him, it felt as if the World-Mother had shed her clay form and revealed Herself in pure spirit. Overcome, he placed a *tilak* of red sandalwood on her forehead. In that instant, his body shuddered. It felt as though he had touched the third eye of the Goddess. Had he hurt Her with that touch?

He bowed low. In a hushed voice, he whispered, 'Bless us, O Mother. Bless all with well-being.'

Kali

The month of Kartik wanes. On the eve of the dark new moon, the sky is a vast chalice of shadow. A hush has fallen upon the earth. In the breath of night, the first chill of winter drifts in, mingled with the delicate fragrance of the night-blooming jasmine. The shrill whisper of crickets stirs the air. Overhead, in the boundless ether, a million stars are strewn. Yet their faint light dissolves into the breast of the Ganga, into fields and forests, into the hushed margins of the world. Nothing is clear. A silence descends that is neither known nor tasted. It is an alien stillness, as though this realm is not of the earth. No light. No wind. Only a dense, death-like darkness unfurling in vast folds—deep, silent, impenetrable.

Before this darkness, seated in meditation, is Swamiji. The temple is alive with preparations for the midnight worship of Kali. The drums throb. Yet none of it reaches his ears. His mind is swept by strange waves of thought—ceaseless waves on a shoreless sea.

In the temple, the worship of the sky-clad Mother has begun. *Sannyasis*, brahmacharis, priests—all have gathered to lay their offerings at Her feet. Yet he cannot bring his mind to join them.

Kali, the ancient source of all power, is not the flute-bearing Krishna of pastoral sweetness. She bears the scimitar, She slays the demon host. The world lies swathed in Her shadow, and yet once, he could not accept Her.

That was a strange moment in life. His father was no more. The family had begun its descent into hardship. Narendra, the eldest son, wandered from street to street, searching for morsels of rice. If food came for his mother and younger siblings one day, it vanished the next. One morning, he awoke with a sudden thought. At Dakshineswar dwells the Mother Bhavatarini, and She listens to Sri Ramakrishna. If Ramakrishna would only speak to Her, surely She would take their pain away. Without delay, he rushed to Dakshineswar. To him, Sri Ramakrishna was like a kin. He said with urgency, 'You must speak to Her.'

Ramakrishna replied with sorrowful eyes, 'I cannot ask for such things. My heart recoils at the thought. You go. Speak to Her yourself.'

Narendra shook his head. 'Why would your Mother listen to me?'

Ramakrishna asked quietly, 'Why wouldn't She? Do you not believe in Her? Have you not said She is but a stone image, like those atheists say?'

But Narendra was not one to yield. 'I don't care about all that,' he said. 'You must make it happen.'

Ramakrishna thought for a moment. 'Today is Tuesday,' he said. 'Go. Bow before Her, and ask whatever you desire. She will grant it. She is my living Mother, the Source of creation. She can do anything. My Mother breaks the bounds of fate.'

So Narendra entered the shrine. Before the world-enchanting form of the Mother, he forgot all poverty, all pain. His heart swelled with devotion. He prayed, 'Mother, grant me wisdom, renunciation, devotion, discrimination.'

He returned to Ramakrishna.

'What did you ask for?' the Master asked with a smile.

'I forgot everything,' Narendra said, his head bowed. 'I asked not what I came to ask.'

Ramakrishna, the knower of hearts, said gently, 'Go again. Steady your mind. Ask what you had intended.'

Again, Narendra went. Again, he could not speak of worldly needs before the World-Mother. The doors of his soul swung open.

This moment marked a profound transformation. He, who had doubted, now accepted the Mother. Ramakrishna teased, 'Naren has accepted the Mother. Good, very good.'

From that day, the rest of his life was suffused with the presence of the Divine Mother. To him, She was at once tender and terrible, compassionate and cataclysmic. She had come to destroy illusion, to crush the demon within. Fierce and mighty, She wore terror as adornment, for Her children, She bore the face of dread.

Years passed. He was no longer Narendra, and was now Swami Vivekananda. With Nivedita as his companion, he journeyed to Amarnath to glimpse the Ice-Shiva, his lifelong deity. But an extraordinary change followed that *darshan*. From Shiva, his mind turned towards Shakti, the Consort of Shiva, the Great Mother. He began to hum songs of *Ramprasad*:

'Dive deep, O mind, dive deep in the Ocean of God's beauty,
If you descend, not pearls but Her grace you will find.'

It seemed to him that everywhere, the Mother's presence was palpable.

Now he was in Srinagar, Kashmir. With him were Mrs Bull,

Miss MacLeod, Nivedita, and others. One day, he was alone in his boat. His heart was a storm of longing. He had not yet grasped the Mother's true form. Tides of ecstasy surged within him. He could no longer restrain himself. A desperate yearning filled his soul, as if in the world of spirit, he had caught the scent of home.

He felt it; his work on this earth was complete. Like a child cradled in his mother's lap, he had nothing more to seek, nothing more to ask. His inner world was now filled with one name, one presence—Kali. Only Kali.

In the midst of that trance, the monk became a poet. In the throes of rapture, he composed 'Kali the Mother.'

The stars are blotted out,
The clouds are covering clouds,
It is darkness vibrant, sonant.
In the roaring, whirling wind,
Are the souls of a million lunatics
Just loosed from prison-house,
Wrenching trees by the roots,
Sweeping all from the path.

But this was no mere poem. It was a vision of the Mother. Swamiji could no longer contain it. In exhaustion, he collapsed upon the boat's floor.

When consciousness returned, he quietly moved to Nivedita's boat. Who else but she could grasp the secret shape of his soul? She was away. He left the handwritten poem on her table.

Nivedita returned and read the verses, an offering to Death-In-Mother-form, a hymn to the Terrible One. Her eyes filled with tears. This was not the cry of a child; it was the cry of the

Mother herself, yearning for her child to return. She knew the time of farewell was drawing near.

Dancing mad with joy,
Come, Mother, come!
For terror is Thy name,
Death is in Thy breath;
And every shaking step
Destroys a world for e'er.
Thou 'Time', the all-destroyer!
Come, O Mother, come!

That Kali. From Kashmir to Belur. There, the Jhelum; here, the Ganga! That day, moonlight bathed the sky. Tonight, it is the deep, impenetrable dark of *Amavasya*.

Within that darkness, the dishevelled-haired Mother spreads Herself across the cosmos. The temple resounds with drums, cymbals, and bells in a rising tide of ritual music.

From the subconscious into waking awareness, Swamiji slowly returns. Soon, the worship of Kali will begin. The officiating monk is the brahmachari Krishnalal.

Sharatchandra enters. Seeing Swamiji sunk in profound absorption, he sits quietly in a corner of the room. A long time passes thus. At last, Swamiji turns his face and, in a calm voice, says: 'Everyone has gone to the shrine, and you're sitting here?'

Sharatchandra, no less serene than his master, replies, 'It feels peaceful here. Too many people in there.'

Swamiji understands the tenor of his disciple's heart. 'So, be it,' he says gently, 'Sit here then. Have you looked outside? How does it feel?'

Sharatchandra rises and walks out onto the veranda. There is dense, unbroken darkness. It is so thick that it seems the blackness of Kali Herself has swallowed the universe. Even a few steps ahead, the eye sees nothing. He returns indoors, murmuring to himself, 'It is *Amavasya*, the night of Kali *Puja*. That is why the world is so dark.'

Swamiji says nothing. He gazes silently for a long time through the open window. His mind drifts upon waves of divine thought. Then he murmurs, almost to himself, 'Do you see what a strange, solemn beauty lies in this darkness?!'

Sharatchandra remains quiet and serene. He senses that Swamiji now floats in another realm. He guards that sacred mood like a silent flame in the wind. From the temple, voices rise, and though distant, they reach even here.

Then Swamiji begins to sing:

'In this dense darkness, Mother, Thy beauty flashes forth....'

The song fades into silence. No one else remains in the room. Alone, Swamiji speaks softly to the air, 'This time, I shall worship the Mother with blood!'

Raghunandan says—

"On the Navami day, the Goddess is to be worshipped with a red, blood-smeared clay." This time I shall do it. Let me offer Her my heart's blood. Perhaps then She will be pleased.

'Her son must be brave, a hero among heroes! In sorrow, in terror, in dissolution, in cosmic annihilation—The Mother's child shall remain unafraid.'

Below, in the temple, the bell rings for *prasad.* Swamiji says quietly, 'Go now. Take your *prasad* and come back soon.'

Sharatchandra descends to the temple.

Latu Maharaj

The worship of the Divine Mother Shyama had concluded. The breath of winter crept silently through the air. Swamiji sat wrapped in a thick quilt, propped up on his bed. Of late, fevers came frequently, lingering a day or two before retreating. His body felt restless, spiritless; nothing seemed to bring comfort. Even when surrounded by people, he often felt alone, deeply, achingly alone. He had never quite been like the others. Perhaps that was why Thakur had left all responsibility upon his shoulders. And now, bearing the weight of so much, he felt utterly weary.

It was now well into the day. The bed no longer offered solace. Swamiji stepped out into the veranda. Morning sunlight lay scattered in golden silence. Two young brahmacharis saw him from below. To the new initiates, Swamiji was a mystery, a figure of awe. They kept their distance, speaking of him in hushed tones. To see him in the morning like this—what fortune! They hurried up and bowed to him. Swamiji gave a faint smile and asked, 'What were you two up to?'

'Sharat Maharaj is going to Mother's house in Baghbazar. We're going with him.'

'Yes, go. Bow before the Mother and seek Her blessing. Know this, when She places Her hand upon a head, that life is sanctified. One finds the Master. The Mother is the Infinite, the Eternal.'

From below, Saradananda's voice rose, 'Where has everyone gone?'

Swamiji gave each boy a gentle pat on the back. 'Go on. Sharat is waiting.'

As the boys left, Swamiji stepped down from his room, heading towards the temple. By the stairs, Bagha lay stretched out, once a proud and unruly dog, now strangely quiet since being driven away. Once, the entire Math had been his kingdom. Now, he seldom wandered beyond the threshold of Swamiji's room. Perhaps he had understood that this boundary was his last refuge. Beyond it, danger lurked.

'Have you eaten?' Swamiji asked.

Bagha did not raise his head. Swamiji understood. It was late; no one had fed him. 'All right, sit here. I'll have someone send food for you.'

He instructed a kitchen hand and continued to the temple. The grounds were silent, and almost no one was around at that hour. In one corner of the temple, he noticed Latu Maharaj seated, chanting softly. Swamiji smiled inwardly. He knew well that Latu observed no set times for prayer or meditation. He was unlike the others, bound by no rule, flowing freely in his own simplicity and innocence.

A memory stirred in Swamiji. Once, he had ordered everyone to rise at four in the morning for meditation. The next day, a bell had rung through the Math at dawn, rousing all from sleep. Latu had grumbled, 'I don't like this rule.'

'This rule is for everyone,' Swamiji had insisted.

Latu's face darkened. 'Then I can't stay here.'

He had packed his few belongings and prepared to leave. Swamiji asked, 'Where are you going?'

'To Calcutta,' Latu replied, his face sombre.

'You'll abandon us and go?'

'You came back from the West and now you're full of new rules. I cannot follow them. My heart doesn't work like a clock. You'll ring a bell, and I must sit in meditation? Who can say when the heart will turn inward? Mine hasn't reached that place yet. Maybe yours has, and good for you if it has.'

Swamiji, amused, had said, 'All right, then, go if you must.'

But he hadn't thought Latu would actually leave. Back in his room, he was told, 'Latu Maharaj is going!'

Startled, Swamiji rushed out. 'Which way did he go?'

'To the gate.'

He ran, breathless, until he spotted Latu at the gate. 'Latu! Wait! Where are you going?'

Latu turned. Swamiji approached him. 'You'd leave us like this? Just walk away?'

'I can't follow your rules,' Latu said simply.

Swamiji burst out laughing. 'I was only teasing you! You don't have to follow those rules. They're for the novices, not for you. You stay just as you are.'

At last, Latu smiled. 'Did you really think I could leave the Math?'

That same Latu now sat in the temple. Seeing Swamiji, he opened his eyes. 'You, here, at this hour?'

Swamiji couldn't resist a bit of teasing. 'Just came to see what you were up to.'

Latu answered with calm solemnity, 'We are small souls. What is there for us to do? Whatever has been done, Thakur has done. We only do as He commands. But you, Noren-*bhai*, what have you done?'

For a moment, it struck Swamiji like a blow. He looked directly into Latu's eyes. 'You think I've done nothing? The work I began, you will understand its fruits later. This is only the beginning. In Europe and America, people have only begun to utter His name. Give it twenty years, you'll see people in those lands embrace Thakur's vision. Now there are only a few. Then, you'll understand what Vivekananda has done.'

Latu stared at him for a while, unmoved. Then he said simply, 'Brother, what new thing have you really done? What Shankaracharya and the Buddha did, you have only traced their footsteps. Nothing more.'

Swamiji was shaken. Latu was right. What pride could he claim? The path he had walked was already lit by the footsteps of the great. He had merely followed.

He stepped forward and took Latu's hand, 'Latu *bhai*, you've spoken truly. I have only drawn lines upon what others have carved. I've done nothing, and yet I go around claiming I've done everything.'

Returning to his room, Swamiji sat in thought. The veil of ego had been torn by Latu's words—gentle, unadorned, true. That evening, he wrote to a friend:

> Action always brings with it the shadow of misfortune. I have lost my health and now taste the fruit of accumulated illness. But I am content. My heart is lighter. A quiet tenderness and peace have come into my life, one I never knew before. I am learning how to remain both attached and detached at once. Slowly, I gain mastery over my own mind.
>
> It is the Mother's Work—She Alone Does It.
>
> The Mother is doing Her work. Why should I worry over

it anymore? Creatures like me, mere moths, perish by the thousands each moment; and yet, Her divine play goes on, undisturbed, unshaken. Victory to the Mother!

Carried by the current of Her will, I have walked alone all my life. Whenever I tried to go against that tide, pain struck me without fail. Let Her will be fulfilled, that alone is my prayer.
I am content now. The storms within my mind have quieted. A deep peace surrounds me. The renunciation in my heart glows brighter than before. Day by day, my ties to kin and kindred grow fainter, while my yearning for the Mother grows ever stronger.

Memories return—those long, silent nights beneath the banyan tree at Dakshineswar, when we sat awake with Sri Ramakrishna. Those hours live again within me.
And work? What is work? Whose work is it, and for whom should I toil?

I am free. I am the child of the Mother. All work is Hers, all is Her play. Why should I scheme and plan? What plans could I possibly make? Without waiting for any design of mine, whatever was meant to come has come, and whatever was meant to go has gone, just as the Mother desired. She is the One who turns the wheel; we are nothing but the wheels turned by Her hand.

Kaligħat

The horse-drawn carriage rolled to a stop before the temple gates of Kalighat. At the front sat the coachman, beside him, Nirbhayananda. With a swift leap, Nirbhayananda alighted and circled to the rear to open the carriage door. First to emerge was Swamiji, then Shuddhananda. Seated within, wrapped in quiet dignity, was Bhubaneshwari Devi. Swamiji extended his hand towards her, and helped her descend.

Not long ago, Bhubaneshwari Devi had been strong and full of vigour. But in recent times, age and affliction had wearied both body and mind. Her steps were slow now. She cast a glance around at the crowded shops and the jostling pilgrims.

As they walked, she murmured, 'Do you remember, Bilu, I once came here with your father? You were a child then. There were no shops, no such crowd. The air was open, quiet. We bathed in the Ganga, and offered our prayers. Your father knew a priest here; he arranged for *prasad* at the temple that afternoo The taste of it! I still remember it.'

Shuddhananda walked ahead and said, 'I've never visi this temple before. But Grandmother made a vow long ago here we are.'

Bhubaneshwari Devi paused, still holding Swamiji's hand. Her voice dropped into a whisper. 'Bilu was four or five, stricken with a fever that would not abate. Doctors, *vaidyas*—none could help. In desperation, I vowed to the Mother of Kalighat, "Heal my child, and I shall come offer worship at Your feet. He will roll on the temple steps in surrender to You." And lo, Bilu recovered. But the vow... amid life's distractions, was never fulfilled.'

Swamiji laughed softly. 'During Kali Puja, Ma came to Belur. I was ill at the time. She grew anxious and said, "You know, I once made a vow for you at Kalighat, when you were sick as a child. Perhaps your ill health now is because that vow remains unfulfilled. Come, let us fulfil it."'

Shuddhananda chimed in, 'It's good we came. You'll recover now.'

Before Swamiji could reply, a group of temple *pandas* crowded around. 'Come, come! You've come to offer worship? We'll guide you; everything will be done properly.'

But before Swamiji could respond, a young man broke through the throng. Broad-shouldered, dignified in bearing, he bowed reverently to Swamiji. 'I am Girin. Sharatchandra sent word yesterday that you were coming. So I've been waiting.'

Swamiji smiled. 'It was our Mother's vow.'

'I heard,' said Girin. 'You must first meet Halder Babu, the temple's chief *sevayet*. He will see to all arrangements.'

Hearing Halder's name, the pandas quickly withdrew.

Swamiji asked, 'Where is your home?'

'Across the main road, within walking distance. My father and grandfather were generous patrons of this temple, so we are held in some esteem here. Let us talk as we walk.'

They crossed the main thoroughfare into a narrow lane flanked by flower shops and stalls. Garlands, *bel* leaves, sweets for offering—all were displayed in vivid colours. Vendors called out, 'This way, Ma! Fresh garlands at a good price! Pure milk sweets!'

Swamiji led the way. Girin, walking beside him, said, 'On special days, the crowd here spills for miles, and people packed, shoulder to shoulder.'

They passed through the alley and entered an old house with its door ajar. Inside was a spacious hall, half-carpeted with cushions. Several men were seated. At one end, an elderly man sat before a wooden chest. Rising at Swamiji's approach, he folded his hands.

'Welcome, welcome, Swamiji. We've been expecting you. I am Bishwanath Halder. Our family has long held the responsibility of caring for this temple.'

Swamiji said, 'I've heard a little of your work.'

Halder Babu smiled. 'But I have heard much of yours. It is my fortune to finally meet you. Please, be seated. Ma, you too.'

Swamiji said, 'I visited here once in my youth, with friends. But the memory is vague.'

A man seated nearby interjected, 'Ours is a very awakened deity. For generations, devotees have come here. And when someone prays with a pure heart, the Mother grants their wishes.'

Shuddhananda, always full of curiosity, asked, 'Were your ancestors the founders of this temple?'

Halder Babu folded his hands. 'No, no. Who can *find* a temple of the Mother unless divinely ordained? Only a great ascetic, a soul of merit, can do such a thing.'

Swamiji nodded. 'You're right. The Kali temple at Dakshineswar, too, was founded by Rani Rashmoni through the Mother's will.'

Emotion welled up in Halder Babu. He paused, then spoke quietly. 'There is a story here as well. Long ago, a spiritual seeker named Atmaram Brahmachari came here. It was wilderness back then. He built a small altar beneath a *bel* tree and meditated day and night on the Mother. One day, while he was in deep meditation, he heard the Goddess speak. She told him, "Here, the toes of Sati's right foot had fallen. This is a Shakti Peeth. The altar where you sit is *Brahmavedi*—once, even Brahma sat here in meditation upon Me. Install My image here."

'Atmaram asked, "But where shall I find such a form of You?"

'She said, "In the Nilgiri mountains lives a sage, Brahmananda Giri. He possesses a sacred black stone pillar. Bring it here, fashion My form, and place it upon the Brahmavedi."

'Atmaram journeyed to the Nilgiris, found the sage, and beheld the vast pillar—twelve hands long, two hands wide. By divine grace, he brought it to Kalighat. Then, the celestial artisan Vishwakarma himself appeared and sculpted the image of the Goddess. That image now sits on the Brahmavedi.'

'And this current temple?' Swamiji asked.

'For long, only a broken shrine stood here. Later, Kali Prasad Dutta of Hatkhola invited Brahmins and donated Rs 25,000. With this, Santosh Roy of the Barisha Sabarna family began the temple's construction. His son completed it in 1809 by the banks of the Adi Ganga.'

Nirbhayananda asked, 'And how did your family become the temple's caretakers?'

Bishwanath replied, 'It's said Raja Pratapaditya's uncle, Basanta Roy of Jessore, came here once. At the time, the deity's image was housed in a humble shed. Basanta Roy built a small temple and entrusted its care to a Brahmin named Bhubaneswar. He had no sons. His daughter married into the Halder family. Through her line, we have served here ever since.'

Just then, a young man—wrapped in a *dhoti* and *chadar*, a

sandalwood mark on his forehead, and the sacred thread peeking from beneath his tunic—approached. Halder Babu looked up. 'Ah, Jatin, you've come. You will prepare everything for Swamiji's worship and *yajna* today.'

Swamiji was a little hesitant. The priests at Dakshineswar had once barred his entry; he had crossed the seas, after all. He wasn't sure how Kalighat would receive him. He had resolved that, if denied entry, he would lie down in the dust outside the sanctum itself.

But Bishwanath's warmth moved him. Folding his hands, Swamiji said, 'You are truly among the Mother's children. You offered Nivedita a place to speak here, and now, you have arranged everything for me.'

Halder Babu's voice trembled slightly. 'Swamiji, you are India's pride. You've taken *Sanatan Dharma* to the world. Those who once mocked us now hang their heads in shame. And Sister, after hearing her speak, I felt though we live beside the Mother, worship Her daily; we have never known Her as she has.'

The priest who had been silent till now, finally spoke. 'Swamiji, come. Soon the temple will be crowded.'

Swamiji rose. Taking his mother's hand, he began to walk. As they crossed the lane, the priest asked, 'Will you bathe before the worship?'

'How can I approach the Mother without purification?'

'Then let us go to the Ganga.'

Nirbhayananda hesitated. 'In this *Paush* winter, will you bathe in the Ganga? The cold may worsen your rheumatism.'

But Swamiji's face glowed with serenity. All the sufferings of life, all the storms of body and mind, seemed to have passed over him like a fading monsoon. He said quietly, 'I have come to the Mother, She who is beginningless, endless, eternal. All that I am is Hers. Why should I think of myself? Let Her do the thinking for I belong to Her alone.'

All stepped out. A narrow alley lay before them—so narrow that even two could not walk side by side. Dwellings pressed in from both sides, their walls leaning close. A short way ahead, the lane ended, opening near the gateway of a Kali temple. The road beyond was earthen, not overly wide, fit for a horse-cart, perhaps, but mostly trodden by foot. On either side, clay huts with thatched roofs nestled close, the humble abodes of the temple priests. Here and there, scraps of garbage lay scattered, whispering of neglect.

Across the road, at last, the river came into view—what the locals called the Adi Ganga, and some, the Kali Ganga. Not as broad as the main Ganga, it looked more like a modest country river meandering through the village. One could swim across, if need be. Boats, lined in rows along both banks, bobbed gently—most loaded with goods, tied fast against the shore.

A built ghat descended into the waters. The tide had come in not long ago; water lapped softly against the second or third step. On either side of the ghat stood two small temples—one of Shiva, the other of Radha and Krishna. Bathers, having completed their ritual cleansing, bowed in prayer and left a coin or two as an offering.

Swamiji now stood at the edge. A cold *Paush* wind blew, stinging but gentle. It was well into the morning, yet the sun had not emerged. A fine veil of mist hovered above the river's surface. Only a handful of people moved silently along the ghat.

Nirbhayananda approached, bearing Swamiji's garments. With calm deliberation, Swamiji removed his shawl and undercloth. His upper body bare, he lifted his remaining cloth above the knee, bent down, and touched the river water, pressing it to his forehead. Then, with quiet grace, he descended the steps into the stream.

From the ghat above, the temple priest Jatin called out, 'Swamiji, do not go beyond the third step! The ghat has weakened.'

Swamiji entered up to his waist. Bowing low, he dipped thrice into the sacred waters. Then, with palms joined, he faced east and saluted the yet-unseen sun.

A mother's heart stirred. In the fierce chill, her Naren stood immersed. A cry burst from Bhubaneshwari Devi's lips, 'Come back, my son! Do not stay in that icy water any longer!'

One cannot disregard a mother's voice. Swamiji emerged. Nirbhayananda stood ready with dry clothes. 'Here, Master, change into these.'

Swamiji paused. 'First, let us visit the temple. I shall see the Mother. After that, I will change.'

His garments still wet, his body exposed to the air, Swamiji walked towards the shrine. Near the entrance, beggars crowded—blind, limping, crippled, aged. Their pleas were soft yet searing, 'A little alms, O Mother, have mercy.'

Bhubaneshwari Devi had brought a small cloth pouch with coins, savings of many months. One by one, she gave each a coin.

They passed the pilgrims' quarters and entered the *natmandir*. Directly ahead stood the sanctum of the Mother. In the southwest corner, a flight of steps led to the veranda of the inner shrine. There, at the heart of the temple, the stone idol of the Mother stood—nearly five feet tall, carved from black basalt. Her eyes were gold, as was her tongue. Her entire form was adorned with flowers. Swamiji gazed, enraptured.

She was the womb of the world, the Divine Mother—Kali.

Stretching out both arms, Swamiji touched the feet of the goddess. A strange tremor passed through his body. Emotions swelled, and his body trembled. With fervour, he recited the mantras of the Devi:

'Thou art Ananda-Mayi Kali, O Supreme Goddess, Bestower of Dharma, Artha, Moksha—salutations, beloved of Shankara!'

There were others inside the temple—several priests preparing for worship. They had been informed of Swamiji's arrival. Clearing the way, they said, 'Swamiji, please offer your salutations.'

Without hesitation, Swamiji fell prostrate on the stone floor, cold and biting. Yet he felt no discomfort. The beloved child of the Mother, at her feet, knew only joy.

From all corners rose the chant, 'Victory to the Mother! Jai Ma! Jai Ma!'

Bhubaneshwari Devi stood aside, tears brimming in her eyes. Her long-cherished desire had finally found fulfillment. With folded hands, she prayed: 'O Mother, keep my Naren well.'

Gaya

Miss MacLeod and Mr Okakura had come to Belur Math. MacLeod was a disciple of Swamiji. Okakura, a Japanese, was famed across the world as an expert in fine arts. A religious conference was being planned in Japan in the near future. Okakura wished that Swamiji would attend. All arrangements would be taken care of. Considering his health, Swamiji said nothing. Who can tell how the body shall behave?

But Okakura had come to India with another dream too—to build a cottage in Bodh Gaya, where he would immerse himself in Buddhist art, literature, and philosophy. He said, 'Come with me, Swamiji. To be near you is no less than to be near the Blessed Buddha.'

A gentle smile touched Swamiji's lips. 'Since childhood,' he said, 'I have been drawn to the Buddha.'

'Have you ever been to Bodh Gaya?' Okakura asked.

Swamiji's eyes drifted towards a far horizon. Some memories shine so fiercely in the mind that they can never be forgotten. Bodh Gaya felt like yesterday. His mind went back to the time when it was the beginning of his monastic life. Sri Ramakrishna was still alive. It was 1886. The Master was gravely ill, living at the Kashipur Garden House. All the disciples were gathered there. By day, they tended to duties, and welcomed visitors. By night, there was meditation, *japa*, and discussions on *dharma*. They often spoke of the life and teachings of the Buddha. Everyone was afire with devotion. At last, it was resolved that they would visit Bodh Gaya, that sacred soil where the Buddha had attained enlightenment.

One day, Swamiji, with two companions, Tarak (later Swami Shivananda) and Kali (later Swami Abhedananda), set out without telling anyone. They crossed the Ganga to Bali station, then took the train via Bankipur to Gaya, and walked from there to Bodh Gaya in their robes of ochre and with blankets over their shoulders. They had no place to stay. As they wandered, they met the *mahant* of a local monastery, a kind man who gave them shelter. A strange exaltation took hold. Swamiji would sit for hours in meditation beneath the Bodhi tree. Such deep fervour would rise within him that he would burst into tears.

He had wished to stay longer. But none of them had clothes for the cold. The bitter chill was unbearable. Their only sustenance was a thick, hard *marua* bread which was so hard that they could hardly eat it. They were forced to return.

Years passed. And now again, they had returned to Bodh Gaya. Okakura sat before him, his eyes fixed upon Swamiji, awaiting his reply.

Swamiji hesitated no more. 'Mr Okakura,' he said, 'I cannot refuse your invitation. I shall go.'

Okakura's face lit up with joy. 'Do not worry, Swamiji. You shall be cared for.'

Seated beside them, Swami Saradananda had been silently anxious for Swamiji. 'Naren,' he said, 'since you're going to

Bodh Gaya, stop by Kashi as well. If the climate suits you, stay there a few days.'

At the mention of Kashi, Swamiji grew still. Kashi meant Shiva, his eternal Lord. For ages, that land had borne the dust of saints' feet. Its very air was a balm to the soul. 'Yes,' Swamiji said softly, 'I will go to Kashi. Perhaps, for the last time.'

Saradananda started in alarm. With a frown, he said, 'Not the last. You'll go many more times.'

A quiet smile formed on Swamiji's lips. 'I know how much you all love me. But I feel it in my bones. The bell of time is nearing its toll.'

Saradananda flared. 'Enough nonsense. You're going. I'll see to everything.'

27 January 1902

Swamiji, MacLeod, Okakura, Swami Nirbhayananda, and two young boys—Gaur and Neda—set out on a night train. Swamiji had chosen five boys to live at the Math and study in outside schools. Gaur, whose formal name was Naresh Chandra Ghosh, and Neda were two among them.

It was quite a group. They had reserved a first-class compartment. The biting cold of Magh was sharp, and all were concerned for Swamiji's fragile health. Nirbhayananda and Gaur laid out a bed for him. Swamiji lay down, softly murmuring his *japa* as sleep approached.

In the dark hours before dawn, a burst of noise awoke them. The train was pulling into Bankipur station. Jo MacLeod's voice called out, 'Swamiji, time to get off.'

Swamiji rose. Bankipur was a small station, with a dim flicker of gas lamps, muffled figures swathed in thick blankets, and wisps of mist hanging low. On a cold bench, Gaur spread a mat to sit. Soon another train arrived, its coal engine loud with hissing steam. Few passengers disembarked. Jo MacLeod asked, 'Where to now?'

'Gaya,' said Swamiji. 'We'll halt there a day, then proceed to Bodh Gaya.'

'No trouble at all,' said Okakura. 'I wrote ahead. Lord Curzon, the Viceroy, gave me a letter. I wired the Collector of Bihar as well.'

Swamiji laughed. 'Such are the privileges of foreigners. We, are the black men, and our letters never reach the Viceroy.'

Both MacLeod and Okakura felt the sting of that truth. There was nothing they could say.

Daylight slowly broke. Through the train's glass windows, the changing countryside unfolded its fields, trees, and distant hills standing tall against the sky. The engine's chuff punctuated the rhythm of the rails. Wisps of smoke curled into the air. Gaur and Neda were wide-eyed with joy; they had never seen mountains before. Swamiji chuckled. 'This? This is nothing. Wait till I take you to Mayavati. There you'll see the Himalayas. Then you'll know what a mountain truly is.'

Green fields, rice paddies, and village huts flew by. The train reached Gaya Junction, a crowded platform with tea vendors calling. They disembarked, one by one. A man in government uniform approached, flanked by two others. On seeing Okakura, he bowed. 'Sir, we've been expecting you.'

Outside the station, three horse carriages stood ready. The rest-house was about a kilometre away. The morning chill had mellowed and golden sunlight bathed the land. They reached a vast garden, and in its midst stood a grand bungalow with many rooms. A cook was arranged for MacLeod and Okakura to prepare foreign fare. All were deeply worried for Swamiji's health. MacLeod asked gently, 'What shall you eat, Swamiji?'

'I'll cook for Guruji,' said Nirbhayananda. 'Plain rice with a light broth.'

'Then we rest today,' said Okakura. 'Tomorrow we set off for Bodh Gaya.'

But Swamiji's heart stirred. Could he leave Gaya without visiting the sacred feet of Lord Vishnu? Was it not here that Sri Ramakrishna's divine advent had been sanctified? He said, 'You all rest. I shall go to the Vishnu temple.'

MacLeod wished to accompany him but knew well that many Hindu temples barred foreigners. Better not to risk insult.

'Go ahead, Guruji,' said Nirbhayananda. 'By the time you return, the food will be ready.'

Gaur summoned a tonga. Neda stood silently by the door, his face wistful. Swamiji caught his gaze. 'Want to come with us?'

Neda nodded eagerly.

Swamiji cautioned him. 'Stay close. There are many bad people out there.'

Neda grinned as the three of them climbed into the carriage. The mist had lifted and the sun shone bright. I was no more cold. Soon, they reached the Phalgu River which was now a phantom stream, dry save for a few silvery traces of water. Its sand shimmered in the light. A boulder glinted here and there. On the banks stood the Vishnupad Temple.

The *Vayu Purana* tells of Gayasura, a demon and ardent devotee of Vishnu, who performed severe penance in the remote wilderness. Fearing he would conquer heaven, the gods appealed to Vishnu. The Lord appeared and asked Gayasura what boon he desired.

'I seek no blessings for myself,' said the demon. 'Let my body become so pure that whoever touches it is freed from all sin and reaches Vaikuntha.'

'So be it,' said Vishnu. And thus, many attained heaven merely by his touch. Yama's realms emptied. Again, the gods pleaded with Vishnu.

This time, Vishnu returned and asked Gayasura for his body. The demon agreed. Vishnu pressed him down with a massive slab and set his foot upon it. 'As long as the sun and moon endure,' he said, 'I shall remain here. Those who offer *pinda* here shall be freed.' And the land came to be known as Gayakshetra.

Swamiji alighted and walked to the temple. Devotees from distant lands had gathered—some offering *pinda*, others seeking blessings. Priests and *pandas* filled the precincts but avoided the *sannyasis* for they hardly got any profit from them. Swamiji stood before the dark stone temple. The original had been small, till it had been rebuilt by Queen Ahilyabai Holkar.

He entered the *sabhamandapa*, where men with shaven heads sat solemnly, offering *pinda* for their ancestors. Crossing the hall, he came to the sanctum. At its heart lay the Vishnupad stone, marked with the Lord's footprint. Flowers lay strewn all around. Swamiji stood still, overwhelmed. His body trembled. Slowly, he knelt down and his hands reached out to touch the sacred stone. Others made way for him, in awe.

'Who is he?' asked a *panda*.

'Swami Vivekananda,' Gaur replied. 'Disciple of Sri Ramakrishna.'

At the Master's name, Swamiji was overcome. Vishnu's holy seat and his beloved Guru, they seemed to merge and become one. He remembered a story he had heard from the Master.

Before Ramakrishna was born, his father, Khudiram, had

visited his daughter Katyayani's in-laws. The girl seemed unwell, possessed, people said. Distraught, Khudiram prayed with deep concentration. 'Who are you, spirit, tormenting my child?'

A voice from Katyayani's lips replied, 'I am a wandering soul, seeking release. I found no refuge but this body.'

'What will free you?' Khudiram asked.

'Give me *pinda* in Gaya,' it said.

Khudiram promised. Instantly, the girl recovered.

It was 1835. In early spring, Khudiram journeyed to Gaya. With heart brimming with devotion, he offered *pinda* at Vishnupad. That very night, he dreamt that he was offering *pinda* again, and his ancestors, radiant and content, received it. Then a divine being, resplendent with conch, discus, mace, and lotus, appeared and said, 'Your devotion has pleased me. I shall be born as your son. You will serve me.'

Khudiram wept, 'But I am poor. How will I serve you?'

'Fear not,' said the radiant form. 'Whatever you can offer will please me.'

He awoke. And in due time, returned to Kamarpukur. In Chandramani's lap was born the god in human form, Gadadhar. Thus was the dream of Gayakshetra fulfilled.

Bodh Gaya

At dawn, they set out once again. From Gaya, they would journey to Bodh Gaya. Two horse-drawn carriages were readied—one carrying Macleod and Okakura, the other bearing Swamiji and his retinue comprising Nirbhayananda, Gour, and Neda. They travelled 15 kms through the countryside, fields of crops, and scattered villages, but mostly through an desolate, arid expanse, unchanged since the time of the Blessed One. The road was hardened earth, and the horses galloped on, stirring up clouds of dust.

Gaur and Neda sat in front of Swamiji, who, with playful laughter, jested with them. They laughed too. Nirbhayananda watched with quiet wonder. Who would believe, seeing Swamiji now display such light-hearted mirth, that this same man, in the stillness of meditation, becomes an image of otherworldly detachment?

After a long ride, the carriages came to a halt. All stepped down to stretch their limbs. The horses, too, took their rest. By ten o'clock, they passed through the outskirts of Bodh Gaya. Trees lined the road. Here and there were ruins of old houses that were now reduced to mounds of stone. Further on, rows of Buddhist temples appeared, ancient and solemn. Swamiji sat still, eyes steeped in reverence. He had returned to the sacred ground where his beloved Buddha once walked. The mirthful man of moments ago now seemed transformed, his soul stirred by some silent exaltation.

The horses pressed forward. After passing a small lake, they approached a two-storeyed house flanked by several smaller buildings. A wrought-iron gate marked the entrance. A few men stood watch. At the sight of the carriages, one raised a hand and the coachman brought the vehicle to a stop. One by one, they alighted.

At the gate stood the *mahant* of the Dashanami Math of Bodh Gaya, Krishnalal Giri, a native of Nepal, no more than thirty years old. He was striking in appearance—fair-skinned, clad in saffron robes, wooden sandals at his feet, a gentle smile on his lips, and palms joined in greeting. At once he stepped forward and bowed low before Swamiji. Swamiji embraced him warmly. One after another, the others too offered *pranam*.

'Come, Swamiji,' said Krishnalal, as he led them into a vast hall. Cushions covered the floor. At one end, a regal seat awaited the *mahant*, draped in crimson velvet, bolstered with pillows on three sides, resembling a throne. As Swamiji bent to sit nearby, Krishnalal rushed forward, face stricken with dismay. 'Swamiji, what are you doing?' he cried. 'Your place is above us all!'

Almost by force, he seated Swamiji into his own seat. The space on either side was left empty for Macleod and Okakura, who sat flanking him like quiet disciples. Krishnalal, still standing with folded hands, murmured, 'By your sacred presence, this ashram is sanctified. Stay here as long as your heart desires. This place is now yours. Two Brahmin attendants will be at your service always. Just speak your need, and it shall be done.'

'How old is this ashram?' Swamiji asked.

'Thirty years,' the *mahant* replied. 'It wasn't always this grand. In the beginning, there were just a few rooms, with no place for devotees to stay. Then came a wealthy patron, a man of faith. I asked for his help, and he built all you see now. We can house hundreds.'

An attendant whispered to the *mahant*, who turned, attentive. 'Swamiji, you've come a long way,' he said. 'Let us show you to your quarters. A Brahmin cook is preparing your meal.'

One side of the guesthouse held rooms, each offered to a member of the party. On the far side were the monks' quarters. There were ascetics of many kinds, dressed in robes of many hues. There was an elaborate kitchen. Outside, rows of bulls were hauling firewood, as labourers moved swiftly. The air was thick with bustle, as if a royal household were in preparation. Yet at the centre of it all was the *mahant*, composed and humble, alert to every detail. He ensured all were fed before he took his own meal. Swamiji, awestruck, said, 'Seldom have I seen a man so scholarly, so pious, so pure of heart.'

After the midday meal and a brief rest, Swamiji said, 'Come, let us visit the Buddha temple.'

Everyone was eager to accompany him. Walking with Swamiji was a joy in itself.

'I will arrange carriages,' offered the *mahant*.

Swamiji replied, 'We'll go on foot. It's better for the body.'

'Then let's visit the Bodhi Tree,' Okakura suggested.

Joy lit Swamiji's face. 'Yes,' he said. 'Let us.'

Across several kilometres stood temples from many lands, each a marvel of devotion and artistry. Soon they reached the Bodhi Tree. Beneath this pipal tree, two and a half millennia ago, on the banks of the Niranjana, Prince Siddhartha had sat in meditation and attained supreme awakening. Hence it was known as the Bodhi Tree. Nearby was the Sujata Tank, where he had bathed before his final vigil.

Swamiji stood in silent awe, his eyes fixed upon the tree. Gaur and Neda stood beside him. 'After enlightenment,' he said softly, 'the Blessed One gazed upon this tree for seven days without shifting his eyes.'

Okakura approached. 'Swamiji, I have heard that you believe deeply in the Buddha's ideals.'

Swamiji fell into a hush. Then, with a voice near breaking, he said, 'Buddha is my chosen deity. My God. I believe he was God Himself. I feel I am not even his servant—but the servant of his servant. Who else has ever lived like him? He did nothing for himself. He gave his whole heart to the world. His compassion was so vast he would have laid down his life for even a newborn goat.'

Tears welled in his eyes.

Macleod, knowing how Swamiji's soul could be stirred like a stringed instrument with but a whisper, said gently, 'Shall we go, Swamiji?'

Swamiji paused. 'Do you have pen and paper, Jo?'

Jo always carried a small notebook and pen in her satchel, for one never knew when inspiration might strike. She handed them to Swamiji, knowing that in Goodwin's absence, no one now recorded his thoughts. Swamiji would write them himself.

'Will you sit here, Swamiji?' Jo asked.

He sat in stillness under the Bodhi Tree.

'I will stay here a while,' said Swamiji softly. 'You all go, look around, take it in.'

The others withdrew, leaving him alone in that sanctified hush. There was no crowd, no sound, only the hush of history, of leaves, and of memory. One side of the Bodhi Tree was paved with stone. Fallen leaves lay scattered. Swamiji brushed a space clear with his hand and sat there. For a long time, he gazed upward at the spreading branches. His soul stirred with a depth of feeling that surpassed thought. He opened his diary and took up the pen.

Namo Sam Buddhāya

Buddha is my chosen one, my God.
He came to me once—into my home, into my life—when I was but a child.
Still a schoolboy, seated in meditation behind closed doors,
Suddenly—he appeared. A radiant being, silent, luminous.
A shaven-headed monk, calm and resplendent,
Carrying staff and alms bowl, light in his face,
His eyes full of speech, gazing at me,
As though he was about to say something profound.
I was overwhelmed. I bowed to him, fully prostrated.
But I was afraid—
I ran out, foolish, without hearing what he came to say.
Yet I know—I know—
It was the Blessed Buddha himself who came to me.
And then—
Years later, I sat in meditation beneath this very Bodhi Tree, here in Bodh Gaya—
And a shiver ran through me.
Can this be true?
That I breathe the same air he once breathed—
That I tread upon the very soil he once walked?
Buddha—
The only one who came into this world
And declared this message:

Death is the great curse—
Life too is a curse.
And the end of death and life alike is Nirvana—
Let that be the eternal refuge of humankind.
Om Namo Bhagavate Sam Buddhāya.

***

Kashi Dham

Later, from Bodh Gaya, they had returned to Gaya again. The next destination was Kashi Dham. The plans were settled long ago. MacLeod had already returned to Kolkata.

Swamiji, Okakura, Nirbhayananda, Gaur, and Neda—two in one tonga, two in another—assembled at the station. The tonga halted just outside. Swamiji alighted and moved towards the platform. Lately, he kept no money himself; all financial responsibility rested with Nirbhayananda. Swamiji's constant companion was a crocodile-leather bag, gifted to him abroad, which had become his cherished possession. Now it rested on Nirbhayananda's shoulder. All travel funds were packed in a pouch inside the bag.

As everyone dismounted, and the luggage was being unloaded, trouble struck. The clasp of the leather bag had jammed shut; no matter how hard they tried, it would not open. If the bag remained locked, the pouch with the money would be inaccessible. The two tonga drivers stood waiting, the fare unpaid.

If Swamiji found out, he would be furious beyond measure. He had only a small sum on him, which was nowhere enough to pay the fare. Nirbhayananda was at a loss. Standing nearby, Okakura sensed the tension and gently asked, 'Is something wrong?'

Nirbhayananda hesitated, unsure of what to say. Asking for help from a foreigner was embarrassing, but there was no other choice. He explained the situation to Okakura, who smiled warmly, lightly patting Nirbhayananda's back. 'No worries. I will pay. How much?'

'One rupee for two,' came the reply.

Okakura settled the fare. Standing beside Nirbhayananda, Gaur murmured softly, 'Once we board the train, there'll be time. We can open the bag then.'

Soon, the train arrived. Its coal-fired engine steamed and huffed like a giant beast as it pulled into the platform. The crowd was sparse. Second-class compartments had been arranged for Swamiji and Okakura. Ordinary carriages lacked bathrooms, which caused some discomfort for Swamiji. He had wished everyone to travel together, laughing and chatting along the way. But that was impossible with Swamiji's needs. So the four had already purchased general-class tickets.

Everyone boarded the train. With plenty of empty seats, finding a place was no trouble. Then attempts to open the bag began again. Keys were tried in every lock, but the clasp was stubbornly jammed tight. Gaur's face grew troubled. If the bag couldn't be opened, what would they do? Swamiji's essential belongings were all inside.

Nirbhayananda's distress deepened. While the journey was smooth, the thought of reaching Kashi Dham and not being able to produce Swamiji's things haunted him. The hope for laughter and ease in the general compartment faded from his mind.

As evening fell, the train pulled into Kashi Dham station. Waiting there were Yamini Babu, Charu Babu, and many others.

Upon stepping down, Swamiji and Okakura were garlanded with flowers. On one side stood Nirbhayananda, clutching Swamiji's locked bag, unsure of what to do.

Suddenly, Yamini Babu emerged from the crowd. Though barely acquainted, Nirbhayananda felt this man might help in a crisis. He hurried forward, voice low and urgent, 'Sir, it's a disaster.'

Startled, Yamini Babu asked quickly, 'What happened?'

'The bag is locked so tight—no key can open it. We must find a way to open it at once. Swamiji does not know yet; if he did, it would be catastrophic.'

'Have you tried anything?'

'We have been trying since Gaya, no luck.'

'I see. The bag must be taken to a locksmith.'

Nirbhayananda's face fell. 'Please, do what you can, but quickly.'

Yamini Babu understood his anxiety and offered comfort. 'Don't worry. Let's get everyone to Gopal Villa first. Then I will arrange everything.'

On the far side of Banaras lay Kali Krishna Thakur's garden estate, Gopal Villa. It was a palatial mansion surrounded by vast gardens filled with fruit trees and exotic flowers from many lands. The group proceeded there in a festive procession. Swamiji's longtime friends, Shivananda Swami and Niranjan Maharaj, were already in Banaras and had visited earlier.

Swamiji settled into the house, weary after many hours. Soon, he realised it was time for medicine. He called out, '*Kanai,* bring my medicine and slippers.'

Nirbhayananda remained silent, but knowing concealment was useless, bowed his head and confessed, 'Your bag's lock has jammed. We cannot open it.'

Swamiji was a calm man, but when angered, he was fierce

beyond measure. Suddenly he shouted, 'Useless fools! None of you is any good! Get out of my sight!'

Yamini Babu quickly interjected, 'Please do not worry, Swamiji. I will take it to the locksmith to open the bag.'

Taking the bag himself, Yamini Babu ran to the locksmith's workshop. An hour later, he returned, smiling. The bag was open. That night passed quietly.

At dawn, Nirbhayananda approached Swamiji with bowed head, only to be met with sudden fury. 'Kanai, you go! Go to Dashashwamedh Ghat and meditate! Beg for your food all day! At night, come back here to sleep. I have no more work for you!'

Swamiji's command was clear. No matter how difficult, it had to be obeyed. With bowed head, Nirbhayananda stepped out of the room. The distance from the villa to Dashashwamedh Ghat was 5 kms. Every morning, Kanai Maharaj set out on this journey and returned by evening. After a few days, Swamiji felt that the punishment had grown too harsh. 'You need not go anywhere anymore,' he said. 'Stay here.'

Swamiji was now settled in Kashi. The devotees were joyful and visitors came all day long, engaging in sacred discussions of the scriptures. The mind was at peace, and uplifted. It was decided he would remain here for a few days of complete rest and would not leave the room except when visitors came.

Winter had set in with a biting chill. The northern winds blew sharp and cold. For long hours, the surroundings were veiled in mist. Dewdrops gathered on every leaf, falling like gentle rain. When the sun rose a little higher, its faint warmth broke through. After lunch, Swamiji would sit with his back to the sun, basking in its mild heat.

Like every other day, he sat on the veranda. The cold wind whipped fiercely, buffeting his face. At last, he went inside and wrapped himself fully in warm garments. A light drowsiness overcame him. Hearing footsteps, he lifted his face. There stood Niranjanananda and Shivananda, with several young men behind them. Though they had met briefly in the past two days, they were not yet well-acquainted.

Niranjanananda and Shivananda took their seats, while the rest spread carpets on the floor and sat there.

Niranjanananda had come to Kashi several months earlier. His deep faith and reverence for Swamiji had already inspired the local youth, awakening them to the ideals embodied by the Thakur and Swamiji. The young men sat on the carpet, their eyes shining with respect. Before them sat Swamiji, a living, breathing divine vision.

Among the youths were Kedar Maulik, Charuchandra Das, Harinath Odedar, Yamini Ranjan, Haridas, and two others.

Niranjanananda spoke: 'Naren, these young men have done much good work in Kashi. They all believe in Thakur's ideals. Every evening, they sit before Thakur's image, singing holy names and reading scriptures.'

Swamiji's face brightened seeing the young men. With a smile, he said, 'I have heard of your work here in service.'

Charuchandra's eyes filled with deep feeling. Bowing his head, he spoke, 'We have just begun, Swamiji. One day, I read your words:

In many forms before you,
where do you seek God?
The one who loves in the soul—
that one serves God.

'Each word struck like a storm within our hearts, resonating deeply with love. We did not know what to do.

'One day, at the Ganga ghat, we found a *sadhu*, sick and unable to move, writhing in pain. Our hearts ached. With Kedar and Harinath, we brought him to an empty house behind Kedar's home. We cared for him until he regained his health. Slowly, our work grew.

'Many spoke ill of us, but we did not heed. We began begging door to door for medicines and food. Two small rooms could not contain us. Then we found a large empty house and started a charitable clinic.

'Alongside, we served the gravely ill. At first, no one stood with us. But gradually, many extended helping hands. Now, our work has greatly increased.'

Swamiji's smile widened. 'You have embodied the ideals of Thakur Sri Ramakrishna. He used to say, "Not compassion, but service. Selfless service to humanity, only then shall you receive God's grace." What have you named this service home of yours?'

Kedar replied, 'We are yet to decide on a name. Please tell us what it might be.'

Swamiji was silent for a moment, then said, 'Home of Service. Selfless service, that too is worship of God.'

Shivananda Maharaj interjected, 'Naren, why not call it Ramakrishna Home of Service instead?'

At once, Swamiji responded, 'Tarakda, this is your one fault—always bringing Sri Ramakrishna into everything. His words and spirit have spread throughout the world. There is no need to attach his name to everything.'

Harinath asked, 'Swamiji, how shall we run this institution?'

Swamiji sat up straight, gravity deepening his expression. 'If you receive a single paisa for serving the poor, consider it the blood of your own heart. Do not let it be misused. Another thing, no institution can last long if run on personal effort alone.

Soon differences and problems will arise.'

Charuchandra bowed, 'You speak the truth, Swamiji. Many will talk. What we have built with such hardship, we do not want to see destroyed soon.'

Swamiji perceived their love for service. 'Such work can only be carried out by those who have renounced all. You must entrust this responsibility to the Ramakrishna Mission.'

Hitherto silent, Haridas, a man of quiet nature who spoke little but worked diligently, asked, 'Then what shall we do, Swamiji?'

'Continue as you have been doing. Only remember you are doing the work of the Thakur.'

A smile spread on Niranjanananda's face. 'Naren has done a great thing.'

Suddenly, Swamiji became quiet. A long silence followed. Then he lifted his eyes and looked about. Within these four walls, there was no view. Just beyond, was the open veranda and the vast blue sky. A solitary white cloud was drifting past. His life's boat, too, was floating towards liberation.

Softly, he spoke, 'This is perhaps the last work of my life.'

A hush fell. Shadows of sorrow settled. 'What are you saying, Swamiji?' Shivananda cried out in anger. 'This is not the last! You still have much to do!'

Swamiji gave no answer. Within, he felt his days were ending. Winter twilight had fallen. Darkness had closed in. Crickets called in the evening gloom and the deep night grew colder. Swamiji sank within himself.

He remembered the young poet of Jorasanko Thakur Bari, Rabindranath, whose poem he had once read:

I waited long for your arrival.
Alone, at the empty ghat,
I crossed the river in a boat.
Broke my flute of play,
Choked with tears and laughter,
In the weary evening's sleep,
Eyes grew covered with mist.
On the other side, in every home,
Evening lamps flicker,
The conch sounds from the distant temple.
Come, come, you weary souls, come—
Come, come, your boat is arriving.

Initiation

Harinath's heart was heavy. A dormant longing stirred deep within—to receive initiation from Swamiji. Yet before the gravity and piercing presence of Swamiji, he could not bring himself to speak the words. What if questions arose for which he had no answers? Moreover, was he truly prepared, both in mind and body, for such a sacred rite? A tempest of anxious yearning raged inside him. There were others, many others, from whom he could have received the mantra. But Swamiji was unlike any other. And in a few days, Swamiji would leave. When he might return was uncertain. Would his hopes and dreams be lost in the pain of incompletion?

Summoning courage, he spoke to Shivananda Maharaj, who was a simple, humble soul, easily mingling with all. Nearby stood Charuchandra, Kedarnath, Bibhuti, and Yamini. 'We too wish to take initiation from Swamiji. Please arrange it.'

Shivananda, ever serene, smiled gently. 'An excellent proposal. You should speak to Naren.'

Charuchandra glanced at Naren but hesitated. Shivananda chuckled softly. 'I, too, have feared speaking with Naren sometimes. Who knows what thoughts dwell in his mind? Even he may not. Alright, I will speak to him.'

Suddenly, Kedarnath's face grew serious. Looking directly at Harinath, he declared, 'You shall not receive initiation.'

Shivananda, surprised, asked why.

'His brother has passed away.'

With profound affection, Shivananda gently patted Harinath's back. 'You have carried such a great sorrow, yet you never shared it with us. You come here, serve Swamiji and us tirelessly. How do you bear it?'

Harinath bowed his head as tears welled in his eyes. 'Here, as long as I stay, I forget all sorrow.'

The pain and yearning in Harinath's heart touched Shivananda deeply. 'During mourning, initiation is not given. Naren will surely return. Otherwise, you will go to Belur Math. Then you shall receive initiation.'

Harinath, thinking not of himself, wished for the others to receive initiation first.

Meanwhile, Swamiji lay reclining on a couch, reading the Upanishads. There was an empty seat beside him. Shivananda came and sat down. Swamiji looked up as if sensing his arrival.

'Seems you've come with something to say.'

Shivananda laughed. 'How did you guess?'

A faint smile played on Swamiji's lips. 'We call it 'thought-reading' abroad. You think thoughts and I read them on your face.'

Shivananda joked, 'I think nothing; I just bring the wishes of Kedar, Yamini, Charu, and others, who desire your initiation.'

'Very good. They have already sacrificed their lives for the country, and are true, pure souls. Such boys are what I seek. Fix the day.'

'Tomorrow is auspicious.'

'Then inform them all. Tomorrow morning, all must be present here.'

'All but one shall receive initiation. Harinath will not. His grief is too great.'

For a moment, Swamiji's face showed some disturbance. A long silence followed. Finally, breaking the stillness, he said, 'Tell Harinath to meet me.'

Shivananda rose. Outside, all were waiting expectantly.

'What did Swamiji say?' a face full of anxious anticipation.

With a smile, Shivananda replied, 'He consented. Tomorrow morning, after your bath, come here. Bring what you can offer your Guru.' Everyone smiled in surprise, for Swamiji's blessing was not easily given. Yet Harinath stood apart, deep in sorrow. Not wanting anyone to notice, he turned away.

Shivananda's gaze followed him. 'Harinath, Swamiji has asked to see you.'

'Who, me?'

'Yes, you. Right now.'

Upon entering, after bowing, Swamiji spoke gently, 'I heard your brother passed away?'

Harinath's eyes overflowed before he could speak. Swamiji called him closer, placing his hand upon his head, as one would on a dear kin. 'You have borne so much in silence. I understand your great pain. Had this happened to my brother, I too would be deeply pained. I could not have endured as you have.'

Harinath raised his face. Every word from Swamiji pierced the depths of his heart—love's balm and profound peace. 'When will your brother's soul depart?'

'In ten days.'

'I understand. I won't be here then. The festival of the Lord's birth approaches; I must go to Belur. Who knows if there will be time for further initiations? Do this, come tomorrow morning, bathed and ready. I shall initiate you.'

Harinath was stunned. Initiation during mourning? He dared not ask more. Outside, the others waited. At the mention of Swamiji's command, Shivananda said, 'Naren has spoken. No further questions. He is a rishi among the seven sages, eternally perfected, a master of meditation. I say, his word is *Veda, Purana*, and *Shastra*. Blessed is the life that bears his blessing. Listen well, initiation is at dawn tomorrow. None shall leave home afterwards.'

Everyone rejoiced and stayed the night. Before sunrise, everyone was up. Outside Swamiji's room, the door was closed but slightly ajar. Inside, the lantern light flickered dimly. Swamiji sat on his blanket-covered bed, wrapped in a thick shawl. In front was a picture of Sri Ramakrishna. He chanted softly. None could grasp what would come.

With a deep voice, he called, 'Mother, Mother, Mother Kali! Ramakrishna, Victory to Ramakrishna!' The call came from the fullness of his soul. Hands joined in prayer, he bowed again upon his bed. Finished, he raised his eyes and gazed upon all present.

'Your baths are done. Now come.'

'Where is Nirbhayananda?'

He stepped forward. 'Your bath water is heating.'

Had it been another day, Swamiji would have said, 'We shall bathe in cold water.' Now, frailty demanded care. He rose and stood on the veranda. Before him stretched the infinite sky—dark, vast, and in the eastern sky, a bright Venus sparkled like a diamond shard. Though summer's light should have already blossomed, darkness still held sway.

Gauri came with a basket full of colourful flowers. Swamiji

instructed, 'Place flowers in the room and prepare seats. Stand guard at the door. When initiation begins, none must enter.'

Swamiji went to bathe. After some time, all returned from bathing and stood hesitantly. Who would go first?

Charubabu said, 'Harinath, you go.'

Harinath entered slowly. Two seats faced each other in the centre. Swamiji sat in one. 'Sit here,' he commanded to Harinath.

All fears within Harinath melted away. He sat before Swamiji. After a moment, the simple serenity vanished. A completely different presence filled the room. The body was still, breath seemed suspended, eyes closed yet glowing with an inner light, as if a divine being was absorbed in *samadhi*. He had risen from the ordinary to the extraordinary. Time passed in silence until normalcy returned.

Extending his right hand, Swamiji touched Harinath's finger. Instantly, a tremor coursed through Harinath's body; those were strange sensations as if body and mind were separate. Desire and aversion vanished. All yearnings dissolved. The cosmos itself seemed calm, steady, slow—filled only with joy, peace, great peace, universal peace. Harinath sat still, drifting in an endless ocean of supreme calmness. No form, no shape remained.

Time slipped by unnoticed. At last, he returned to consciousness. Swamiji gave the *mantra* and spoke further, 'From this day forth, all your burdens are mine.'

Harinath's heart and soul overflowed with joy. He took a handful of flowers from the vessel and scattered them at Swamiji's feet, his humble offering of reverence.

The Song at the End of the Day

At twilight, a crimson glow spreads across nature. Swamiji was quietly singing to himself.

No sun, no light, no beautiful moon.
A shadowy image floats across the vast sky,
The world drifts like a vague reflection—
A restless flow, rising and falling without end.

His eyes were heavy with fatigue. In the upper-floor room of his home, he lay stretched out comfortably on the reclining chair. His feet rested on a small stool in front of him. He looked terribly swollen, like a delicate lantern swelling in the wind, ready to burst. It felt as if he could no longer hold himself together, waiting for the eruption of a fiery volcano within.

At the door stood his disciple, Sharatchandra. It was their first meeting since Swamiji's return from Kashi. Softly, Swamiji called out, 'Come, sit.'

Sharatchandra came and sat down by Swamiji's feet. He tried to ask how he was, but stopped himself. It felt like an unnecessary disturbance, only causing embarrassment. His gaze swept over Swamiji's entire frame; just a simple loincloth covered him, nothing else. His skin had shrivelled, his face pale and drawn; it was a sorrowful sight. A silent sob rose deep within Sharatchandra's chest, but he restrained himself.

Swamiji sensed his disciple's pain and spoke simply, 'I got a good rest in Kashi. Towards the end, my body was a little weak.'

Sharatchandra gently stroked Swamiji's feet. In a slow, tear-choked voice, he said, 'But coming here, it feels as if your health has worsened.'

'Are you suffering?' Swamiji asked calmly. 'Why? What are you thinking? The body is born, and it will surely die. If I can pour my thoughts into you, then I will know that coming into this world in a physical form has been worthwhile. Remember one thing always—the only way to be free from the bondage of the body is renunciation. Renunciation is truth. Renunciation is *dharma*. Renunciation is *Brahman*.' He spoke these few words and then gasped for breath.

'Please, don't speak any more,' Sharatchandra said.

There was a long silence. Swamiji, lost in himself, said softly, 'I do not want to speak. I do not like the pointless crowd of people. Yet, I still speak. Do you know why it feels bad? I have spoken all these years for hours and hours, in this country and abroad. I have never grown tired.'

Sharatchandra nodded. 'I know, Gurudev. People in America call you the "Cyclonic Monk", the storm-raising ascetic. It's all the magic of your words.'

Swamiji was deeply melancholy. 'The Cyclonic Monk has quieted down now. Except for a few people, nothing else pleases me. So many people come twice daily, yet they do not understand my condition. I fear the festival in two days; how many will come?'

'I say, arrange guards at the door. Not everyone will be allowed in.'

Sharatchandra's words echoed in Swamiji's mind. There was only one person for this task, Niranjan.

Sharatchandra rose. 'I will call Maharaj now.'

Soon, Niranjan Maharaj appeared and greeted them, 'Tell me, Naren *bhai*, what do you need?'

Swamiji smiled faintly. 'The festival will be in two days. So many people will come to Belur. Everyone wants to come to me. I used to manage, but now it's very difficult. I cannot bear it.'

Niranjan's eyes lit up. 'Don't worry, Naren *bhai*. Just as I guarded Thakur, I will not let anyone enter your room. I will stand guard with a stick.'

'Only a stick? Won't you wear your turban too?'

Niranjan laughed. 'If you say so, I'll wear the turban. How strange that Sharatchandra finds it odd! The same Thakur Sri Ramakrishna, whom we called *Ishwar-koti*, perfect from birth, will have such a great soul as Naren's elder brother standing guard at his door, stick in hand. No pride at all. Such genuine respect for Naren *bhai*—this is what love truly means.'

The day of Thakur's birth anniversary arrived. Crowds gathered from dawn. People had come from far and wide. The monastery grounds were packed with men and women alike. A group of *kirtan* singers played cymbals loudly as they chanted. Bamboo fences were set up, and behind them, the kitchens buzzed with activity. Four large ovens glowed, and massive iron pots bubbled with food. *Khichuri prasad* would be handed out by the handful.

The sunlight was gentle, the air pleasant. The harsh days of winter were over, and tender green leaves sprouted on every tree. The monastery courtyard was never empty; there was a gathering of people everywhere. Some arrived by boat, some by horse-drawn carriage along the main road, and others on foot. Many sat on the fresh grass chatting with familiar faces. Numerous men and women had completed their holy bath in the Ganga, seeking a little extra merit by attending the festival. At one spot, young girls changed clothes behind a cloth screen. The number of older attendees far exceeded the young.

That morning, Swamiji had managed a brief visit to the temple. Just that short walk had exhausted him; he had supported himself by resting his arms around the shoulders of two men. Back in his room, he had settled into his recliner and not ventured out again.

The sounds of the crowd filtered faintly into the room. It was time for the midday *prasad* distribution. The busy hum grew louder. With such crowds, there was no chance to receive the offering if one did not come early.

Rakhal Maharaj came to visit Swamiji's room. 'How are you today, Naren?'

Swamiji smiled gently, 'My body is not well. All the machinery seems to be breaking down. But I am fine. What news of the festival?'

Rakhal Maharaj said with enthusiasm, 'Good. Very good. More people have come this year than last.'

Swamiji shook his head. 'What people do you see! The way Thakur's name is spreading everywhere, soon the crowd of devotees will reach GT Road[23].'

Brahmananda said nothing but deeply believed in his heart that all this fame and spread of Thakur's name was because of Naren. If Thakur was the Ganga, Naren was Bhagiratha.

Afternoon came, and the noise downstairs swelled. Swamiji

23 Grand Trunk Road

understood that the crowd had gathered to see him. It pained him. Though a renunciate, detached from worldly life, he had not been able to shed the attachment to his flesh and blood. His heart longed to call everyone inside, but he could do nothing. At the door stood Niranjanananda, tireless guard, hearing endless pleas and requests. His face showed no change.

Someone brought *prasad*. It was the first offering to Thakur. It was touched lightly to Swamiji's forehead, then placed on his lips.

'How is everything going?' Swamiji asked.

'Very well,' came the reply.

'When will the religious assembly start?' Swamiji inquired.

'After the *prasad* distribution.'

A furrow formed between Swamiji's brows. After the distribution of prasad, who really listens to religious discourse? Everyone would be half-asleep over their food, or dozing off on their benches.

Sharatchandra chuckled. 'Once, I went to hear a saint's sermon in Dhaka. It was at a landlord's house; a grand feast was laid out. The saint was giving a fine talk. But after a while, I noticed people in the back rooms were snoring away.'

Swamiji smiled faintly. 'You put it well.'

Just then, Niranjanananda entered the room. Swamiji glanced at him briefly and asked, 'Are you still unable to keep the crowds at bay?'

Niranjanananda laughed quietly. 'As long as I'm here, no one will bother you, Naren *Bhai*. Someone just said Nivedita is coming, along with two or three others.'

Swamiji's attention sharpened instantly. Wearing only his loincloth, he knew it would not do to meet any woman in this state. Rising, he said, 'Bring me my shawl.'

Sharatchandra carefully took down the shawl hanging on the wall, a deep maroon cloth, and draped it over Swamiji's frail body. Settling back in his reclining chair, Swamiji prepared to receive his guests.

Soon, Nivedita arrived, accompanied by Jo MacLeod and two other foreign women. Leading the group, Nivedita was clad from neck to foot in a pristine white sari. Around her neck hung a *rudraksha mala*, giving her the serene aura of a meditative ascetic. Her hair was not quite golden but neatly tied up, and though she wore no adornments, the moonlight falling on her face atop the hill made her glow with a tranquil beauty. Beside her stood MacLeod, with her familiar stern, rugged face.

Seeing these dear friends, a faint but complex joy lit up Swamiji's tired features as if he had been waiting for them all along. Nivedita bowed respectfully, and Swamiji returned a gentle smile. 'How are you, Nivedita? It's been a long time since we met.'

'Yes, Swamiji.'

MacLeod, standing nearby, offered some flowers to Swamiji. 'I heard you've been having difficulty breathing, and your legs have swollen. That's why you couldn't come to the festival.'

Swamiji laughed softly. 'Oh, MacLeod, pain is the eternal truth; if the body remains, there will be suffering. It can't be denied. The only sorrow is that after giving away everything, I am now utterly destitute. I once had much, but I gave it all away. Sometimes I wonder what I will do if I need something....'

MacLeod understood the depth of Swamiji's suffering. Such a man, so incomparable in her life, her friend, teacher, and God, all at once. She spoke kindly, 'Don't worry, Swamiji. As long as you live, I will send you $50 every month for your expenses.'

Swamiji joked, 'Will that money even be enough for me?'

MacLeod smiled back, 'It will be enough. Though maybe not enough for cream.' She pulled out $200 from her bag and placed it in Swamiji's hand. 'I'll send more later.'

Nivedita stood nearby. Seeing Swamiji's fragile condition, a lump rose in her throat. She spoke softly, 'I have opened a school for girls in Bosepara Lane. You must come visit us someday.'

Swamiji nodded in a detached manner. 'I will come. Very soon.'

'I want to seek your advice on a couple of matters.'

Lately, Swamiji had had little interest in attending weddings or social functions. He found little harmony between Nivedita's thoughts and his own. He sensed that beneath her serene exterior, Nivedita was withdrawing behind a shadow cast by Okakura. When he first met Okakura, he had liked him; he was a scholar and a devout man with a love for Dharma, art, and the Buddha. But now, he saw that despite all his talk of renunciation, Okakura was a man of the world, one who wanted to enjoy every pleasure life had to offer, be it money or women. Swamiji felt that the sooner he could pull Nivedita out of Okakura's influence, the better, for otherwise, all her dreams would be lost.

Perhaps Nivedita sensed this. Calmly, she said, 'Come whenever you feel like it. I will wait for you.'

Swamiji looked up, eyes filled with worry. 'What will become of my body? I do not know....'

'You will recover,' Nivedita said, her eyes glistening with tears. Struggling to hold herself together, she added, 'We will come, Swamiji. You must rest now.'

They all left, and Swamiji sat quietly for a while, feeling the day's pain and the body's ache. Everyone's presence had briefly distracted him from it. After seeing them down the stairs, Sharatchandra returned. Swamiji looked at him and said, 'Did you see how civilised these foreign women are? If they were Bengali, they'd have talked to me for at least half an hour despite my illness, and no one else would be allowed in. Now, prepare my tobacco properly. Roll it nicely. Take a good puff.'

Nivedita

In the soft glow of the lamp-stand, Swamiji sat writing a letter. Diabetes had stolen much of his vision; one eye was now sightless, the other dim and faltering. His brother disciples teased him fondly, 'You've become the great *Asura-Guru* Shukracharya, blind in one eye.'

Swamiji, laughing, would reply, 'So be it! Shukracharya was a man of immense wisdom.'

Slowly, his hand moved across the page. A young brahmachari stood nearby. These days, someone was always by Swamiji's side. The youth noticed the room was too dim, the lamp's faint light barely revealed the page; shadows clung to every corner like silent sentinels. And yet, by long habit, Swamiji wrote on, untroubled. Quietly, the brahmachari lit another lamp. A smile lit Swamiji's face. 'Well done. Sit here. I'll finish this quickly.'

He had written two pages of careful writing. When he had finished, he read it to himself.

It was a letter to Mrs Ole Bull, whom he addressed tenderly as Dhira Mata, the Steadfast Mother.

Beloved Dhira Mata,

Belur Math, 14 June 1902

It would have been better had I replied sooner to your affectionate letter. A book by Dr Jess has reached me, and though there may have been some request to write about it, I dared not express any opinion without a clearer invitation, especially concerning a work from such a revered friend. Still, as per your present wish, I shall write to Mr Fox as soon as I am able.

I am as I am—holding on. All else is well. Nivedita is in the mountains. Okakura has returned to the city and is staying with the Honourable Surendra Tagore. He came to the Math one day, but I was away. I hope to see him soon and learn more about his future plans.

The young Japanese man, Herry, fell ill with a fever here, but he recovered in a few days and has now gone to spend time with Okakura. His religious spirit has endeared him to all. His ideals of brahmacharya are lofty indeed, and he aspires to found a monastic order rooted in true celibacy in Japan. Yet I feel, for a nation to rise to the ideal of perfect brahmacharya, it must first sanctify the bond of marriage and see in motherhood something sacred and inviolable.

The Roman Catholics and Hindus hold marriage to be holy and indissoluble, and so have nurtured many powerful souls rooted in brahmacharya, men and women both. But among the Arabs, marriage is a contract, or worse, an imposed right that is easily discarded. No wonder, then, that neither the ideal of virginity nor of spiritual celibacy could flourish there.

Modern Buddhism, too, has passed into the hands of nations where the sanctity of marriage has not fully flowered. As a result, monasticism among them has become a mockery.

So, unless the Japanese awaken to the sacredness of marriage, beyond mere physical attraction, how can great monks or nuns be born among them? I do not know.

You, who understand that chastity is life's sole true glory, must know too, as I now do, that to bring forth a few such mighty souls, we must root a vast portion of the people in this profound purity.

I had meant to write much more, but my body is too weak. Mary Louise has come here, now as a devotee of Chaitanya. I hear some wealthy people have taken her under their wing. May she gain much; this is my hope. 'In whatever form one worships Me, I return to them in kind', she worshipped wealth; may the Lord grant her abundance.

...This pomp of the West is but a hollow show, a finer chain for the soul. Never before have I so starkly felt the futility of the world. May the Lord free all souls from bondage. May all be released from Maya. That is my constant prayer.

Yours ever in boundless affection,
Vivekananda

For a long while, Swamiji sat still in silence. Today, thoughts of Nivedita surged in his heart with unrelenting force. He had wished to entrust her with his full spiritual legacy, the sacred inheritance of India's eternal wisdom. In this land, radiant with the dawn of divine truth, once walked women of divine stature—Sita, Sati, Savitri, Gargi, Maitreyi. In later times, Ahalyabai, Rani Bhavani, Rani Rashmoni, and in their living presence, the holy mother Sarada. Their teachings bore the fragrance of selfless love and lofty nobility. Life not for the self, but for the joy of others.

Nivedita had come, drawn by that sublime call. And yet now,

she seemed torn in many directions—entangled in the ideals of the Brahmo Samaj, later drawn towards the Tagore household, and presently captivated by Okakura. She dreamed now not of love, but of armed revolt. She yearned for weapons, not worship, to drive the English from this soil.

'But who shall give us these arms?' Swamiji had once asked.

And Nivedita had answered, 'Japan, Korea, many lands. If need be, soldiers.'

Swamiji had laughed gently. 'Borrowed strength,' he said, 'can never win the war against tyranny. What we need is inner strength, *Atmashakti*. The day this nation awakens, the chains of bondage will fall of their own accord.'

'Must we wait until then?' she asked.

'Waiting and patience are the eternal lessons of our land,' he replied.

Nivedita gave no answer; perhaps, in her heart, she could not accept his words. Yet how vividly Swamiji remembered the first time he had seen her, back in England, in Lady Margesson's drawing room. She was still Margaret Noble then, one among many. After his lecture, several had remarked, 'What new truth did you really say today? All your words are old.'

But much later, Nivedita had told him, 'You had quoted a verse from the Gita—*"Mayi sarvamidam protam sutre manigana iva"*—"All this is strung in Me like pearls upon a thread." Your every word entered me like those sacred pearls, strung into my soul.'

When her stay in London ended, she returned to America. Then, one day, Margaret came to him and asked, 'What would you advise me?'

Swamiji had only said, 'Never accept anything without judgement.'

With deep reverence, she had replied, 'Swamiji, you seem to me a messenger from a distant world, bearing tidings of another realm. Your words still ring in my ears like a sacred chant: *Hē divyalokavāsī amritasya putrāh*—O children of immortality, hear ye all! You are the sons and daughters of the Divine, heirs to the Eternal. You are holy, perfect, divine. You are gods walking this earth. Sinners? Impossible. To call man a sinner is the greatest sin. Man is sacred—a free, ever-blissful soul, ever pure, ever awakened, eternal being of truth, consciousness, and joy.'

A year passed. Swamiji returned to London. There was a great stir, a throng of people. One day, Margaret came again. She had changed. In one meeting, Swamiji appeared clad in a long black alpaca robe, a crescent-shaped black turban upon his head. He seemed like a radiant being risen from the depths of the night.

He began his lecture, a tale from the Upanishads. Margaret sat before him. His voice rose—grave, luminous, and yet profoundly sweet. He spoke of Rishi Gautama, the sage of supreme wisdom, who longed for the unending joy of heaven after death. To please the gods, he performed the *Viswajit Yajna*, a harsh sacrifice.

The air grew heavy with the fragrance of a sacred fire. The land resounded with chants of the *Samaveda*. When the *yajna* ended, the sage prepared to give away all he owned.

His son, Nachiketa, watched as his father, running out of possessions, began gifting feeble, dying cows to the priests. Innocently, the boy asked, 'Father, to whom will you give me?'

Gautama ignored him. But the child persisted—once, twice, thrice. Annoyed, the father uttered, 'Unto death, I give thee.'

And a rishi's word, once spoken, cannot be unspoken. Believing his father's words as truth, Nachiketa walked unafraid towards the realm of Death. He arrived at Yama's abode. The Lord of Death was away. For three days and nights, the boy fasted, waiting in silence.

When Yama returned, he was moved by the child's resolve and offered him three boons. Nachiketa asked for two worldly boons, and for the third, he said, 'Grant me knowledge of the Self.'

Yama was astonished. 'A child asking for Self-Knowledge? Even sages fail to grasp it after lifetimes of penance. Take instead riches, pleasures, palaces—anything you desire.'

But Nachiketa remained unmoved. 'All these are fleeting,' he said. 'Give me the truth of the Self.'

Then, recognising his purity, Yama whispered into the child's ears the secret of the soul—*Tat Tvam Asi*—Thou art That. O man, thou art That.

The lecture ended. Margaret stood before him, as though awakened from a dream. 'Who am I, Swamiji?' she asked.

To Swamiji, it seemed as if Nachiketa of a new age stood before him. He looked at her with deep affection. 'You,' he said, 'are that Supreme Truth. A knower of Brahman.'

With bowed head, Margaret whispered, 'You have turned my whole life upside down.'

Swamiji smiled. He felt her soul's burning yearning. 'We shall meet again,' he said.

At another gathering, filled with critics and doubters, Swamiji stood serene, and unmoved. In a voice that rang with command, he cried out, 'What does the world lack today? Twenty men and women who can rise and say with fearless faith, "God alone is our refuge!" Who among you will answer this call?'

The hall fell silent. None responded. Swamiji rose, scanning the faces before him. Was there none?

Then his gaze fell on Margaret. Was she about to speak?

Later, in solitude, she came to him and unburdened her heart. 'I wish to dedicate myself to the service of humanity.'

Swamiji looked with wonder at the young Irishwoman. 'I

have plans,' he said, 'for the upliftment of India's women. Will you help me realise them?'

'I will,' she said.

'There will be many sacrifices.'

'I am ready to renounce all. Only accept me.'

'Then you must go to India.'

'I shall go. I await your command.'

At last, Margaret arrived in India as a changed being. Swamiji sent her to Holy Mother Sarada. For if the Mother did not accept her, neither would society.

At the threshold of the Mother's abode, Margaret stood. The Mother saw her and said, 'There, my daughters have come.'

Though they spoke no common tongue, all barriers fell. The two hearts met, melted, and merged into one.

On 25 March came the most sacred moment in Margaret's life. At the monastery, before the deity, Swamiji led her to the shrine. Before them was a vessel of flowers and *bel* leaves. Swamiji placed them in her hands.

'Offer these at the feet of Mahadeva,' he said. 'With a mind gathered into stillness, surrender all to the Divine.'

Margaret did so. Her trembling hands placed the offering at the Lord's feet.

'Restrain the mind,' said Swamiji. 'Offer your very soul. This life is no longer yours; it belongs to God. It is now consecrated to the service of the world.'

Margaret's whole body quivered. In that holy moment, Swamiji initiated her into the life of the spirit.

The purest flower of her inner self was laid at the Lord's feet.

And Margaret became Nivedita—'The Dedicated One.'

The Farewell Sounds

17, Bose Para Lane

In the northern quarter of Kolkata lies Baghbazar, an old neighbourhood, aged in its silence and memory. Nestled within it is a narrow winding lane, Bose Para, where lay scattered homes, patches of open land, and little gardens blooming in solitude. A single road runs straight to the north, which is quiet all day, save for the murmur of the Ganga's morning pilgrims. A little farther flows the sacred Bhagirathi. There's a stone ghat where women, after bathing, offer *pranam* at a roadside shrine before returning home. As the day ripens, the rhythm of life begins to stir. The residents are mostly native, born of this soil, shaped by its time.

At one end of this lane stands Number 17. Not far off is the famed residence of the dramatist Girish Ghosh. Across a sparse patch of land beyond this, you will reach the area's boundary. A lone, one-storeyed house sits there. Its exterior bears the age-worn grace of the past. On one side is a pond; along its raised bank are tall palms, *bel*, and coconut trees that sway in the breeze.

To the people of the Para, this house holds a quiet reverence. For here lives Nivedita. In one room, she has opened a school for young girls. One afternoon, she sat in her chamber, writing. School had ended early; it was Saturday, a time for solitude, for study, for the stillness she so dearly loved. The maid was in the next room. Outside, the neighbourhood slept in peace.

A soft knock is heard at the front door. A visitor at this hour? She called for the maid but paused. She had dozed off. Nivedita rose and went herself to open the door.

When the door opened, a mist of wonder clouded her gaze. There, before her, stood Swamiji, Vivekananda himself, with two brahmacharis by his side. The joy of an unexpected grace filled her. For a moment, she was stunned, then, breaking through the daze, she cried aloud in ecstasy, 'Victory to the Guru! Victory to the Maharaj!'

Then, quickly gathering herself, she said, her voice trembling with awe, 'Swamiji… You?'

Swamiji smiled a sacred, radiant smile. 'I came to see your school, Nivedita. I had some work nearby. It's done. I thought I'd visit you as a guest.'

She folded her hands in deep reverence. 'Then today is my day of great fortune. Please, come in. You too, brothers.'

They crossed the veranda and entered the house. There was a line of rooms. In the front were two rooms made into classrooms. Swamiji removed his shoes and stepped in. The room was neatly arranged with a carpet on the floor, bright pictures on the walls, and wooden shelves with a few books. In the corner was a basket of toys, a wooden horse, and a chariot. With childlike glee, he turned them over in his hands.

'So beautiful,' he murmured.

Nivedita said softly, 'Do you remember, Swamiji? It was three years ago, on the night of Diwali. Every home was adorned with lamps, making the darkness fall away. The Mother, in her form as Kali, descended to the world. You came. With you were Swamis

Saradananda and Brahmananda. The entire school was decorated with flowers and leaves. Then came Sri Ma, and she took her seat as priestess. First, she worshipped Sri Ramakrishna, then offered the sacred fire. She marked the girls' foreheads with the ash of blessings. You named this school, Nivedita Balika Vidyalaya.'

As she spoke, Swamiji sank into a reverie. Slowly, he walked ahead. A map hung on the wall. He stood before it. Then he said softly, as if to himself, 'If I had lived a few more years, Nivedita—how many more lands I could have seen.'

She knew of his failing health. The worn frame, the waning strength—worry gnawed at her heart.

'Why do you say such things, Swamiji? If you so wish, you can live many more years.'

He drifted into deep thought.

'Do you still remember Amarnath?' he asked.

A soft glow of joy lit her face. That journey… one of life's holiest memories. They had travelled to Kashmir. 'I shall go,' Swamiji had said, 'to the snowy shrine of Amarnath. Will you come with me?'

'Yes, Swamiji.'

'It's a perilous path. Will you not be afraid?'

'You are with me; how could I fear?'

So, the journey began—sometimes on horseback, sometimes on foot. Uphill after uphill. The road to Amarnath's cave was blanketed in snow. Just before the entrance, the snow vanished. Pilgrims pressed forward in fervent joy. Exhausted, Nivedita sat down, waiting for Swamiji to reach this point. Near the cave was Panchatarini, where pilgrims bathed in the glacial waters. Swamiji bathed too. One by one, people entered the great cave, a vast hollow crowned by the icy Shiva-linga. It was as if Lord Mahadev himself had sat upon his throne.

The crowd wept, shouted and sang with wild devotion. There was no elaborate worship, just raw, burning faith.

Swamiji stepped into the cave, bare-chested with only a loincloth on his body. His face glowed with rapture. He was transformed. His entire frame smeared in ash, he prostrated fully before the linga, touching the sacred feet of Shankara. Then, there was stillness. As if in a trance, he remained motionless. Nivedita, too, was silent. She saw no longer the man, but Shiva himself, deep in cosmic meditation.

It was a moment that stood apart in time.

When he emerged from the cave, he spoke, his voice deep with mystery, 'Do you know, Nivedita, what I received at Amarnath?'

'What?'

'The boon of death at will.'

Her soul shuddered. Then his tone turned soft again, intimate, urgent. He grasped her hand and said, 'Tell no one else of this.'

From memory, she returned to the present. Swamiji stood now in her schoolroom. In a voice like a whisper of eternity, she said, 'You are the conqueror of death. Even death yields to your will.'

He raised his face to hers. In his eyes, there was a peace beyond time. 'Death is inevitable, Nivedita. It comes. And when it does, we must open our arms and receive it. This body, this shell, has grown too worn. It is time to cast it off.'

Just then, the two brahmacharis entered. 'Gurudev, come to the roof. It looks beautiful from up there.'

Swamiji turned to Nivedita, smiling.

'No more talk of death, my child. Come. Let's go to the terrace, and let us look upon the life all around.'

'Yes, let us go.'

The Passenger of the Infinite

The sky of July bore the first whispers of the monsoon. Clouds and sunlight danced in a game of hide-and-seek across a horizon stained with blue and black. Yet all across the fields and riverbanks, a desolate dryness still lingered as remnants of summer's fever. In the drowsy hush of the afternoon, across the Ganga, chimneys from a distant mill belched out smoke that curled upwards, merging with the sky. The green of the grass had burned into pallor, bleached by summer's cruel heat. Beyond the plains lay the river, wide and languid, like a streak of water fallen upon a sun-seared earth. It moved, yes, but it no longer seemed alive. The vision faltered between illusion and reality.

In front of Swamiji's room stood a palash tree, stripped of its leaves. Only here and there, a solitary crimson blossom clung to the bare branches like a torch of remembrance. Swamiji stood by the window, his gaze fixed intently on the tree. Beside him, Shuddhananda waited in silence. Swamiji murmured as if to himself, 'You've seen summer now, how devouring it is, like death itself.'

Shuddhananda had noticed it for some time, how everything

seemed to Swamiji to echo death's shadow. He understood well that death is an inevitable fate, yet he wondered, what was it that had brought this quiet obsession? Trying to lift the air, he said gently, 'Summer is ending. The rains are almost here. The earth will be green again.'

'Perhaps,' Swamiji said, 'but I may not be here to see it.'

The words startled Shuddhananda. 'Why say such things, Gurudev?'

'Can everything in this life be explained?' Swamiji replied, his voice low. 'Come. Let's go downstairs. This room oppresses me.'

'But it's still hot outside,' Shuddhananda protested, worried for his master's frail health. His mind was riddled with fear.

Swamiji paid him no heed. Clad only in a *kaupin*, he threw a light cloak over his shoulders. 'You people worry too much,' he said with a faint smile. 'I'm quite well. Why, the medicines your Mahananda Kaviraj prescribed would bring the dead back to life!'

Thin clouds drifted lazily across the sky. The light had softened. The sun's fury had waned under the shadow of those silent messengers. From the wall clock came the chime of three. Swamiji and Shuddhananda walked along the banks of the Ganga. A steamer floated down the river, bound for some distant shore. Its whistle pierced the air. Swamiji paused, his eyes following the vessel. The memory of his first voyage to America stirred within him. It felt like a lifetime ago.

They walked on. A cluster of flowering shrubs stood by the path, now shrivelled in the heat. A touch of rain, and they would bloom again. Far ahead, the grass grew thick, but dry and coppery from thirst. Near the river's edge stood a *bel* tree, heavy with young fruit. Swamiji stopped there, still and silent.

'What are you looking at, Naren?'

Neither of them had noticed Saradananda approach. Swamiji

turned, as if waking from a dream. He looked at his brother-disciple with solemn eyes. 'Sharat, since you're here, let me tell you, when my body is gone, perform my cremation here. One side, the sacred *bilva* leaves. The other, the Ganga. No place could be more fitting. The municipality may object at first, but it will be resolved.'

Saradananda frowned. The words displeased him. 'Don't speak like this,' he muttered.

But Swamiji, perhaps to escape his protest, turned to Shuddhananda, clasped his hands, and said, 'Come, let's walk a little further.'

They had barely taken a few steps when a brahmachari came running towards them. 'Swamiji, two people have come asking for you. One of them says he is your brother, Habul Dutta.'

'Habul has come to see me?' Swamiji repeated, surprised. 'I wonder what brings him.'

In the office room sat Habul Dutta, a cousin, and beside him, another relative, Tamu Dutta. As Swamiji entered, they stood up respectfully.

'We came to see you, Dada,' Habul said.

For a fleeting moment, Swamiji's heart clenched. Was it news of his mother? 'How is Ma?' he asked, hurriedly.

'She is well. I saw her before coming here.'

Relieved, Swamiji gestured for them to sit. 'What brings you to me today?'

Habul hesitated. 'It's about the lawsuit with our great-aunt, Gyanadasundari. It's been going on too long. She no longer wants to fight.'

Swamiji understood at once. The old woman, stripped of means, had once begged him for help. Now, exhausted, she was willing to let go. He, too, had grown weary of the endless case. If there was a chance for peace, it must not be lost.

'What does she want?' he asked.

'Rs 1,000,' Habul said. 'She'll withdraw the suit. Everything will remain as it was.'

It felt to Swamiji like a boon from heaven. 'Wait here,' he said. 'I'll return shortly.'

He went straight to Brahmananda's quarters. 'Rakhal,' he said, 'Aunt wants to settle. She'll withdraw if we pay her a thousand rupees.'

Brahmananda, who had long been entangled in this family dispute, stood up at once. 'That's excellent news. I'll arrange the money.'

'Habul is here. Go with him and meet our lawyer today. Have the papers prepared and get her signature within the next couple of days.'

'I'll handle everything,' Brahmananda assured him. He knew what quiet suffering this ordeal had brought to Swamiji. 'You don't worry about a thing. I'll see it through.'

The three men set out. Down at the ghat, a boat waited. The wind off the Ganga rose, fresh and fragrant. Swamiji inhaled deeply, his chest lifting with calm delight.

What quiet joy stirred in him then. What relief. What clarity.

Sharatchandra had arrived, still clad in his office attire. Upon seeing Swamiji, he stepped forward and bowed in reverence, asking softly, 'How is your health?'

Swamiji's mood was light that day, his face aglow with quiet joy. A longstanding problem had finally found resolution. Smiling, he replied, 'I'm quite well. Looks like you've come straight from the office, haven't you?' Then, noticing something amiss, he added with a curious glint in his eye, 'You're in coat and trousers, but where is your collar?'

Sharatchandra hesitated a little, visibly awkward. Swamiji caught on at once and said gently, 'I understand. I'll tell Sharat (Saradananda) to give you a couple of my collars. But remember this, never forsake your national dress or your native food. In abandoning them, you diminish the honour of your homeland.'

Sharatchandra lowered his head. 'At work,' he said with quiet resignation, 'wearing Western dress is mandatory. It's the rule.'

Swamiji nodded. 'Then wear it there. But once home, become the Bengali gentleman again, with your gathered *dhoti*, flowing *kurta*, and a shawl upon your shoulder. Do you understand?'

A smile broke across Sharatchandra's face. 'I'll go and change,' he said. Swamiji turned and entered his quarters.

The day had waned. The early darkness of evening descended upon the world like a veil of mist, gentle and soundless. The temple bells chimed softly. One by one, the brahmacharis and monks emerged from their rooms and began making their way to the temple. All heads were shaven, some clad in ochre, others in white—each one serene and composed.

Sharatchandra entered the temple. The evening arati preparations were underway. The young monks and ascetics had begun to gather. Cymbals, bells, and conches resounded in unison. A hymn began, Swamiji's own composition, sung as the evening devotional:

'Destroyer of the bondage of the world, adored by the universe, To thee we bow.

O Formless One, who wears the guise of man, Beyond attributes—yet full of all divine qualities.'

A monk with a shaven head stepped forward, carrying the five-flame lamp. The arati began. When it ended, a profound stillness enveloped the hall. All sat motionless, steeped in silence. Only the faint rhythm of breath stirred the air.

Time passed. Gradually, the monks rose, one by one, and departed. Sharatchandra made his way to Swamiji's room and paused at the doorway. Inside, Swamiji sat in meditation, facing west, serene and absorbed. His eyes were closed, his face bathed in a tranquil glow, like a deity sculpted in stillness, a still flame, immersed in endless contemplation.

Not wishing to disturb him, Sharatchandra sat quietly by the door. Nearly half an hour passed. Then a tremor ran through Swamiji's frame. Like the seated Buddha, his hands resting on his lap quivered slightly. Slowly, he opened his eyes. The light of the heavens retreated from his gaze as he returned gently to the mortal world. Seeing Sharatchandra, he asked softly, 'When did you arrive?'

'Just a little while ago,' Sharatchandra replied.

'Good, good. Bring me a glass of water,' Swamiji said. 'You know, today's meditation was deep, and truly absorbing.'

'Then teach me, won't you?' Sharatchandra said.

With effortless simplicity, Swamiji replied, 'Just practise daily—that's all it takes.'

Sharatchandra smiled and shook his head. 'No, even that won't do. What's needed is your company; only that will make it possible.'

A wistful shadow passed over Swamiji's face. The earlier brightness vanished as if a curtain had been drawn over a flame. He seemed to slip from the warmth of the living world into a colder, distant realm. Turning to Sharatchandra, he said quietly, 'My company won't last much longer. I shall not live past forty.'

Sharatchandra protested gently. 'You are a follower of the Buddha. Remember, his greatest deeds were done between the ages of forty and eighty.'

Swamiji looked away. 'Not everyone's path is the same. What

I had to give, I have already given. Now, I must go.'

'Why must you go?' Sharatchandra's voice trembled with emotion, the ache in his heart laid bare.

Swamiji remained silent for a long while. A profound detachment rested on his brow, in the stillness of his eyes, and the quiet of his lips. At last, he spoke, gently like wind passing through ancient trees, 'The shade of a great tree does not let the saplings beneath it grow. I must depart… to give them the light and space to rise.'

Sharatchandra sat wordless, motionless. His eyes brimmed with tears.

He descended the stairs slowly, the heaviness in his chest pressing down like twilight. He would return home. Tomorrow was yet another day at the office. But of late, such comings and goings, the routine of daily toil—all felt strangely hollow, emptied of meaning. Life, he now knew, was far vaster… like the sky. It was only in Swamiji's presence that he had come to feel this truth. And without that nearness, he felt a quiet helplessness. Life demands much even from those who wish for little.

He drifted into thought. A soft touch brought him back. He looked up. Before him stood Shuddhananda, a fellow disciple, young, but held in deep respect by Sharatchandra for his brilliance, scholarship, and quiet strength. One day, surely, he would carry great responsibility in the Order.

'How are you, brother?' Sharatchandra asked with affectionate warmth.

Shuddhananda bowed, smiling. 'Well, *Dada*. Are you leaving now?'

'Yes. I had come to see the Master. But I leave with an ache… it felt as if he is withdrawing, pulling away from all that binds one to this world. Something is changing, I can feel it.'

'Life has its tides,' Shuddhananda replied softly. 'All will be well again.'

'May it be so,' said Sharatchandra, and turned to go. He did not know that this would be his last meeting with his Master.

Shuddhananda ascended the stairs. Swamiji sat upon his bed, his eyes closed. Shuddhananda stepped forward, and waited. Then he whispered, 'Guru Maharaj....'

Without opening his eyes, Swamiji spoke: 'Could you bring me a *panjika* (an almanac)?'

'A *panjika*? Yes... I'm sure someone has one. I'll find it.'

Downstairs, he asked around. No one had it. Then someone recalled, 'Yogin Maharaj had a new one.'

Yogin Maharaj, disciple of the Master and dearly beloved by the Holy Mother, was a simple, gentle soul. Shuddhananda offered his *pranams* and said quietly, 'Guru Maharaj is asking for a *panjika*.'

'Naren? Why would he suddenly ask for an almanac?' Yogin Maharaj's voice held wonder, and a sudden shadow passed across his face.

'I don't know,' Shuddhananda replied.

Yogin Maharaj grew solemn. 'I don't like this. Long ago, Thakur once asked me to bring him the *panjika*. It was the 30th day of *Shravana, Krishna Pratipada*. I brought it. He asked me to read the last days of that month. I did. Then he asked for the planetary conjunctions and the star alignments. I read them out to him. At one point, he raised his hand and stopped me. "What needed knowing has been known," he said. That very night, he left us all. I do not know what to think. But if Naren asks, then take it. Take the *panjika*.'

Shuddhananda returned with it. Swamiji had turned up the light himself. He leafed through the pages slowly, as though seeking something hidden deep within time. The effort strained his eyes. At length, he closed it.

'Let it remain with me,' he said. 'I'll return it later.'

Though the wind from the Ganga was cool, beads of sweat glistened on Swamiji's brow. Shuddhananda began to fan him gently. Night wore on. Eventually, Shuddhananda retired to his room. A young *sevak* lay asleep on a mat upon the floor. Swamiji could not sleep. He stepped out onto the veranda and sank into a chair. Then he lifted his face to the sky.

Moonlight streamed across the heavens. In the northern sky, the constellation of the *Saptarshi* glimmered—*Kratu, Pulaha, Pulastya, Atri, Angiras, Vasistha, Marichi*—seven ancient sages, seated in quiet meditation. Their silent summons seemed to echo in his soul. The spirit within, caged in this body of clay, longed to soar to the realms of nectar-light. There was no fear, no burden of thought. Only a single yearning remained—to journey to the land of stars, where the supreme consciousness, the *Para-Brahman*, resides.

A deep stirring arose within. Was this the awakening of divine knowledge? Do disembodied souls, through such silent blossoming, ascend from one realm of spirit to another? Is this how the worlds of the mortals and the worlds beyond intertwine? Perhaps this consciousness gives birth within us to an unknown feeling—one that opens petal by petal, like a lotus blooming in scent, form, and radiance, leading the soul into the realm of supreme bliss.

Perhaps this was what Buddha glimpsed beneath the Bodhi tree and what Jesus beheld in the silence of Gethsemane...what Chaitanya, Nanak, and Sri Ramakrishna touched in their ecstasy. Was this the nearness of the Divine? Where there is nothing to gain, nothing to ask, only an infinite peace, an unwavering trust, and the irresistible longing to surrender all at the feet of the All-Good, the Supreme.

A profound contentment descended upon Swamiji. His soul withdrew inward, merging into the luminous pathways of the stars, voyaging towards distant nebulae, an unseen Nirvana-world, where the spirit rests in silence, in light, beyond all form and shadow.

Salutations to the Master

Ashadh is drawing to a close, yet the sky remains barren of rain. The earth smoulders beneath a cruel sun; the wind itself seems scorched, rushing across the land like a fevered breath. Sister Nivedita, born of colder climes, feels her limbs grow listless in the unrelenting heat. Through the hushed noon hours, the entire neighbourhood lies mute and parched, each moment heavy, languid, and wearisome.

It was Wednesday, 2 July. Nivedita awoke with an inexplicable restlessness. Her heart ached to see her Master. Only two days earlier, she had visited him. Swamiji, himself, had welcomed her. Young monks had gathered around, and he had said warmly, 'Nivedita, speak to them about your school.'

With quiet passion, she had shared her visions and dreams. Yet Swamiji soon realised that many among them could not grasp her words. Gently, with loving clarity, he had translated her thoughts into simpler speech. As the sun climbed higher, it was time for her to return to Baghbazar. When she bowed to take her leave, Swamiji placed his hand upon her head, a touch from which streamed such profound affection that her soul trembled.

'On the day of my school's celebration, will you come and bless it?' she had asked. With a smile radiant and serene, he replied, 'I am always blessing you. There is boundless strength within you, I long to see it manifest.' Filled with joy and a deep inner fulfilment, she had returned home. Yet even there, every breath echoed with his presence.

Days passed. Nights turned their pages. The calendar shifted quietly on the wall. And through it all, a quiet pull, deep and inexpressible, kept drawing her back to her Guru. Like the hidden current of a river—unseen, yet irresistible.

Her morning duties done, she set out across the Ganga at Baranagar, towards Belur. It was Ekadashi, a day of sacred fasting. As she stepped into the stillness of the monastery, she heard the sound of the chanting of sacred texts drifting from within. No one loitered in the blazing heat. A gardener lay asleep on a veranda mat. Somewhere nearby, a dove cooed gently. Peace blanketed the world.

Standing near the temple were Nirbhayananda and two brahmacharis, just returning with Ganga water for worship. At the sight of Nivedita, smiles broke like sunshine across their faces.

'How are you, Sister?'

'I'm well. And all of you?'

'We're fine too. How goes your school?'

'It's new. It needs a little more time to take shape. You must come visit. It will do you good.'

'You're doing so much for the girls of this country,' said Nirbhayananda admiringly.

Nivedita paused. Turning, she said quietly, 'This land is vast, India. So many girls, so many sorrows. What can I really do? My power is small. Whatever I attempt, it is by Guru Maharaj's blessing.'

One of the brahmacharis nodded gravely. 'There is none like

Guru Maharaj. At first, we were afraid, and we kept our distance. But he drew us near, and then we felt his love.'

Nivedita agreed gently, 'Yes. Those who only see the surface may not understand. But those who truly know him, know.'

Just then, Nirbhayananda pointed, 'Look, there he is, on the second-floor veranda.'

Nivedita looked up. Swamiji sat still, his gaze cast elsewhere. Of late, he could no longer see distant things clearly; the world seemed a haze, a drifting mist. At the foot of the stairs, Nivedita hesitated, then turned to Nirbhayananda and said, 'Let him know I am here. I'll offer my *pranam* at the temple first.'

The temple was empty. She sat in the silence for a while. As always, that sacred place poured tranquility into her heart. Rising, she knew her Master waited.

Swamiji sat upstairs. At the sight of her, his face broke into a smile.

'Come,' he said. 'Since morning, I had the feeling you would come today.'

She bowed. He felt, as always, that in that act, she surrendered herself utterly. In a voice hushed with benediction, he said, 'May all be well.'

A cushion had been placed before him. Nivedita sat there, dressed in her white silk robe, hair tied in a soft knot, *rudraksha* beads around her neck, and a second rosary of crystal. Her face glowed with joy, a quiet radiance.

There was no rain. The heat pressed down. Sweat streamed down their faces. A young *sevak* stood by, fanning Swamiji. Nivedita gently asked for the fan and began fanning him herself.

'How are you today, Guruji?' she asked.

His smile deepened. 'If I said I was unwell, you'd grow sad, wouldn't you? The joy of your morning would vanish. Now that you're here, I feel well in body and mind.'

His joy was her own. Uplifted, she began to speak with the eagerness of a child. 'Do you know, Guruji, I want to introduce a new science course at the school. Without science, the girls will never rise out of ignorance. I've discussed this with Sir Jagadish Chandra Bose. We're planning something new. May I tell you?'

She poured out her thoughts. Swamiji listened, saying nothing. When she asked softly, 'What do you think, Guruji, of this new education plan,' his silence deepened.

Then, calmly, he said, 'You may well be right. But I can no longer speak on such matters. For some time now, I've felt a great *tapasya*, a deep meditation, rising within. I am preparing for death. It is time to bid farewell to all things.'

Her heart stirred. In Kashmir, she remembered, he had once held two stones in his hand and said, 'When death comes to me, all my weaknesses fall away. Fear, doubt, worldly thought—none remain. I only ready myself for death.'

And now she understood. He was readying his soul for the flight beyond.

Swamiji sat still. His lips trembled slightly, and each word that left his mouth seemed to carry the weight of a sacred utterance. There was a difference in his voice that day, something that was deeper, more solemn. Nivedita sat near him, overwhelmed. She could sense his body was fatigued under the burden of his illness. If it had been possible, she would have taken that suffering upon herself without hesitation.

Swamiji looked at the wall clock. It was late. 'You'll have your lunch here today,' he said gently. He called a brahmachari and spoke to him briefly. Nivedita sat down at his feet. He began to speak of so many things; so many memories of the past. A few monks dropped in to see him, and all of them shared a warm bond with Nivedita. Brahmananda, Saradananda, Shivananda—they all held her in deep affection.

'If I'm not here someday,' Swamiji said, 'speak to them. Seek their guidance.'

Nivedita protested. 'Where would you go?'

'I don't know. Maybe far away,' he replied.

These days, she often struggled to grasp the full meaning behind his words. They seemed layered, and distant.

A brahmachari came and announced, 'Swamiji, lunch is ready.'

Swamiji suddenly became active. He stood up. 'Come, Margot,' he said, calling her by the name he sometimes used with affection. The meditative man of a moment ago now appeared light-hearted, almost playful. 'Come, come, Margot! The food will get cold. You can't follow religion on an empty stomach!'

As they entered the dining room, Nivedita noticed it was empty. 'Where is everyone?' she asked.

The steward, Maharaj, stepped forward. 'It's Ekadashi today, Sister. Everyone is fasting. So not much has been prepared.'

Soon, a brahmachari arrived with a tray. It held only a few small bowls—some rice, boiled potatoes, jackfruit seed curry, yogurt, and a little fruit.

Swamiji turned to the attendant. 'You may go. I will serve Nivedita myself today.' He began serving with a smile, making light remarks as he did so.

Nivedita felt uneasy. Swamiji, so unwell, was serving her with his own hands. 'Why are you doing this?' she asked softly.

He looked at her calmly. 'You all serve me all the time. Sometimes, I too wish to serve you.' His voice was warm and sincere. The quiet note of affection in his words moved her deeply.

Everything about him seemed different today, almost unreal. She ate with satisfaction. To her, it felt like more than a meal. It was as if he was offering her *prasad*, sacred food with the taste of something far beyond the ordinary.

When the meal was over, Nivedita got up to wash her hands. A young attendant stood nearby with water and a towel. Swamiji took them from him. Nivedita held out her hands. Swamiji poured the water gently, then set the vessel aside and dried her hands with the towel.

Nivedita was stunned. She looked at him in disbelief. Her heart swelled with emotion. In a hushed voice, she said, 'What are you doing, Swamiji? It is my duty to serve you.'

Swamiji's tone was calm, almost scriptural. 'Did not Isha, Jesus, wash the feet of his disciples?'

Nivedita was startled. A chill ran down her spine. She remembered it had been on the last day that Jesus had done so. The thought tried to form on her lips, but she could not say it. A silent pain rose within her. Had the moment of final farewell come?

A suppressed grief stirred in her chest. But she didn't cry. She couldn't. She didn't want to cause him sorrow.

The Deathless Soul

In the final hours before dawn, Swamiji awoke. In the next room, his attendant Brajendra lay asleep. All night, the small oil lamp had flickered faintly. Its flame had now dimmed to a whisper, its strength nearly gone. At any moment, it would vanish into darkness. Swamiji rose from his bed, opened the door, and stepped out onto the veranda.

A grey, fading darkness lingered. Soon the light would return. The Ganga, drawn back by the ebb tide, glimmered in the distance, far from the shore. A gentle breeze stirred the stillness. Birds rustled their wings in the mango tree.

An armchair waited on the veranda. Swamiji sat. All around him was silence. A vast, solitary stillness. How many times had he stood alone, asking himself the unending question: why this birth? Why this passing away? That eternal mystery stirred again in his mind, swelling like a rising tide.

Boats returning from a night of fishing drifted towards the banks. Amid them, life flowed quietly. A lone boatman's song floated on the wind, melancholy and wistful. So many dear ones, had now vanished into some unseen realm. Faces remembered in heart-stirring melodies were now fading into silence. The world, once vivid, was now a pale, dissolving painting. And yet, suddenly, in that deep darkness shone one luminous face, meditative and still. The half-closed eyes were suffused with bliss and love. It was a face that shone with the radiance of a timeless spiritual striving of a deathless, heroic soul.

Slowly, Swamiji opened his eyes. In them, glowed a light not of this world. As if it was calling all beings to his side, 'Come. I am waiting for you.' Something within the heart surged—waves of feeling, mysterious and profound. Even the atoms of his body seemed touched by a sweetness like the scent of flowers, like a call from the unknown.

'Your work is done,' whispered that silent call. 'Now come. The Helmsman of the Beyond awaits you.'

The heart quivered. The music of Krishna's flute stirred the soul. A deep yearning rose—'I must go to Him.' On Swamiji's luminous face, a smile bloomed. Like a song dissolving into light, he seemed to merge with something vast. Moments passed like waves, endlessly flowing.

Gradually, he returned to ordinary consciousness. He opened his eyes. What did he see? He plunged inward again, into an infinite sky. A light breeze passed over him. There, curled beside his feet, sat Bagha, the faithful dog. Swamiji smiled, reaching down to gently stroke its back. Bagha was a mute creature, yet one so deeply dear.

The darkness of night had lifted; morning had come. The tide was low. The monastery stirred to life. Bells rang in the temple. Soon, the courtyard would fill with monks and novices. But lately, crowds no longer pleased him. He had drawn inward, into quiet. He softly sang to himself:

'Mind, return to your own true home—Why wander in

the world, a stranger in a foreign land? Return, O mind, to your own true home.'

The day grew. Brajendra entered. 'Master, shall I bring your tea?'

Swamiji usually took tea and breakfast in his room. But today, he smiled and said, 'No, I'll join everyone in the dining hall.'

There, others were gathering—Premananda, Niranjanananda, Virajanananda, Sadananda, Shuddhananda. Swamiji's presence lit up the room like a moonlit night. Niranjanananda laughed, 'Naren has come today! Let there be a proper breakfast!'

Swamiji laughed too, 'So other days we get improper breakfast?'

Premananda joked, 'It's always good. But today, it will be even better!'

The cook entered. 'Maharaj, the potatoes are done. Shall I fry the *luchis*?'

'Yes, and make some chutney. That will be perfect.'

Two novices were in charge of the morning shopping. Suddenly, everyone turned, someone had entered carrying a large fish. This led to an uproar of joy, 'Hilsa! Hilsa! The first hilsa of the season!'

Swamiji beamed. 'Wonderful! Hilsa curry, hilsa in mustard, fried hilsa, and sour hilsa stew!'

Premananda widened his eyes dramatically. 'What does it matter if the fruit is ripe and the crow sees it? You're not allowed to eat it, your doctor forbids it.'

Swamiji laughed. 'I won't eat, just smell it. That's half the meal already.'

Then, turning to a young novice from East Bengal, he asked playfully, 'Bengali, isn't there a custom in Dhaka to worship the first hilsa of the season?'

'Yes, Master. It's a proper celebration in every household!'

'Good. Then perform the worship here, too. But what will you use for the offering?'

Everyone burst into laughter. Soon the food arrived, and the meal began with laughter, stories, and joy. When they finished, all returned to their duties. Swamiji bathed and entered the shrine.

The temple was usually empty at this hour. Most people simply offered *pranams* and left. Swamiji sat in silence before Sri Ramakrishna's image. Lately, memories of the past overwhelmed him. How many years had passed since their first meeting? Now, having entrusted all burdens to him, Sri Ramakrishna had returned to the spiritual realm.

Who can worship such a one? God, avatar, man—he had taken all forms. Infinite love, infinite compassion, infinite wisdom. What form could contain it all? Even now, doubt remained. Who would truly recognise his greatness unless he allowed them to see it?

Tears welled up and rolled down his cheeks. His vision blurred. Yet he knew that it was Premananda approaching. That familiar footstep. Swamiji rose.

'I want to sit in silence today. Prepare a seat for me in Thakur's bedroom,' he said.

Premananda sensed Swamiji drifting into the world of spirit. Wordlessly, he arranged the seat. Swamiji entered the room, closed the windows and doors, and sat for meditation.

The temple courtyard lay silent as morning advanced. A light shower had fallen the night before, but the summer's heat still scorched the air. Near the temple, the *kadamba* tree bloomed in fullness.

At last, Swamiji emerged. He had meditated a long while. The veranda lay dappled in light and shade. In that quiet rhythm, something stirred, an echo of divine presence. Gently, he began to sing:

'Is my Mother dark? She is dark indeed—dark as the thundercloud. Her hair is unbound, yet lighting the heart's lotus with divine radiance....'

His voice, noble, resonant, full of sweetness, filled the air. Premananda, busy in the shrine, stood still. Many sang in the monastery, but none like him. Had he been only a singer, he would have been great even then. Two novices ascending the stairs paused, not wishing to disturb the song. How they longed for such a voice.

Finishing the song, Swamiji raised his eyes towards the Ganga. The tide had risen. The waters swelled, and waves crashed against the ghat. A strange, exalted stillness filled the world. Life itself was like the Ganga's tide, rising and receding—in so many forms, so many hues, but how many truly grasped its essence?

His own life, yes, that too, was like the Ganga's tide—from spark to flame, from drop to ocean.

No one knew, no one understood. He murmured to himself, 'If only there were another Vivekananda, he might have understood what this Vivekananda has done.'

In the shrine, Premananda was startled. *What was that he said?* Was he preparing to leave the world?

He finished his chores and went to Swamiji, placing a hand on his back. The bell rang for lunch.

In a soft voice, Premananda said, 'Come, let's go to the dining hall.'

As they returned to the dining hall, Swamiji seemed transformed, different from before. He laughed and joked with everyone. After the meal, all gathered on the temple's adjoining veranda. Every day at this hour, they shared stories, exchanged words. The ascetics, shed their austere shells, and sat in simple companionship.

Suddenly, Swamiji said, 'Tomorrow is *Amavasya*.'

Shuddhananda responded, 'Yes, *Amavasya*, Saturday, a very auspicious day.'

Swamiji's face brightened with delight. 'Then tomorrow night we shall have Kali *Puja*.' A *puja* meant enthusiasm for all.

Niranjanananda reassured, 'No worries. By tomorrow afternoon, everything will be arranged.'

Nirbhayananda, sitting beside Shuddhananda, was particularly eager. 'Behind Belur Market, there is a potter who makes clay idols. He usually keeps two or three ready. Whenever one needs an idol, he can get it easily.'

Premananda asked, 'Then tomorrow morning, will you fetch the idol? Who will perform the puja?'

Swamiji replied, 'Shashi's father, Ishwar Chakraborty. Just tell him; he will take care of it.'

Many rose, as afternoon is the time for their customary siesta after lunch. Premananda raised his hand twice to greet, but Swamiji sharply interrupted, 'Are you going to sleep?'

Premananda laughed, 'What else can I do? There's no work now.'

'But to sleep,' Swamiji said with a gentle admonition, 'is a grave sin for a monk during the day. Shuddhananda, bring the *Shukla Yajurveda* from my room. Today, we will discuss some of its verses.'

Swamiji would teach. Everyone was delighted. His simple explanations made even a child understand. The whole afternoon was spent in scripture study. Time slipped by and evening tasks awaited. One by one, they all departed.

They played; he fed them. Swamiji sat quietly by the wall clock. Nearby, a few fireflies flickered. The clock struck five.

Swamiji looked at Premananda. 'Do you have any work?'

Premananda nodded. 'Do you need anything?'

'Let's go for a walk. After many days, the body feels quite well.'

'Where to?'

'Not far. Just a little walk.'

Descending from the temple veranda, the two stepped outside. The heat of the sun had lessened. Ahead stretched a field and a pond, surrounded by countless trees. In the distance, grazing cattle wandered over the pasture. A few houses stood nearby, their crops ripening. Beyond, partly hidden behind foliage, was Nilambar Mukherjee's home. The sky was veiled in a thin layer of clouds, soft as milk. A gentle breeze whispered.

Two figures walked side by side. Passing through the monastery gate, they entered an open expanse. Swamiji halted, gazing with steady eyes. Small grass, wild shrubs, and a few mango trees stood on one side.

Premananda watched. It seemed as if Swamiji was not fully present. His gaze pierced beyond the open field, crossing its boundary into the infinite. For a moment, he seemed to forget the presence of the companion beside him.

Placing a hand on Swamiji's shoulder, Premananda asked softly, 'What do you see?'

Swamiji turned his face away, glanced briefly around, and then took Premananda's hand into his own—there was such warmth in that touch!

In a low voice, he said, 'For the past thirty years, I have only laboured. I never thought of myself. Whatever I learned and understood, I have tried to share with people, both near and far. Many think it was all easy. It was not. Sometimes I worked twenty hours in a day. Sometimes I slept for only an hour at night. Often I toiled through entire nights. At times, I stayed in places so silent they could almost be called soundless. After all that effort, what I have gained, I have poured out for you all.'

Premananda nodded. 'I know, brother. Like Dadhichi, a sage who gave up his life for god, you have given yourself completely, sacrificing all for the sake of others. This Belur monastery, the community of monks, all are because of you.'

Swamiji said nothing for a while. A mild excitement flickered in his eyes and on his face. He seemed to want to say more. A serene glow enveloped him, like moonlight soaked in soft radiance.

He walked on again, speaking as they moved. 'This Belur monastery, the spiritual power it has begun to manifest here, will endure for fifteen hundred years. One day, it will become a vast university. Don't think this is mere imagination. I see it clearly before my eyes.'

Premananda felt as if Swamiji were glimpsing far-off days yet to come.

The hues of dusk spread through the landscape. The evening light faded; the sky grew pale.

Swamiji moved forward again. A herd of cattle passed by, their footsteps breaking the stillness. Then silence returned.

To Premananda, the familiar companion of two decades felt suddenly strange. They walked a while more together. The day was ending. Now it was time to return home.

It was a summer day. The evening twilight began a little late. On the veranda, three brahmacharis sat sipping tea. Swamiji stood up. 'You are having tea. Bring me a cup as well.'

'Please sit down. I will bring it.'

One of the brahmacharis hurried inside and returned with tea. Premananda was not fond of tea. Seeing Swamiji take it, he quietly returned to his room.

Swamiji looked at the brahmacharis. 'Do you know how we became addicted to tea? After Sri Ramakrishna passed away, we, the brothers at the Baranagar monastery, had endured many hardships. You cannot imagine those days of pain. But there was joy, too. The whole day was spent in meditation and chanting. The greatest difficulty was when visitors came. Guests were Narayan, and we had nothing to offer them. In the mornings, there was only one cup of tea. Afterwards, we brewed as many cups as we wished. You could not bear that hardship. Actually, Thakur Sri Ramakrishna gave us strength.'

One of the brahmacharis said, 'You give us strength.'

Swamiji looked up in surprise, his face turned towards the sky. Then he said, 'I have given all I could. Now it is time for me to go.'

'Where will you go?' someone asked.

'I do not know,' he replied, standing.

Darkness had fallen. The temple bells tolled. It was the first quarter of the night.

Swamiji returned to his room. Brajendra had lit the lamp. He had walked quite some distance, and his feet throbbed. He settled comfortably on the couch. The sound of evening devotional music drifted in from the temple. The room was filled with the scent of incense.

After a while, Swamiji said to Brajendra, 'Sit outside with the *japa mala*. Come when I call.'

Brajendra sat on the veranda. The temple music was clearly audible. When it ended, Swamiji called him in. Sweat dotted Swamiji's brow. He felt hot. 'Open the window,' he instructed.

A mat was spread on the floor. Swamiji lay down. Brajendra immediately began fanning him.

'Are you in pain, Gurudev?'

Swamiji gave no reply.

Brajendra fanned more briskly. The Ganga breeze blew gently. The heat had lessened, perhaps rain was coming.

In a soft voice, Swamiji said, 'No more fanning. Just press my feet a little.'

The wall clock struck nine. In Swamiji's hands, the *japa mala* slipped quietly, fingers turning the beads, or perhaps lost in trance, immersed in the depths beyond time's silent currents. Outside, the stars bloomed in the velvet night, their distant light traversing a thousand leagues of space to descend gently into the earth's embrace. From Swamiji's lips came a faint murmur, scarcely more than a sigh, like a newborn's fragile cry, rising from the innermost sanctuary of the soul.

'O Keeper of the Beyond, You have come. I have waited, ever patient, for Your arrival. Now shall sound the final flute of farewell….'

His right hand trembled slightly. A deep breath escaped him. His head slipped softly from the pillow, stillness enfolding all around. Peace reigned in the vast expanse.

Beside him, Brajendra sat, bewildered, calling out gently, 'Gurudev… Gurudev…' But no answer came, only the whisper of the passing breeze.

Again Brajendra called, heart pounding, fear rising. Unable to comprehend the stillness, he ran downstairs, crying out like a madman, 'Come! Everyone, come! Gurudev Maharaj does not speak….'

A crowd gathered, rushing in as if the world had broken apart. Bodhananda took his pulse; there was no movement. No breath. Only the eternal quiet.

Tears surged forth in waves, flowing into the silent folds of nature itself, into the infinite vastness where one great soul dissolves, merging with the boundless cosmos. Around them stretched only infinite emptiness, serene and eternal.

Beloved Friend Eternal

A hush of sound, a barely audible knock, brushed the door like a whisper from the void. A few moments passed. Then, once more, a gentle rap, like a breath against wood. Sister Nivedita stirred. Her sleep broke, not with clarity but with a fragile sense of disquiet. Eyes still heavy-lidded, she looked around as the first pale light of dawn begun to thread its way through the shutters, pouring a dim gold upon the floor.

For a moment, she was uncertain. Who could it be, so early, before even the birds had stirred the silence?

She rose. Every day, her soul awakened before the world, in the sacred hush that precedes sunrise, when the city is a temple of stillness and prayers are whispered to the sleeping sky. But last night had been unlike any other. She had had a strange dream, a dream that clung to her like mist. Long did she lie, eyes wide open, her mind adrift. Sleep only came in the final hush before the world's awakening.

'Sister.'

A muffled voice came from the other side of the door.

She opened it slowly.

A young brahmachari stood there, solemn and still. Though his name escaped her, she knew his face; he was one of the quiet ones from Belur Math. But what brought him to her threshold at this hour? Some shadow, some urgency trembled in the air.

He spoke not a word. From the folds of his bag, he drew out a single sheet of paper and held it out with reverent silence.

'What is this?' she asked, her voice a bare whisper.

He did not answer.

Only tears fell, silent, steady, as if the soul itself were weeping.

A tremor passed through her. An unspoken foreboding settled over her. Her fingers grasped the paper and unfolded it with trembling hands.

A few lines only.

'All is over. Last night, at nine, Swamiji went to sleep. He will not awaken again.'—Saradananda

4 July 1902.

A silence vast as the sky descended within her.

He is gone. A storm broke inside her breast.

Grief, raw and thunderous, surged without warning; it was as if the heavens themselves had torn open. Her body shook. The paper slipped from her hand. Darkness rushed in from all sides. She clung to the doorframe as though to the edge of a crumbling world.

A cry escaped her, deep and primal, rising from the ruins of the heart. *He is gone.*

The monk stood just outside the door, his eyes lowered, his presence a quiet compassion.

'The others are waiting for you, Sister,' he said softly. 'At the Math.'

Still she wept. As though the world's last light had been

extinguished. As though the very meaning of the world had drained away.

And then he murmured, almost to himself, 'Do not fall like this, Sister. What shall we do, then?'

She stood motionless for a long, silent moment.

Then, gathering herself from the storm, she stilled her breath and composed her limbs. The pain remained, but it was wrapped now in purpose. She would go. She must go to him.

Dawn had scarcely broken. Baghbazar still lay under the veil of early morning. The streets were hushed, and misty. A few figures slowly walked towards the river, brass vessels in their hands. The shops were shuttered. From some roadside shrine, a temple bell chimed faintly. The lamp posts flickered like dim stars holding on to the last threads of night. But she saw none of it and heard nothing. The world, to her, was hollow. Only one echo tolled through the silence, over and over again: He is gone. My Master. My lamp upon the path. My friend. The hand that had guided her through shadow and fire—now stilled.

'Sister,' the brahmachari's voice called her gently back. They had arrived at the ghat.

The Ganga, in full tide, shimmered under the pale morning.

The water murmured as it kissed the stone steps. Two or three boats drifted slowly, lost in thought. One was moored at the side, waiting.

A few souls stood waist-deep in the river, bathing in silence.

The monk raised his hand. A boatman steered near. 'Come, Sister,' he said.

Wordless, like one moving through a sacred dream, Nivedita stepped into the boat. The oars dipped. The current cradled them.

Silence, vast and unbroken, wrapped them as the boat drifted gently.

Then, like a wind stirring fallen leaves, she spoke softly, 'Was he very ill... last night?'

'No,' came the reply, quiet as the river's breath. 'He spoke to us all. He laughed. He sang. At noon, he said, "Let us all dine together today." We were so happy. There was something... luminous about him. It was a brightness not of this world.'

She turned her gaze to the horizon, as if looking for the place where memory touches eternity.

'In our last meeting, only two days ago, he was radiant. Like one lit from within.'

The monk nodded, his voice thickening.

'Yesterday... hilsa fish was cooked. There were so many dishes. The doctor had forbidden it, but he tasted a little of each.

'He smiled like a child. And in the afternoon, he taught again.

'The hardest truths, and he made them simple. Clear as morning. Even a child would have understood.'

Tears brimmed in his eyes.

She felt them rise in her own. She said, with a tremor of wonder, 'Yesterday morning, a sadhu came to my house in Baghbazar. He brought a small loaf wrapped in paper. "Swamiji has sent this for you," he said. My hands trembled. I touched it to my forehead. It was no mere bread. It was *prasad*, his sacred gift. A blessing.

'I asked, "How is he today?" And the sadhu replied, "He is well." My heart filled with joy. All day I felt him near, watching over me. I had planned to visit the Math soon.'

'But that night, Sister....'

'I had a dream. I do not know why. But I saw Sri Ramakrishna again, upon his deathbed. The disciples had gathered, their hearts breaking. A tide of unending sorrow, unfolded. I awoke in anguish. I looked out of the window. The stars lay scattered like prayers across the heavens. One star, one alone, blazed brighter than all the rest. A strange heaviness gripped me. I could not name it. But I knew...something was coming. My eyes filled with tears. And then...in the last hours before morning, sleep took me. Then came the knock. And now, he is gone.'

The young brahmachari broke down, his sobs rising like waves against the hush of the morning. Nivedita, steadying her grief, reached out with quiet strength. 'You must gather yourself, dear one,' she said softly. 'Great burdens lie upon you now. You must be strong—for all our sakes.' Her voice, though gentle, carried the weight of awakened purpose.

'What was Swamiji doing yesterday evening?' she asked, her tone hushed and reverent.

The brahmachari, his breathing slow with remembrance, began to speak, haltingly at first, then with the slow unfolding of pain as he spoke of yesterday's events.

'Everyone knew,' he said. 'We felt it. We could not name it, but we knew. One of us was sent to Baranagar to bring Dr Mazumdar. He came swiftly and examined Swamiji. Tried—oh, he tried. Then, bowing his head, he said, "It is over".'

Nivedita's voice was barely a whisper. 'Where were Maharaj Brahmananda and Maharaj Saradananda?'

'They were at Balaram Babu's house. When word reached them, they came at once. Maharaj Brahmananda entered Swamiji's room. He seemed…undone. As if something inside him had been torn away. He flung himself across Swamiji's chest and wept like a child. Maharaj Saradananda had to pull him back almost by force. He would not be restrained. "Before my eyes, the Himalayas have vanished!" he kept saying, crying all the while.'

A cry tore through Nivedita's chest, a sound more music than grief, like a flute breaking its heart upon the wind, caught in the swell of the Ganga's morning tide. But only for a moment. She composed herself swiftly, her sorrow cloaked in dignity. Quietly, she said, 'Just thirty-nine years and he is gone. Returned to his Master, Sri Ramakrishna. I saw it in his eyes the day before yesterday. He was preparing… preparing for departure. And yet—'

She could say no more. Tears coursed down her cheeks in silence.

It had not yet been forty-eight hours.

Still, the presence of her Master clung to every atom of her being, like incense to cloth, like moonlight to a dream.

So many memories surged, so many words, so many glances, so many silences. In these last days, his body had grown frail, burdened with a hundred ailments. At times, he had seemed dazed with pain. At others, he soared above suffering—serene and luminous with joy. She had poured her soul before him—her thoughts, fears, and hopes for the future. Always, he had listened. Sometimes he would counsel. Sometimes he would smile and say, 'Do as you think best.'

Once, he had spoken of himself.

'I am glad I was born. I am glad I suffered so much. And now, as I drown in this peace of Nirvana, I am glad still. Whether freedom comes by the death of the body, or while it still endures, know that the old Vivekananda is no more. He is gone, forever. He will not return.'

The words rang now with haunting clarity.

Nivedita lifted her face. The boat had reached the ghat at Belur. A few figures stood waiting. The brahmachari stepped off first, then turned to help her down. She heard fragments of whispered speech, his name… his passing….

Only two days ago, she had walked these very steps. Then, the world had been full. Now, it was stripped bare.

She walked forward with silent purpose. Rain had fallen lightly in the night; the earth was soft beneath her steps. The Math lay wrapped in a deep and aching stillness. Not a sound was heard. A few monks stood scattered here and there. Not one of them smiled.

Where once they would greet her warmly, today their faces were etched with sorrow.

As she neared the staircase, a voice said gently, 'Go upstairs, Sister.'

Without pause, she ascended to Swamiji's chamber on the upper floor. The Ganga flowed beyond, but her eyes did not turn to it. She stepped through the open doorway. The room was dim, and the windows were closed. In the muted light, she saw Swamiji, lying upon the carpet, clad in ochre robes. A silken turban was upon his head. His face turned west, and his feet were towards the river. His body was strewn with flowers. Hands folded upon his chest, a rosary was resting between his fingers.

She sank beside him, speechless. The stillness of a great yogi, absorbed in supreme *samadhi*, lay before her. Slowly, reverently, she reached for a hand fan placed nearby, and began to fan his face with quiet devotion. At his feet sat young Nandalal, a brahmachari. Others entered in time—Chandrashekhar, the Mother's disciple, with his friends Nibaran and Dulal Shashi.

They seated themselves near Swamiji's feet, their heads bowed low.

Devotees began to arrive one by one. They paused at the threshold, folded their hands in silent *pranam*, and left. The monks sat below, on the veranda. None spoke. The silence was complete. At length, Nivedita turned to Chandrashekhar and asked softly, 'Will you sing the songs Swamiji loved?'

Chandrashekhar shook his head. 'I do not know them, Sister.'

She turned to his friend. 'Do you, Nibaran?'

'Yes, Sister,' he replied gently.

And then, in a clear, bare voice, he began to sing. *'Yatane hridoye rekho adarini Shyama…'*—Cherish her within your heart, O tender one, Shyama.

One song followed another. *'Ke bole Shyama amar kalo… Gaya Ganga Prabhasadi Kashi Kanchi—keba chay?'*—Who says my Shyama is dark? What more does one need than Gaya, Ganga, Prabhas, Kashi, or Kanchi?

Tears streamed down Nivedita's face, like the river below—silent, endless, full of longing.

Her mind returned to their first meeting.

It had been November 1895. England's journals overflowed with his name. Some compared him to the Buddha. Others, to Christ. But Margaret had not yet heard of him then.

One day, a friend had invited her, 'A Hindu monk is coming to Lady Isabel Margesson's house. He will speak on religion. Will you come?'

Out of mere curiosity, Margaret had said, 'Yes.'

And thus, began the journey that led to this moment of holy silence beside her fallen Master. That Sunday afternoon, Margaret arrived at Lady Margesson's home. In a large, curtained drawing room sat a small group. Every seat was taken, save one, at the front. She hesitated, then took her place. Lifting her gaze, she saw before her a monk clad in ochre robes. His face bore the radiant calm of a child. Behind him, a fire flickered gently in the hearth, and against that warm light, his presence seemed almost otherworldly.

Lady Isabel said softly, 'Swamiji, all our friends have gathered.'

A slight smile touched the monk's lips. With palms joined in prayer, he murmured, *'Om Shivaya Namah.'* And then, he began to speak. His voice rose like a sacred chant—lofty, open, and tender. He spoke of religion, renunciation, and liberation. Margaret could not accept all he said. And yet, something deep within her stirred, something ancient and nameless. She felt, against her will, that to ignore this presence would render life barren. That day became a beginning. The river of memory surged. Each wave bore joy, sorrow, anguish, love, all fused into one.

Time passed. Upstairs, Swami Saradananda entered. In a quiet voice, he said, 'Chandrashekhar, we must take Swamiji down now.'

Chandrashekhar hesitated. 'Shall we carry him?'

In a broken voice Saradananda replied, 'It feels as though all my strength has left me. I don't know how we will manage.'

'Do not worry, Maharaj,' said Chandrashekhar gently. 'We will carry him with our own hands.'

From below, a hum of voices reached them. The last rites were about to begin. Three householder-devotees and Nandalal carefully lifted the sacred body. Outside, a flower-laden bier awaited. They laid Swamiji down upon it, his form surrounded by monks, each with tears glistening in their eyes.

Swami Advaitananda, the elderly Gopal, brought a few fruits and said to Nandalal, 'Swamiji loved you dearly. You must perform the final offering.'

With trembling hands, Nandalal placed the flowers and fruits upon the Master's chest. Sister Nivedita stood silent, her eyes fixed on his serene face. A man of thirty-nine, who had never asked anything for himself, who had poured out his whole being in service to others, was snatched away, too soon, by the divine.

One devotee suggested, 'Let's take a final photograph.'

But Maharaj Brahmananda replied, 'There are so many beautiful photographs of Swamiji. Why must we remember him like this, in parting? It will only cause pain.'

A young brahmachari took the imprint of Swamiji's feet in vermilion on cloth. Nivedita bent and gently touched his feet with her handkerchief, her last relic of her Master.

The hour moved on. A lamp was lit. Conch shells sounded. Monks approached, one by one, offering their final *pranams.* Some broke down weeping. To Nivedita, the flower-covered form seemed no longer of this earth. It was as if Shiva himself now journeyed towards Kailasa. From every side rose the cry—Victory to Guru Maharaj*!*

She stood beside him. Someone spread a familiar shawl over his still body. Nivedita recognised it. He wore that shawl often. She thought, *If only I could keep it, even a small corner—just something....*

Swami Saradananda stood near. She asked softly, 'Will the shawl also be consigned to the fire?'

'Would you like to have it?' he asked gently.

But the words stuck in her throat. She couldn't ask. Only the thought burned—*if only a piece remained with me.*

The procession began. Upon their shoulders, the monks bore Swamiji towards the banks of the Ganga, beneath the ancient *bel* tree, just east of the Math, his chosen resting place. There the bier was placed.

Crowds had gathered—Girish Ghosh, the writer Jaladhar Sen, Mahendra Nath, and many others. Even people from Simla in Kolkata had come, their grief breaking forth in sobs.

Then came his mother, Bhubaneshwari Devi, holding the hand of her young son Bhupendranath. A mother's heart shattered by loss. 'My Naren is gone! I am left desolate. Come back, son…come back once more!'

A cry of anguish rose from the banks. All hearts ached. Saradananda said, 'Take Mother away. She must not witness this.'

Almost by force, she was led away to a waiting boat. It moved out slowly. Her weeping voice faded into the distance.

The pyre was arranged. A monk brought a sacred torch. Nivedita stepped forward and touched the flame to the sandalwood. One by one, others followed. The fire roared to life.

Nivedita stood transfixed. In those fierce tongues of flame, all that was left of her Master was dissolving into the sky. She felt herself unmoored, as if sanity teetered on the brink. How could she bear this sundering? It was a grief deeper than death. She moved closer, encircling the fire. Sparks flew with the wind, brushing against her, but she did not flinch. The heat touched her face and her garments.

Suddenly, Brahmananda called out, 'Nirbhayananda, take Nivedita away. Her gown might catch fire.'

Nirbhayananda approached, took her hand gently, and led her to the riverside. There, she sank upon a stone.

The flames leapt high, licking the sky. Twisting smoke curled upward like blackened clouds. The chant rose again—Victory to Guru Maharaj!

Nivedita sat still, her soul asking only one question—*He has left me. But the burden he gave, the mission he entrusted—can I fulfil it alone?*

The sun dipped westward. The fire, once a towering blaze, now dimmed. The Ganga flowed quietly past.

Then suddenly, she felt a tug at her sleeve. Startled, she turned. A piece of cloth fluttered to her. It was a part of Swamiji's shawl, the one that had been draped over him.

In that supreme sorrow, a strange joy lit her heart. Her

unspoken wish was fulfilled. A silent message from beyond the pyre—*This is for you.*

The fire died. Water was poured over it. The last trace of the mortal form dissolved into the sacred river.

It was time to return. Nivedita lifted her face to the sky. A few stars had bloomed. In those stars, she saw him, her Master, her guiding light. He was like the Pole Star, fixed and eternal. The time had come to walk forward, carrying the torch he had passed to her. For the last time, she bowed to him. Then, without a word, she turned and walked on.

Behind her, the monks chanted by the river's edge—*Om Shanti, Om Shanti.*